HELPING FAMILIES CARE

HELPING FAMILIES CARE

Practical Ideas for Intergenerational Programs

James McGinnis

A Joint Publication of

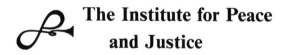

The Institute for Peace and Justice

and

BOOKS

© 1989 by the Institute for Peace and Justice

Special thanks to Nanette Ford for her illustrations
and to Discipleship Resources, Nashville,
for permission to include worksheets from
Christian Parenting for Peace and Justice Program Guide.

Published in the United States by Meyer-Stone Books,
a division of Meyer, Stone, and Company, Inc.,
2014 South Yost Avenue, Bloomington, IN 47403
Telephone: 812-333-0313

and

The Institute for Peace and Justice
4144 Lindell Blvd., #122
St. Louis, MO 63108
Telephone: 314-533-4445

Cover design: Carol Evans-Smith

Typesetting output: TEXSource, Houston

Manufactured in the United States of America
93 92 91 90 89   5 4 3 2

Library of Congress Cataloging-in-Publication Data

McGinnis, James B.
    Helping families care.

    Bibliography: p.
    1. Church work with families.   2. Family — Religious
life.   3. Intergenerational Christian education.
4. Family life education.   I. Title.
BV4438.M38   1989   259   88-43049
ISBN 0-940989-44-1 (Meyer-Stone Books)

Contents

CHAPTER 1

Vision, Principles, and Expectations

Vision

Helping Families Care attempts to address some of the most pressing needs of our age — the needs of individual families as well as the needs of the whole human family.

First of all, individual families want to be caring at home. They keep working at it, hopeful on some days, despairing on others. This guidebook, like all other "Parenting for Peace and Justice" resources, is designed to help families grow in caring for one another and to become a more loving community.[1]

Second, despite, or perhaps because of, the tremendous mobility characteristic of the last quarter of the twentieth century, family members often feel less rooted, more cut off from one another. The extended family traditions, common to so many of the ethnic roots from which North American families come, are vanishing from this continent. Feeling this sense of loss, many families have begun to search for alternatives. Some of the most vital family situations today are the communities of families being created out of this need. Whether they are called "basic Christian communities" or "family support groups" or something else, these groups of families are together discovering wholeness, or, to use the term taken from the Hebrew scriptures, *shalom*. This guidebook offers suggestions and models for promoting this kind of cooperative living and mutual support.

Third, families are discovering that together they can make a difference in the world. At this moment in human history, when for the first time humankind has the power to destroy God's creation, the human family and the earth urgently need committed agents of that *shalom*. Precisely because of the

---

[1]The Parenting for Peace and Justice resources referred to throughout this book are available from the Institute for Peace and Justice. See below pp. 147–153.

love they experience within their family communities, families have a special responsibility to be those agents and to share that love and concern with the world around them — their neighborhood, their nation, their earth. As recipients of God's *shalom*, we are called to share that *shalom* in ever-widening circles. This guidebook provides practical suggestions on how to be agents of God's *shalom*.

PPJ Assumptions

Underlying this program are twelve assumptions that characterize all the Parenting for Peace and Justice (PPJ) resources and programs:

1. Parenting is a guiding and a nurturing process that includes immediate and extended families. "Families" come in many varieties — for example, single-parent, two-parent, blended families, extended families. "Family" can be further extended to include "church family," as in Lola Mavor's Australian program (see chapter 14).

2. Families of faith believe that we are not alone in the process of parenting, that God is a partner in this process.

3. Relationships need to be developed on the basis of acceptance and forgiveness. Affirmation, a sense of self-worth, and cooperation are crucial for family life.

4. Communication skills (for example, listening, owning and sharing our feelings) and conflict resolution skills are essential for parenting.

5. All family members have a right to participate in family decision making, according to their ability.

6. Just as the earth's resources are meant by the Creator for the well-being of all persons and gen-

erations, so too our own possessions and talents are not ours in an exclusive sense; they are gifts meant for the well-being of others as well.

7. The richness of the human family is expressed in the diversity of races and cultures. Each person and family should seek to be enriched by this diversity.

8. Each family member should be encouraged to develop as full a range of emotional, intellectual, and physical responses and skills as possible, regardless of sex, age, or disability.

9. Families are communities with not only an internal mission to love one another and help each family member grow, but also an external mission: to help build the human family and to challenge those forces (for example, racism, sexism, militarism, materialism, ageism) that undermine our fundamental human unity.

10. Families are part of a global family and are called to express active concern for those in need in other parts of the world as well as in their own communities and nation.

11. Families do all this best by working together with other families.

12. Families of faith do all this best when they integrate these concerns explicitly with their faith and worship.

Religious Principles

Complementing the twelve "PPJ Assumptions" are the following religious principles. Because Parenting for Peace and Justice is evolving in its understanding of itself, these principles reflect current understandings rather than unchangeable tenets.

1. We embrace a diversity of religious and moral traditions. Because we experience the richness of the human family in the diversity of races and cultures (see Assumption 7 above), we want PPJ to be articulated explicitly within a variety of religious and moral traditions. Rather than seek a religious statement that applies to every tradition and offends no tradition, we encourage people and groups involved in PPJ to express PPJ's assumptions, principles, and goals according to their own language, culture, and religious or moral tradition.

The originators of PPJ share as a common heritage the Judeo-Christian understanding that marriage and family life are a covenant in which God the Holy Spirit is also a partner calling forth faithfulness (Hosea 2:3). The specific suggestions for family action are equally applicable to the various religious communities although they will often be flavored — and enriched — by the various traditions from which people come.[2]

2. Shalom is our unifying value. Because all the originators of PPJ come from a Judeo-Christian tra-

dition and most of the early outreach was to families within the various Christian traditions, there has been a predominantly Christian flavor to PPJ. To be as ecumenical as possible within this context, *shalom* was identified as that overarching value that best expressed the vision and concerns of PPJ.

We understand *shalom* to encompass many values: harmony, wholeness, sharing; peace and security; justice and integrity; material well-being; above all, unity or oneness, the oneness of the human family with the rest of God's creation. *Shalom* is God's will for the world, especially as expressed in Isaiah 65:17–25, Amos 8, Ezekiel 34, 2 Corinthians 5, and Revelation 21. And this vision of *shalom* is to be realized at all levels of human community — in the home, the neighborhood, and the world.[3]

---

[2]Thus three new versions of the PPJ *Families in Search of Shalom* filmstrip have been created — to reflect Jewish, Black Christian, and Hispanic Christian perspectives.

[3]See *Christian Parenting for Peace and Justice,* Program

This vision has three major implications for action. First, we believe that God calls each person to share in the building of *shalom,* to be co-creator, as it were, with God. Whenever and wherever *shalom* is frustrated, contradicted, or denied in creation, we are called to denounce this denial of God's will and work to change the situation. If we see the sword coming, as expressed in the prophet Ezekiel (33:1–11), we are to sound the alarm to alert the people. Each of us is called to be a "sentry for God's people," to share in prophetic ministry. We cannot use inexperience or youth (Jeremiah 1:6) as an excuse for not responding.

Second, we are called to hope. God's will for the world is *shalom.* In the face of rampant injustice, we are called to persistent action, to fidelity to our prophetic mission, no matter how complex or overwhelming the problems seem and how insignificant our actions seem. In the face of the "dragon" of Revelation 12, we are to be like the woman who looks the dragon in the eye and gives birth in the face of the dragon despite the seemingly inevitable destruction of the infant.

We are called to "hope against hope," to be faithful to the small actions for *shalom* we can perform, believing that God will take these actions — combined with millions of others — and will realize the "new heaven and earth" of Isaiah 65:17 and Revelation 21, the "new creation" of 2 Corinthians 5:17.

Third, we are called to pay a price. Discipleship — fidelity to our prophetic mission — is costly. The Hebrew prophets paid a price. The message of the Suffering Servant of the Jewish scriptures is that liberation, *shalom,* the Reign of God are purchased through suffering love. For Christians, the core of our faith is the cross of Christ — Jesus crucified and then raised from the dead as Christ by God.

Ephesians 2:14 says that it is through the blood of Christ (his redemptive suffering) that the barriers of hostility are broken down and *shalom* secured. The apostles of Jesus paid a price. Christian and Jewish martyrs (witnesses) throughout the centuries have paid a price. Our " seed," too, must fall to the ground and die in order to bear fruit.

3. PPJ themes are considered in relation to *shalom.* Affirmation, cooperation, nonviolent conflict resolution, mutuality in decision making and

_____
Guide, "Overview: Families in Search of Shalom," pages 1–4, for an elaboration of this vision with specific suggestions for action at all three levels.

home responsibilities (see Assumptions 3–5 above) are all ways of realizing greater harmony or unity (*shalom*) within the home.

Developing healthy racial attitudes in children, promoting greater appreciation for cultural diversity, and challenging racism (see Assumptions 7 and 9) are all ways of realizing greater harmony (*shalom*) in our neighborhoods as well as countries (see the book of Ruth) and the global family. They help reflect more adequately the infinite richness of our Creator.

Celebrating human diversity and potential by challenging stereotypes of women and men (Galatians 3:28), of the elderly (Psalm 92:14), and of people with disabilities; promoting the full human development (emotional, physical, intellectual) of girls and boys; and challenging sexism and ageism (see Assumptions 8 and 9) are all ways of realizing wholeness (*shalom*) in individuals as well as in society as a whole.

Promoting conservation of the earth's limited resources, nurturing a sense of reverence for God's cre-

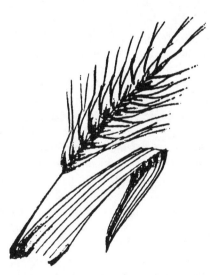

ation, encouraging a sense of stewardship of our personal talents and possessions as well as the earth's resources, and challenging materialism and wastefulness (see Assumptions 6 and 9) are all ways of realizing our oneness (*shalom*) as a human family and with the earth.

Exploring nonviolent means of resolving intergroup and international conflict and challenging the threat or use of violence and military force as an appropriate means of resolving human, social, or political problems are ways of realizing greater harmony (*shalom*) within the larger human family. Encouraging families to link with families in other parts of the world and to respond to hunger and poverty in the Third World as well as in our own communities (see Assumption 10) are ways of realizing our oneness (*shalom*) as a global family.

Implicit in this understanding of *shalom* and explicit in the scriptures of all religious traditions is the sacredness of each human life. Created in the image and likeness of God, each person is sacred. No one is expendable.

4. This call is to families also. Families as well as individuals live by grace and forgiveness. Families as well as individuals are called to share in social ministry. For many, "family" or "family responsibilities" has been an excuse for noninvolvement in social or prophetic ministry. While we affirm the importance of family responsibilities and family involvement in social action, we also recognize another twofold responsibility.

First, family love exists not just for its own sake. It is also a gift to be shared. Precisely because of the support that this love can bring to families, families have a responsibility to share that love with others and to be willing to take risks in that sharing.

Second, such risks may entail suffering, but we are sometimes called to put discipleship before "family" (see Luke 3:41–50, 14:25–27).

5. There are a variety of valid family models. We find in the Jewish and Christian scriptures no single model of family life, but, instead, a plurality of models.

There is the clan or tribal family headed by a patriarch in the early Hebrew scriptures; the "good wife" of Proverbs managed the household and was the primary income producer, freeing her husband for political activity "at the city gate where he takes his place with the elders of the land." In Paul's letters there are seemingly conflicting models of family life. In Ephesians 5:21–33, there is a patriarchal view where wives are to be subject to their husbands, but there is also the notion of "mutual submission." Galatians 3:26–29 stresses the equality of members in the Body of Christ.[4] Finally, there is the Christian community as a new kind of family or volun-

tary community, often in tension with the natural family (Matthew 10:37–39; Luke 14:26–29; Mark 3:31–35).[5]

Finding such a variety of family models in the Bible and recognizing the cultural conditioning of the biblical authors and the cultural adaptations of biblical values, we do not consider a patriarchal model of family life to be *the* biblical model to be imitated (see Assumption 1). Instead we find biblical values — for example, authority as service rather than giving orders, family and community as a body in which each member participates according to its function — that point toward a *mutual* mode of family life, where decision-making power is a shared responsibility among all family members (see Assumption 5) and where child-rearing and household tasks are also a shared responsibility (see Assumption 8).

How to Use This Guidebook

1. Who is the guidebook for? There are three main groups for whom this guidebook will be most helpful:

- *program leaders,* such as directors of Christian education, adult or family Sunday School leaders, family camp directors, and others who conduct family enrichment or social concerns programs for adults and children in intergenerational settings;

- *groups of adults,* such as family support groups, Bible study or social action groups, PET (Parent Effectiveness Training) or STEP (Systematic Training in Effective Parenting) groups, Marriage Encounter and other family enrichment groups, and others who want to involve children with them in a process of integrating home and family concerns with larger social concerns;

- *individual families* or any group of children and adults who nurture children (which includes teachers, social workers, grandparents, aunts and uncles) and who want to integrate their efforts at *shalom* into the larger world.

---

[4]Jesus' commitment to the discipleship of equals (women and men) is developed at length in Elisabeth Schüssler Fiorenza's *In*

Memory of Her: A Feminist Reconstruction of Early Christian Origins (Crossroad, 1983).

[5]See Rosemary Ruether's excellent article, "An Unrealized Revolution: Searching Scripture for a Model of the Family," in *Christianity and Crisis,* October 31, 1983.

2. Settings and formats. This program has been designed:

- *for large groups*, generally in a church, camp, or community center, with adequately prepared program leaders;

- *for small groups*, generally meeting in participants' homes, led by the participating adults themselves, perhaps with the assistance of an additional program leader;

- *for individual families* looking for personal enrichment, selecting those activities most appropriate for their needs, interests, and talents as a family.

The themes and activities outlined in chapters 4 through 8 can be combined in any number of variations. They can vary from one- and two-day programs to a series of three or four or more sessions.

There is no expectation that all the activities or even all the themes can be incorporated into any one program. Leaders and participants need to select those most appropriate to their situation, needs, and interests. Activities that cannot be incorporated into formal program sessions can be offered as "take home" possibilities.

When the program is a series of sessions rather than a concentrated day or weekend, participants can try some of the activities at home and then report back at the following session.

Expectations of Program Leaders

While individual families and already existing family groups or clusters can use this book as a self-

guided learning experience, it is probably a more valuable resource for persons who want to lead a larger intergenerational group through the themes.

While this guidebook, like all the other Parenting for Peace and Justice leader resources, is designed to simplify the role of program leaders, there are still expectations that program leaders should consider. We do not call them "requirements," but our experience has shown that the following are important:

1. Background reading. Chapters 2 and 3 below present detailed suggestions for PPJ programs, the various program options, and all the planning and preparatory tasks essential for a good intergenerational program.

2. Further preparation. Before the program begins, preferably even before recruiting participants for the program, read the book *Parenting for Peace and Justice* (Orbis Books, 1981). It is preferable to read this with other parents and experiment with your own family situation. It is also highly recommended that you view the *Building Shalom Families* video program on Parenting for Peace and Justice. This unique resource is both for leader preparation and for the participants themselves.[6]

3. Input. The content input expected of you as leader during the program is minimal. The audiovisual resources, the information provided on the participant worksheets, and the use of the *Parenting for Peace and Justice* book or tapes provides the bulk of the input.

4. Group process skills. This is probably the most essential expectation. This program calls for a lot of group interaction, both in small groups and large. It treats some difficult issues, touches the emotions deeply, invites shared prayer, and necessitates community building within the group. Those without group process skills or uncomfortable leading a group through a variety of activities should not lead this program or should seek out someone else to help.

5. Personal experience in "parenting for peace and justice." No one has "arrived." All of us are in process, on a journey, in search of *shalom*. Parents or couples should not feel that they can be leaders only if they have done most or even some of the actions and activities suggested. But it is important

---

[6]Both the book and the video are available from the Institute for Peace and Justice. See the ordering information on p. 153.

that you as leader see the need to explore this dimension of family life and have begun to do so. If so, you will have more credibility with the group, will have some experiences to share (failures as well as successes), and will learn more while leading the program.

6. Contact with the PPJ Network (PPJN) — and your denomination's Family Life Office:

- Though not essential, it is helpful to have participated in a PPJ program, workshop, or training session prior to leading a group. The *Building Shalom Families* video program can serve as a training alternative.

- Become a member of the PPJN and receive and use the program leader mailings for ongoing nurture. $20 a year covers both regular membership services, including the bimonthly newsletter, and three program leader mailings. Members are also entitled to a 15 percent discount on purchases of resources.

- Whether or not you participate in a prior PPJ workshop, it is important to contact the PPJN for the names of others in your area who have been program leaders and for the name of your local PPJ coordinator. They can be of great help as you plan and conduct your program.

- Relate on a regular basis with a "partner" program leader, a family support group, or the local PPJ coordinator or team for support and growth. If possible have at least one person from these support systems evaluate one of your presentations or programs each year; in addition there is a yearly self-evaluation sent to the PPJN office.

- Please complete a "Report Form" following each PPJ program you conduct. Send it to the PPJN office to help the PPJN listen to and support you and other program leaders. Contact PPJN for these Report Forms.

CHAPTER 2

Conducting Intergenerational Programs

Based on our own experience as teachers and program leaders for over twenty years and on the experience of other program leaders in our Parenting for Peace and Justice Network, we have identified guidelines for both *shalom* programs in general and intergenerational programs in particular.

General Guidelines

1. Affirm where people are as well as challenge them to next steps. Before people can act on social issues, especially when these actions involve a degree of risk, they need to feel good about themselves.

Further, people are more open to new challenges when they know that the challenger is aware of and appreciates what they have already done.

Finally, giving participants in a PPJ program a chance to share with other participants what they are already doing, before the leader has surfaced new possibilities, provides a dynamic through which new possibilities for action emerge from the group itself. Often participants are more open to new possibilities that come from their peers rather than from the leaders — whom they sometimes expect to do more because they are somehow different or more expert.

2. Be facilitators rather than experts. Precisely because of the "expert" category into which program leaders are often slotted, much emphasis is placed upon small group sharing and "what we are already doing."

Second, much of the content — both data about issues and suggestions for action — in the various sessions in PPJ programs is communicated in the form of audio-visuals and worksheets. This is to take the burden of content off the leaders and allow them to focus on their role as facilitators.

Third, when audio-visual presentations challenge — and sometimes even threaten — the participants, the leaders can act as facilitators and help the group process the content. But if the challenges come from the leaders, then it can be more difficult — both for participants who are sometimes inhibited about challenging leaders and also for leaders who react defensively when personally challenged.

3. Personalize the content. While the leaders are not responsible for all the input, it is important for the leaders to share examples from their own lives, especially examples of struggle rather than a series of "success stories."

Beginning each session with a personal example personalizes the theme, lightens the atmosphere, establishes some credibility, and enables participants to relate more personally with the leaders.

Sharing our brokenness and failures with participants helps them to relate more honestly with the content and with one another.

4. Move from awareness to concern to action. PPJ is more than a consciousness-raising program for families. It is designed to lead to action to change those situations and structures that hurt people, that undermine family life, that frustrate the further realization of *shalom* in our world. Because our experience has shown that people generally move from awareness to action on a sustained basis to the extent that they develop a growing sense of concern, PPJ programs include this middle element.

We promote this desire to act in a number of ways, four in particular: (1) by allowing ourselves and others to be touched by the lives of the victims of injustice and war and also (2) by the lives of those taking risks in working for change; (3) by allowing ourselves and others to experience the call to action as a call from our God; and (4) by providing for ourselves and others a community of people who support and challenge us to act consistently and courageously.

5. Encourage a variety of action options. The action goal of PPJ is broadly defined. Individuals and families are at different points and what is appropriate for one person or family is not necessarily appropriate for others. The range of suggestions includes:

- actions of direct service as well as social or structural change;

- actions that focus on local issues as well as global issues, or on both the local and global dimensions of the same issue;

- actions in the home as well as in the community and larger world. Because action is so essential, we build into PPJ programs opportunities to act on the spot rather than wait until returning home. This tends to give participants more satisfaction, reinforces the importance of action, and generates a sense of solidarity among the group.

6. Make decisions within sessions. Similarly, our experience has shown that participants are more likely to make and implement action decisions if they are made during the sessions themselves. We encourage taking the last five or ten minutes of each

session, before the concluding reflection, for each participant or family group to decide on their next step regarding the issue being considered. With family groups, this means having a "mini" family meeting. Personal and family decisions should be written down and put in the "Shalom Box" (see Worksheet 1 below) or recorded in some other way, for example,

on individual "hands" (see p. 26 below), written and kept in an envelope, or logged in a personal journal.

7. Provide a process. The PPJ programs focus on specific issues, but always from the point of view of their impact on families and how families can address these issues.

The issues have included peace, cooperation, and conflict resolution in the home; helping children deal with the violence in the world around them and with the threat of nuclear war; racism and developing healthy racial attitudes in children; sexism and counteracting sex-role stereotyping within the family; stereotyping of other groups in society, for example, the elderly, people with disabilities; stewardship and helping children deal with materialism and peer pressure; developing a concrete sense of the global family.

Other issues are also frequently addressed in PPJ programs: peace and the arms race, media violence and consumerism, food and hunger. Further, the PPJN newsletter addresses itself to issues like domestic violence, multicultural celebrations, and participation in the electoral process.

But the primary concern in PPJ is not to mobilize families around specific issues; rather it is to provide families with a process and the necessary tools for acting consistently and courageously about whatever issues concern them.

8. Encourage family support groups. Individuals and individual families are empowered to action, in large part, when they come together with others. Children as well as adults need peer support; they need to see these values lived out in other families, to know that others struggle with simpler living, with more nutritious eating, with more constructive uses of television, with nonsexist family patterns, with multiracial and multicultural living.

The long-term goal of PPJ is the formation of family support groups — regularly coming together with other families for discussion of PPJ values, for joint action, for prayer and worship, for celebration and play, for sharing resources and talents. Guidelines and models for the formation of family support groups are described below (pp. 64–71).

9. Reflect and pray. Our experience has convinced us that, in large measure, people find the inspiration and courage to act for peace and justice through their personal relationship with their God.

Silent reflection and group prayer are essential to PPJ programs. But because participants often come from a variety of faith or ethical traditions, we consider it equally important to pray out of a wide range of such traditions.

Two excellent sources for such diversity of prayer and worship services are *Peacemaking Day-by-Day* (Pax Christi USA, 348 E. 10th St., Erie, PA 16503), a book of meditations on peacemaking from numerous sources, and *More Than Words: Prayer and Ritual for Inclusive Communities* (Meyer-Stone Books, 2014 S. Yost Ave., Bloomington, IN 47403), a collection of prayer services incorporating inclusive images, language from a variety of cultural traditions, and social concerns.

To promote personal reflection during PPJ programs, we encourage participants to bring and use a journal. Mary Joan Park suggests distributing to children what she calls "Just Me Notebooks." These are notebooks with pockets and 3-ring clips that children can decorate (for example, a symbol on the front cover that says something about themselves). The notebook serves as a binder for papers used during the program as well as a diary for thoughts, feelings, questions, and drawings. See also chapter 9 below, "Worship Suggestions."

10. Pay attention to feelings. A journal is an excellent way for participants to be in touch with their feelings. It is also helpful to provide time for the participants to share their feelings aloud. This gives the leaders as well as the rest of the group a sense of where people are.

To avoid lengthy statements, invite participants to describe their feelings in one word, for example, exhausted, scared, excited, hopeful, angry, sad, anxious.

It is also helpful for participants to reflect on their feelings "in pairs" after input that stirs their emotions. This is especially true when audio-visuals challenge, threaten, or inspire participants. Sharing in pairs, even if just for a minute or two, often diffuses feelings that, if expressed to the whole group, could dominate group discussion time.

Guidelines for Intergenerational Programs

1. Provide a mix of activities. Each person has a different learning style. Some learn best through visual experiences, others through words or auditory experiences, others through tactile or manual experiences. Everyone is enriched by a variety of learning experiences. Few people get bored when programs incorporate such variety. This is especially true in intergenerational programs, where the key is to keep the children interested and involved.

We recommend a balance of substantive input, craft activities, small and large group discussions, silent reflection, group prayer, outside time, play time, free time, singing, humor, "talent show" time, story time, and ample sleep and eating time.

Activities that engage all family members together, particularly activities where adults and children are both learning — for example, learning to make origami paper peace cranes (see Worksheet 15) — are essential. So are times and activities in which different age groups meet separately — adults, teens, children.

2. Don't overprogram the content. The greatest temptation for PPJ program leaders is to try to squeeze in too much. Limit the number of issues. Allow open time for reflection and play.

While the number of activities described in this guide enables leaders and families to spend days on each theme, tailor the number and type of activities to the needs of your group or family. Start with the issues most relevant to the participants. Sample formats and issue combinations are provided in chapter 3.

3. Share leadership. It is impossible for one leader to meet the expectations of adults, teens, and children. Team leadership provides different teaching styles. A balance of male and female leaders is important. Sharing leadership roles with as many participants as possible, including children and teens, is equally important. Such roles include song leaders, readers, MCs for talent shows, distributors of hand-outs, operators of audio-visual equipment, worship leaders, helpers with younger participants, game organizers, storytellers.

Even in terms of the program content, it is important to have participants serve as resources for one another. Leaders should more often throw questions back to the whole group rather than answer questions themselves. Participants can display or describe resources they have found helpful on tables or newsprint.

4. Beware of leadership training in your programs. Sometimes groups want a leadership training component in the program in addition to family enrichment. Adults will be challenged by the program content itself. Since they are also trying to pay attention to the needs of their children, it will be difficult to add a third component. Difficult, but not impossible. Chapter 3 discusses how to add this dimension.

5. Meet the needs of four age-groups simultaneously. This is the real challenge of intergenerational programs. Adults, teens, "over-6's," and "under 6's" have very different needs and expectations. Besides the mix of activities recommended above, separate time for each group is essential.

"Under 6's." For the most part, all children under 5 or 6 should be in child care during the content sessions. If an occasional activity involves preschoolers, then adults can be given the option to include their preschoolers. If mothers are breast-feeding, they should be assured that their children's presence is not discouraged. Generally, however, parents should be strongly encouraged to place their preschoolers in child care.

Child-care workers should be competent, adequate in number, and have appropriate programs for the different age groups in their care. These programs should integrate the themes of the overall program. Several samples are provided in chapter 12 below. Parents should be encouraged to suggest changes in the child-care arrangements if the planned arrangements are not helpful to their children.

"Over 6's." Elementary school-aged participants need a mix of activities and need to have their time with adults in content sessions move quickly. Strategies that have worked well over the years include:

- having drawing, coloring, and construction materials readily available on a side table;

- having a "peace book" or "peace toy" table and a corner of the room for children to visit or borrow from;

- having nutritious and tasty snacks available during mid-morning and mid-afternoon breaks;

- having place mats for meals or "peace game" sheets that offer children creative alternatives to listening during content sessions;

- having leaders speak in language that children understand; speak to the children directly, engage them in problem-solving situations, invite their reactions first before turning to adults and teens;

- using images, visuals, and phrases that will stand out and be remembered; recall these images throughout the program, for example, "Jumping Mouse" as an example of discipleship (see p. 25), an inflatable globe or "hug-a-planet" earth ball (see p. 36), a theme song like "We've Got the Whole World in Our Hands," the "Peace Pal" Bunny (see p. 37) and North American and Russian Bears (see p. 39), cut-out hands for "helping hands" (see p. 26), a chant as a definition of stewardship (see p. 46, no. 2), a light bulb attached to a handle as an imitation microphone when soliciting "bright ideas" from participants during brainstorming sessions;

- incorporating puppets, stories, or a clown into the content sessions;

- using songs that include motions;

- pairing each child with an adult or teen (but not someone from the child's own family) for occasional activities, for example, reading a story together;

- trying to end one-day programs at 3:00 p.m.

Teens. Teens are probably the toughest group to satisfy, for several reasons. First of all there are differences in maturity between 12- and 13-year-olds and 17- and 18-year-olds. Second, teens will often find present only one or two other participants their own age. Some are reluctantly present and often have no idea what to expect. Many are self-conscious and are going through stages of adolescence that can occasion attitudes and behavior not always helpful. On the other hand, teens are often wonderful participants with a lot to add to PPJ programs. Some strategies for eliciting their cooperation and behavior include:

- providing ample social time, particularly after evening activities, during which they can interact in informal and enjoyable ways;

- providing good audio-visuals for both content sessions and after-session times, for example, films like *Amazing Grace and Chuck* or *Karate Kid II* offering a wonderful image of nonviolence and "enemy love" as well as of Japanese culture; rock-videos for discussion-starters (the PPJN has a video presentation entitled "Videos and Values" that can be rented);

- having teens meet one another as a separate group as early as possible in the program;

- focusing this initial meeting on teens sharing expectations (and worries, doubts, fears) they might have concerning this program; include enjoyable ice-breakers; allow the teens to introduce themselves in creative ways, for example, through the "peace book" they each brought, or as the kind of animal or color each thinks would best symbolize him or herself;

- providing leadership opportunities during the program and explaining these at the initial meeting, asking for volunteers but giving them the opportunity to consider the possibilities and decide later. These leadership roles could include reading stories or reading at worship, assisting an "over 6" participant or group during "adult time," leading music, MC-ing the talent show, teaching or leading a cooperative game, handling logistical responsibilities such as campfire starting, setting up AV equipment, assisting with meal preparation or recreation equipment distribution. Solicit the teens' gifts, the talents they are willing to share during the program;

- having something for teens to read during the program and being prepared to discuss the material; introduce them, via this reading, to written resources they can continue to use after the program, for example, articles in magazines like *The Other Side, Sojourners, Salt, Ebony, Jr.*

- during content sessions, mixing adult-teen small group discussions with some teen-only groups;

- assuring teens, in a pre-program mailing to all participants, that there will be activities specifically geared to their needs and interests; let them know the number of other teens to expect;

- involving some teens in the planning of the program itself in order to increase the likelihood of its meeting their needs.

Further tips have come to us from Canada:

- Although many teens are interested in issues and very involved with the peace movement, the United Farm Workers movement, and other peace and justice related activities, teens need more than issues to attract them to a community. They are attracted largely by social involvement with others of their own age group.

- Teens are very connected to music, so having both live and taped music throughout the week-

end is a powerful attraction. Music can provide a wonderful background for the entire weekend. Opening each session with live music in which everyone can participate and having music to wake people up in the morning and in the background during mealtimes are ways in which not only teens, but everyone, is made to feel relaxed.

- In the opening session, it is effective to have some type of dramatic presentation, usually comic, based on the theme of the weekend. This is a good way to introduce a theme and to "break the ice."

- In planning a weekend where teens are involved, it must be recognized that there has to be a partially separate program for teens alone. This does not mean excluding teens from the regular program but recognizing that, if workshops are being given, one or two must be especially attractive, but not exclusive, to young people. One way to do this is to have teens do the workshop. After the opening session, it is beneficial to take teens aside and outline their program.

- Teens must be directly incorporated into every aspect of planning the weekend. They have perceptions and energy that can often revitalize a program. Also, when teens are involved in planning a weekend, they can set an example and get other teens to participate.

- Co-op games, which introduce the teens to one another and allow them to have fun, give the weekend a good start (see pp. 32–35). Organized sports are popular, but cooperative sports help build a community atmosphere and will make youths more receptive to the core themes.

- Other activities popular among teens are T-shirt painting, tie-dying, and leather craft. All you have to do is set up a table with some leather, sharp scissors, and beads and materials for bracelets, anklets, and other trinkets. Lay out some dyes in buckets, provide lots of rubber bands or string, and non-aerosol spray paint. Since each T-shirt comes out differently, the teens express their individuality. But they also share an activity with the rest of the group. This can occupy youth for hours while adults are in sessions or workshops elsewhere.

- One of the best ways to attract all ages is a dance. A well-chosen selection of music that pleases both young and old can be the highlight of a weekend.

- Finally, since teens are social beings, provision must be made for them to interact. Lots of free time should be provided and an atmosphere formed that allows them to go on long walks and to talk and form relationships. They might be allowed to stay up all night if they wish. So they don't disturb others, provide a place where they can go. For teens, the relationships they form are often more important than the weekend itself.

Adults. While our experience has shown that if their children are satisfied with the program, the parents will also be satisfied, there are some additional strategies that increase adults' satisfaction. These include:

- providing at least 30 minutes of "adults only" time, toward the end of each content session, for extended discussion of the theme (large-group discussion time when children are present has to be quite short);

- providing small-group discussion options according to similar family situations — parents of primarily preschoolers, parents of primarily teens, single parents, adults not parenting at home, etc.

- providing as much information as is possible ahead of time, especially about accommodations and what to bring (the less parents are taken by surprise, the better);

- soliciting ahead of time any dietary, child-care, or accessibility needs;

- making it as easy as possible for the whole family to participate, for example, providing child care for preschoolers, giving price breaks for additional family members (see p. 17, no. 3);

- making sure whole families can sleep together (one family camp group "revolted" when it turned out that the cabins were divided into "males only" and "females only"!).

CHAPTER 3

Program Planning and Preparation

From trial and error, we and other leaders have learned the importance of the guidelines and strategies that follow.

These cover a range of concerns, from the formation of the planning team itself up to the last-minute details of the preparation and the arrival of the participants. The success of any intergenerational program has at least as much to do with the thoroughness of the preparation as it does with the experience of the program itself.

Planning Team

1. Recruit a broadly-based team. No one person or couple can do it alone. But more than just additional members are needed. The team should represent a diversity of age groups. One or two teen representatives can help ensure the program's relevance for teens. An ecumenically diverse team is preferable to a single-denomination team. If the program is open to a geographically diverse population, the make-up of the team should reflect this diversity as well.

2. Recruit a committed team. "Committed" should mean at least the following:

- team members should each take some area of responsibility (for example, music, worship, finances, liaison with the program leaders, child care, registration, accommodations and food, publicity — including brochures, news releases, mailings);

- team members member should commit themselves to a specific recruitment goal, for example, ten participants from each member's denomination;

- team members should be committed to participating in the program itself. This significantly enhances follow-up to the program.

3. Select an overall coordinator. No matter how committed team members are, no team functions well without an overall coordinator for the meetings, the person to whom other members report between meetings, the one who "holds things together."

Program Focus

1. Choose between family enrichment only or family enrichment plus leadership training. As mentioned above, adding a leadership training component is difficult but not impossible. Generally, leadership training within an intergenerational format is limited to the following:

- conducting the sessions as a model that participants can adapt for their own group;

- providing leadership resources for interested participants (for example, copies of this guide, leadership membership in the PPJ Network, access to the *Building Shalom Families* video program; see p. 149).

- taking the last half-hour of each session or an hour in the open afternoons of a several-day program for leaders to explain why they did what they did, what they might do differently in different settings, the content of the various leadership resources; give time for the leadership training participants to comment or ask questions about the sessions, to suggest resources and strategies of their own, and to explain how they have conducted or might conduct a similar session.

This additional time also requires additional child care to free parents to participate. Leadership training requires program leaders who are competent as trainers as well as leaders of a family enrichment program. Consult the PPJN office for a list of such leader-trainers.

2. Focus first on participants' felt needs. Generally, this means the following sessions: at least some of "Families in Search of Shalom" (chapter 4), "Shalom in the Home" (chapter 5), "Consumerism and Stewardship" (chapter 7), and often some aspects of "Shalom in the Global Family" (chapter 6). The more that participants feel their needs have been met, especially in the "Shalom in the Home" session, the less resistant they tend to be toward some of the other, potentially more threatening, issues.

3. Don't attempt too much, especially in an initial program. Limit the length of your initial program: one day instead of two days, or a series of three or four sessions instead of six or seven sessions. Call your initial program "Part I," if you wish. People are less resistant to shorter programs. A relatively safe "Part I" can give hesitant participants a taste of what you and PPJ are all about, can establish a level of trust in you as program leader, can expose them to the benefits of a group experience, and can thereby lay the foundation for their going further into the PPJ themes.

At the conclusion of a "Part I" PPJ program, invite participants to a follow-up "Part II" program. This might be a second whole day or series for the same group. If so, invite potential participants to identify those PPJ themes not yet covered, or not sufficiently covered, that they would like to see as the focus of the program. As much as possible, design this second program according to the participants' needs.

4. Use an effective title. "Parenting for Peace and Justice" has generally not proven to be an effective title. "Parenting" tends to limit the range of adult participants. "Nurturing children," on the other hand, suggests a broader range: teachers, social workers, grandparents, aunts and uncles, and youth ministers all nurture children and would benefit from such a program.

"Peace and justice" generally scares away all but the already committed. Unfortunately, these words raise red flags for many. On the other hand, listing the specific topics or themes (see chapter titles in this guide), or putting them in question form, can be quite effective. For example,

> "Adults, do you want to reduce conflict at home, to help children deal with violence or the pressures of consumerism, to develop healthy racial attitudes in children, to help children become caring persons, to make a difference in the world...then you will want to participate in our ——— program."

More generic titles have included the following:

- "Nurturing Children in a World of Conflict"
- "Developing Caring Families"
- "Families Peace-ing It Together"
- "Becoming Peacemaking Families"
- "Families Making a Difference"
- "Peacemaking at Home and in the Church, Community, and World"

Program Format Options

As pointed out above, the program format should be tailored to the needs of participants. For an initial program, shorter rather than longer is generally more attractive and thus more effective. The themes and activities described in this guide have been used in a variety of settings and with different lengths of time. Any number of combinations is possible. Program planners should consider the strengths of the leaders and resource persons and the needs and interests of participants. Some of the more effective combinations of themes and formats are the following (see pp. 97–99 for a sample schedule):

1. One-day program at a church or community center. The most effective combinations have been a morning on "Shalom in the Home" (chapter 5) and the afternoon on either "Shalom in the Global Family" (chapter 6) or "Consumerism and Stewardship" (chapter 7).

2. Weekend at a church or community setting or a family camp. If the setting is a family camp, then the program should be intergenerational throughout.

Friday evening can focus on the introductory theme of "Families in Search of Shalom" (chapter 4), with Saturday morning on "Shalom in the Home" (chapter 5). Depending on the needs and interests of the group, Saturday afternoon can either be free for fun (see chapter 11) or can be focused on all or part of "Shalom in the Global Family" (chapter 6).

But much of this theme can be the focus of the evening meal and program afterward, thus freeing the afternoon for fun. Sunday morning can complete "Shalom in the Global Family," but generally "Consumerism and Stewardship" fits better there. "Where Do We Go from Here?" (chapter 10) can be part of the noon meal or one or two hours afterward.

3. Three- to five-day family camp. These longer experiences allow more flexibility and time for more of the "lighter elements." In order to accommodate participants who cannot take much time from work, some programs have devoted the first day to fun and begun the formal program the second evening. Also, this longer format makes the additional leadership training component less difficult.

4. A series of one- to three-hour sessions. Many options are possible here. A series of Sunday school classes, even if only one hour each, can cover as

many themes as participants and leaders desire. But keep in mind the "Part I, Part II" recommendations above. A series of Sunday or evening potluck suppers and sessions has been a popular and generally effective format. This is especially true in Christian churches during Lent or Advent, when church members are accustomed to faith enrichment programs. Other leaders have found a series of after-school sessions on peacemaking at home or cooperative games an effective format for younger children and parents.

Recruitment Strategies

1. Choose an appealing title (see p. 14, no. 4).

2. Build an effective list of potential participants. This is done in several ways. First, any time you make an initial presentation on PPJ or any of its themes, be sure to distribute copies of the "Interest Form" to participants (Worksheet 34 below). Collect and collate these forms.

Second, offer to make initial presentations on PPJ, or extended announcements about PPJ resources and programs, to already constituted groups at one of their regularly scheduled meetings. The *Families in Search of Shalom* filmstrip (10 minutes) is an especially effective resource for a short preparation. Part or all of the video cassette "Phil Donahue Show on PPJ" (45 minutes) is also quite appealing. PTO's (Parent Teacher Organizations), PET (Parent Effectiveness Training), or STEP (Systematic Training in Effective Parenting) groups, Marriage Encounter groups, Renew groups, adult Sunday school or Bible study groups and social concern groups, are all good places to recruit.

Third, contact the PPJN office for the names of the nearest local PPJN coordinator and of leaders and members of the PPJN in your area.

3. Get commitments from planning team members — and start early. As mentioned above (p. 13, no. 2), specific recruiting goals for each team member are crucial. Beginning the recruiting six to nine months before the program is not too soon, especially if it involves nurturing relationships with local church or community leaders who are not familiar with PPJ.

4. Recruit in person rather than through the mail. Mailing thousands of flyers will generally net only a handful of participants. There is no substitute for personal contact. Visit church and community leaders and educators, show the filmstrip, or leave copies of the pamphlet *Nurturing Children in a World of Conflict* or the book *Parenting for Peace and Justice* (both available from the Institute for Peace and Justice). Ask each leader to recruit a team from their church or group or at least give you the names of others who would do this or the names of possible participants themselves. Visits and phone calls to these persons are essential. Follow-up calls or mailings (of the program brochure and other PPJ pamphlets and booklets) are generally necessary.

5. Get denominational sponsorship. Team members should get their own denomination or group to sponsor the program. This can mean

- advertising the program in bulletins or newsletters, mailing program brochures, announcing the program at appropriate gatherings, having the group's name listed on all program publicity;

- getting a commitment to recruit a specific number of members from the group;

- getting a financial commitment to the program, either as an outright grant to cover costs or scholarships for participants from that denomination or group. Getting these sponsorships should be done at least six months before the program, if at all possible.

If denominational representatives are not familiar with PPJ, the "Religious Principles" for PPJ (pp. 2–4 above) is a good piece to share, along with the pamphlet *Nurturing Children in a World of Conflict.* Also, contact the PPJ office for the names of the representatives of the appropriate denominations that serve on the PPJN board of advisors. These representatives can not only legitimate the PPJ program but may also help with funding.

6. Contact the PPJN office for sample brochures and resources. In addition to names of local PPJN leaders and members and of PPJN denominational representatives, the PPJN office can provide sample program brochures and a variety of written and audio-visual resources. These resources can be used in recruiting and they can be sold during the program. Consignment purchases can be negotiated.

7. Make sure that participants know what to expect. This includes an appropriate title and description of the program (see p. 14, no. 4 above). Also it can be helpful for participants to read the "PPJ Assumptions" ahead of time (see pp. 1–2). If the program includes a leadership training component,

we have found it very helpful to have these persons read the book *Parenting for Peace and Justice.* Further, especially if the program is in a family camp setting, participants need to know what the facilities are like and what to bring (everything from sleeping gear to mosquito repellent). We suggest having the participants bring the following, but the list can vary according to themes addressed and preparation and participation encouraged:

- a Bible for personal use as well as for use during sessions;

- a "peace toy" or "peace book" from each child or family member (favorite toys or books that promote *shalom* in some way);

- a family "Shalom Box" (see Worksheet 1);

- other helpful peacemaking resources the participants want to share;

- musical instruments or other materials for a talent show and campfires;

- construction supplies (for example, scissors, magazines) that will be needed beyond what the planning team can provide;

- information or display materials about peace and justice groups that participants want to promote during the program.

8. Make sure the leaders and planners know what to expect. Design the brochure to solicit at least the following information and share the data with the program leaders far enough in advance to assist their preparation (one or two weeks is generally sufficient):

- the ages of the children coming and the number who will require child care;

- special dietary or medical needs;

- accessibility needs (for persons with disabilities) or communication needs (for persons with hearing impairments or persons speaking a language other than English).

9. Keep costs for participants as low as possible. Denominational grants and participant scholarships are the key for weekends or longer programs where outside leaders are brought in. Asking participants to bring snacks or potluck meals can reduce costs.

Costs can also be reduced by housing out-of-town participants in local homes if the program is conducted at a non-resident facility.

Finances

1. Denominational or community group sponsorship and scholarship support. Incentives to denominations are often helpful, for example, a set of the PPJ resources for a $300 to $500 contribution, a commitment from a church-sponsored team to help conduct at least one PPJ program for the church or group.

2. Materials fee. Often it is helpful to provide all participants with a set of PPJ publications as well as workshop handouts. PPJ participants are also offered first-year membership in the PPJN for only $5 per family (see pp. 63–64 below). For leadership training, a copy of each of the leader resources is essential. These can be purchased at a group discount from the PPJN office.

3. Family and team incentives. As a way of encouraging whole families to participate, fees for spouses and children should be less than for individual participants (for example, $15 per person, $20 per couple, $5 each for children, maximum $30 per family). Similarly, teams coming from the same church or community group could be offered the same discount. Promoting "team" participation increases the likelihood that participants will do something with the program afterward (see the sample publicity letter, p. 81).

Environment

1. Appropriate setting. An adequate play area, areas of natural beauty, and attractive or comfortable facilities and furnishings do make a difference. Areas of natural beauty — even if only a flower garden — enhance the experience, particularly in relation to worship and to the "global family" and "stewardship" themes. Outdoor space for some activities provides a welcome change from indoor confinement. Children especially need ample space to run and burn off their pent-up energy.

2. Adequate and comfortable meeting space. A series of sessions for a small group could be conducted in participants' homes. For a larger group, however, the following elements are essential:

- one large room for most of the sessions, with enough space for tables with 4–10 chairs around each table;

- enough blank wall space for hanging murals and sheets of newsprint;

- enough space for several display tables (for "peace books," "peace toys," material for sale, participants' own resources) and for a "peace toy" and "peace book" area (for play and reading);

- an additional room (two, if possible) for dividing the group into adults, teens, and children, for separate activities;

- the possibility of darkening the rooms for audio-visuals;

- an area for drinks and snacks;

- an area that can serve as a stage for the talent show, pantomiming, or puppetry;

- a worship area where murals can be built or displayed (a chapel or sanctuary can be used for worship, but most of the prayer and worship needs to be where the murals are);

- child-care facilities near enough to be convenient but far enough away that preschoolers do not disturb the sessions by crying or running in to get their parents whenever they want;

- all rooms accessible to people with disabilities.

3. Satisfactory sleeping and eating arrangements.
Participants of all ages are more likely to be satisfied
if their sleeping and eating needs are taken care of.
This can mean:

- whole families staying together in the same
  cabin or quarters;

- when pairing or clustering participants, putting
  together those with like-aged children or with
  other similarities (for example, putting disabled
  persons closer to the bathroom and other facilities);

- ending the program early enough in the evenings
  so that younger children can be put to bed on
  time, providing nap time during the day for
  those needing it, encouraging older participants
  to get adequate rest, being sensitive to those who
  do not sleep well the first evening (which often
  happens at family camps);

- modelling nutritious and ecologically sound eating practices (for example, alternatives to meat),
  but also providing food that is — at least somewhat! — appealing to participants, especially
  teens and children who are not completely comfortable with "alternative diets"; options like
  multiple ingredients for making salads or sandwiches generally work well;

- if assistance is required for preparing and cleaning up after meals, rotating helpers so that everyone contributes; if assistance in meal preparation includes cooking, having different groups
  prepare special meals as a way of bonding within
  these groups (for example, a teen-prepared meal
  or a Latino-prepared meal).

Worship and Music

See p. 8 (no. 9) and chapter 9 for principles and
examples of prayer and worship; see the thematic
chapters (4–8) for specific music suggestions. See
also Lola Mavor's Australian program (p. 97, no. 7)
for a process for creating worship by the participants
themselves.

Program Supplies

While assembling the following items takes time and
increases program costs, these items make enough
difference in the quality of the program to be worth
the extra cost and effort. If planning starts early
enough, many of the items can be borrowed or ob-
tained free. Waiting until the last minute stifles creativity and reduces options.

1. Construction materials.

- Specific activities require specific materials, but
  strips of colored construction paper are useful
  for various activities, as are materials for creative building by children during sessions; extra
  whole sheets of construction paper are also useful.

- Scissors, tape (scotch or masking), crayons or
  marking pens, and glue are all necessary. If a
  pair of scissors for each participant is not feasible, ask participants to bring their own.

- Sheets of newsprint are essential for each participant or family, as well as for leaders, to post
  agendas, build murals, and make posters and petitions.

- Have a table for supplies in the main meeting room so that the materials are accessible
  throughout the program.

- Shoe boxes can be provided for participants
  who did not bring their own "Shalom Box" (see
  Worksheet 1).

2. Magazines. Participants can be asked to bring
their own magazines if activities require multiple
magazines, but program planners can supplement
these with:

- magazines like *Sojourners, The Other Side,
  Maryknoll, Salt,* to encourage ongoing reading
  by participants;

- magazines with ads for critique in several sessions (for example, consumerism, militarism,
  sexism);

- magazines with pictures or stories about our
  global family and people from other countries
  or cultures.

3. Audio-visuals and equipment. The sessions described in this guide make considerable use of audio-visuals. Reserving those chosen for a program is best done several months in advance to assure their availability. Contact the PPJN office for a list of what is available through them. Keep the following suggestions in mind:

- When a VCR is required, make sure the TV monitor is large enough for all to see; sometimes more than one monitor is needed (if the group numbers more than 100 and many cannot be bunched closely in front).

- make sure all the equipment has been tested and is working; have back-up equipment, at least bulbs, readily available;

- have additional audio-visuals, especially videos, available in case bad weather eliminates outdoor activities or for late afternoon or evening viewing.

4. Worksheets, pamphlets, packets. Having a packet for each participant or family with all the worksheets, pamphlets, and other written resources is a helpful extra. These packets can double as containers for other handouts, purchases, and reflection sheets.

5. Roster and schedule. If a program schedule is not included in the program brochure, it needs to be printed for each packet. Having as complete a list as possible of participants (names, addresses, phone numbers, and church affiliation) in the packet when people register helps participants to get to know each other. This also increases the likelihood of continued contact after the program.

6. Name tags. Creative options for name tags are numerous. Participants should create their own name tags as they register. One effective version has been a 4″ × 6″ piece of construction paper and a pin. Each participant is asked to add other items besides their name to their name tag — for example, where they live, a peacemaker they admire, a group with whom they have a special affiliation, their favorite movie or book in the last month or year, their favorite main dish or dessert or ice cream flavor. These can be developed throughout the program — for example, the first night put the funnier items on the front side; the second day, turn it over and add

some of the more serious items (as the people in the group get to know one another). Remind participants to keep their name tags on whenever possible; this increases opportunities for participants to get to know one another.

7. Resources for display and sale. Besides encouraging participants and leaders to bring resources they have found helpful, planners can get PPJ sources on consignment from the PPJN office. Also, local peace and justice groups and progressive bookstores often have appropriate resources and welcome the opportunity to have them available at a PPJ program.

Arrival and Welcoming Suggestions

If planning team members and program leaders have prepared ahead of time, they can be more available to focus on the participants as they arrive. Feeling

welcomed makes a significant difference in participants' attitude toward the whole program. Welcoming suggestions include the following:

1. Arrival time. Make sure there is ample time for participants to register, move in (if overnight accommodations), get their children settled (if child care is required), and catch their breath before the opening session.

2. Packets with rosters at the registration table (see above p. 19, no. 5).

3. Greeting. There must be people to greet people. Always have a smile, handshake, or hug if appropriate; be helpful and understanding of the needs of those arriving. Help them to unload their cars, give friendly directions for parking, help set up their tents, show them how to register, direct them to their rooms, post a note of welcome on each family's door, have a piece of fruit on each participant's bed. In short, show by your actions that you are glad that they are there and that participants are indeed welcome. All too often, people are left to fend for themselves. Often they are unsure, somewhat confused, and take a "let's see what's happening" attitude. Teenagers especially need to be assured that they are genuinely welcome.

4. Music. Play taped music during the welcome and registration period. Once participants are assembled, music is a good way to break down barriers. No meeting should start without it. Naturally, the music should be happy, perhaps related to a theme, and fairly well known.

5. Name Tags. There is no nicer sound than your own name. It's like music. It is therefore essential that people in a group setting be able to see a name so that a greeting can easily be extended in a personal way. Accordingly, ensure that at registration a name tag, or the materials to make one, are prepared and handed to the participant. Be sure that at least the first names are written large enough and clearly enough for people to read them at a short distance (also see above p. 19, no. 6).

6. Opening meal. Starting after dinner is appropriate if there is significant financial or logistic reason, but generally programs work better if the first activity is a meal. This allows participants more time to get settled in and begin to know one another. Also, the opening meal can be the time for announcements and participant introductions; this reduces the amount of time necessary for the opening session.

7. MCs (Leaders, Facilitators). Participants need to know what is going on or what happens next. This information "sharing" should be done by session leaders or MCs in a positive way. This can be done, for example, by posting ongoing announcements or written agenda on the wall. Always make sure that there is a specific person available to answer questions.

CHAPTER 4

Introductory Session:
Families in Search of Shalom

While components of this session could be incorporated into the morning session of a one-day program, usually the session introduces a weekend, other multiple-day programs, or a series of three or more sessions.

As with subsequent chapters, the format here provides several options for each theme. We begin with how we (the McGinnises) have most recently presented each component. There follow alternatives that other PPJ program leaders have used. Footnotes identify these leaders. Chapter 13 provides further description of their programs.

Lola Mavor presents a quite different model for the entire opening session, in which she organizes "extended families" that work together throughout the entire program (see chapter 14).

Goals

In the opening session, the biblical basis for PPJ is shared: God's promise of *shalom* and God's call to us to be agents of that *shalom*. Participants are put in touch with their own experiences of *shalom* and with God's working in their lives.

This is also a time for participants to meet each other, for them to share their own experiences and understanding of *shalom*, and for the group to have fun together. All the activities are designed to build a sense of hopefulness, of community, of playfulness, and of prayerfulness.

Components

1. GATHERING SONG OR GAME

As a way of calling participants together and energizing the group, have the music leader lead some singing, simple songs that most know. A quick cooperative game could also be played, especially for early or on-time arrivals (see pp. 32–35 for some possibilities).

2. CREATIVE INTRODUCTIONS

Even before introducing the program content and goals, we want people to introduce themselves in an enjoyable, engaging way. For example:

Finding Partners: Especially if the name tags have been made as suggested (see above p. 19, no. 6), have all participants move about the area (in the main meeting room, outdoors, or in the eating area, if that is where everyone can most conveniently assemble), finding other participants who fit the following categories called out by the leader. Allow one or two minutes for each category, asking participants to introduce themselves to whomever they find that fits the category. The categories can include someone:

- whose first name begins with the same letter as yours;
- who lives within 10 miles, or further than 50 miles, from you;
- who likes the same flavor ice cream;
- who liked the same movie;
- whose peacemaker you have never heard of;

- who is the same size as you;

- who is the same age as you;

- who has the same colored hair (shirt, shoes, etc.).

Personal Trees: As a variation on "Finding Partners," have participants prepare as follows. Pass out sheets of paper and colored pencils. Ask each person (regardless of age, children under three or four may wish to assist parents) to draw a tree that has some special significance to them. Then each person draws five decorations on the branches of the tree. These decorations should be symbols of things that are important in their lives or tell something about them. Participants then share with their partners why they chose their tree and symbols.[1]

Values Clarification: Adults and older youth gather after the little ones are settled in. In an informal gathering around the fireplace or another focal point

explain the values clarification game. Beginning with simple decisions, give the total group choices on specific topics. In the beginning, they are simply asked to raise their hands if they like one answer or the other. As the time goes on, have them get up and move to one side of the room, or, if they are undecided, to place themselves along the space between the two extremes. Design the choices to fit the group and the local and national issues. For example, participants make a choice for:

---

[1]From "Family Church Camps"; see below, p. 84.

- apples or oranges

- picnic on the beach or dinner in an elegant restaurant

- mountain climbing or walking on the beach

- mandatory seat belts or not

- optional military taxes or not

Each side might develop a statement as to why they feel the way they do. After each controversial issue the groups can be divided so that three or four from each opposing group get together and share their views.[2]

3. WHOLE FAMILY INTRODUCTIONS

As an alternative to whole group introductions, if the group is large, families could limit themselves to introductions among two or three other families. Such introductions can be done in several ways:

Shalom Box: Each family explains the various items in their Shalom Box, if they've been asked to prepare this prior to the program (Worksheet 1). At this time you might explain the purposes of the Shalom Box for the program. Not only is it a way for participants to introduce themselves but it also serves as a reminder of our all being agents of God's *shalom,* as a reminder to pray for *shalom,* as a centerpiece for our worktables and dinner table, and as a container for items constructed during the program as well as for ideas and decisions to follow up on.

Peace Books, Peace Toys: Each family member describes his or her "peace book" or "peace toy."

Time Capsule: Each family writes or draws something that explains what their family is like to people in the future or people from another planet. Use large newsprint. One person in each family shares their family time capsule with the group. A large decorated box can be made beforehand and labeled "Time Capsule"; each family puts their picture in the box after they talk about it.[3]

Centerpiece: Each family brings something that can be used as a centerpiece that helps tell more about

---

[2]From "Family Church Camps"; see below, p. 84.

[3]From "Events on Cooperation and Competition"; see below, p. 83.

the family: a symbol of a special vacation, a family memory, a special hobby, another country or group with whom they are linked.[4]

Family Name or Crest: Read the information about family surnames on Worksheet 6. The families fill in the Family Certificate, adding information on the meaning of each family member's first name. Parents share information about their surname. Has it changed through the years? In what country did it originate? Locate the country on a map or globe. Parents share with their children how they chose their names. Draw a family crest on the bottom of Worksheet 5. This could also be done at home after the program.[5]

4. GOD'S PROMISE OF SHALOM

We communicate this component first through visuals, then through Scripture, and finally through participants' own pictures, ideas, and sayings.

Visual Biblical Reflection: Leaders select visuals (slides or pictures) to illustrate each line of Walter Brueggemann's reading on *shalom* (see Worksheet 3). Or use the themes that emerge from the Shalom Box descriptions (see Worksheet 1). Project slides on a screen or use a flashlight to highlight each picture on a shalom mural or banner prepared ahead of time. The mural or banner can be expanded by participants. This AV reflection is included in the *Building Shalom Families* video program (see p. 149) and as a filmstrip/cassette tape in the *Hope Springs from God* program (see p. 63).

Shalom Mural or Shalom Banner: A large mural can be created during the program to serve as a focal point for an opening session on *shalom,* for subsequent sessions, especially ones on "Shalom in the Global Family," and for the closing worship. The leaders should have the "foundation" in place before the program begins. One effective mural was constructed as shown on p. 24.

- The first third is used during an opening session on "families in search of *shalom*." Participants draw one way they have been peacemakers and given themselves for others (like Jumping Mouse, if that story is used; see p. 25).

---

[4]From "Families Covenanting for Peace"; see below, p. 83.
[5]From "Families Covenanting for Peace"; see below, p. 83.

- The second third can remain blank and serve as a screen for AV's, if it can be located in a suitable place, especially for an AV on Sadako (see p. 40). It can also house any petitions created by the group, especially in the session on "Shalom in the Global Family."

- The last third can be used during the concluding worship or at the conclusion of the "Shalom in the Global Family" session for participants to post their decisions on their next step for peace.

This mural can be flanked with one or two side panels: one for participants to post peace posters they have created during the program and the other for children to use at random for drawing peace pictures or sayings. Having several peace posters and children's drawings already on side panels adds both visual attraction and creative encouragement.

Shalom Covenants: In the opening sentence of the Ezekiel passage quoted by Brueggemann (Worksheet 3), God proclaims: "I will make a covenant of

peace [*shalom*] with them...." Participants might be asked what "covenant" means, as well as what *shalom* means. The word "covenant" is most important in a family, just as it is in our relationship with God. When the Israelites did not live up to the covenant they had made with God, God still loved them and was still willing to allow them to try again.

The family is very much like this. Within our family covenants we often disappoint one another, but that does not mean love is absent. It simply means that our expectations of one another need to be examined, and perhaps new agreements need to be made about the details of our living together as a family. See the optional "Family Covenant" activity

SHALOM MURAL

Peacemakers,
like Jumping Mouse,
give themselves for others

Sadako Sasaki:
"I will write peace on your wings
and you will fly all over the world."

Next Steps for Peace

in the "Shalom in the Home" session below (p. 31 and Worksheet 11).[6]

Further biblical reflection is sometimes desired, although children may grow restless if this goes on for very long. Worksheet 4 contains several passages that can be prayed over at home. At this point in the session, each table can be assigned one passage. The passage is read aloud at least twice before table members are asked to share what they think it means.

5. PARTICIPANTS' INSIGHTS AND EXPERIENCES OF SHALOM

Family Shalom Sheet: Families create a family *shalom* sheet (Worksheet 2), which can be posted on a large piece of newsprint (at least 18″ × 24″). The larger newsprint enables family members to draw pictures rather than be limited to word descriptions of their family's *shalom*, both as receivers and givers. As on Worksheet 2, use the top half of the newsprint for identifying God's gift of *shalom* to the family.

First list how each family member is a gift, how each contributes uniquely to the family's *shalom*.

Then list some of those other special moments or experiences when each family experienced God's gifts of *shalom*. If "shalom" language is confusing at this point, a simpler way to describe such moments would be to call them "favorite family moments."

On the bottom half of the newsprint, have participants describe (draw, if possible) ways the family has been God's agent of *shalom* for others in the family, church, neighborhood, and world. These *shalom* sheets should be shared with at least one other family (having at least two families per table facilitates this sharing). Then they are taped to the walls of the meeting room as another way of giving ideas and inspiration to one another.

Family Puzzle: As an alternative to writing the unique contributions of each family member on the Shalom Sheet, each family is given an envelope in which they find their "family puzzle pieces," one piece for each family member.

Each member writes his or her name on one piece and the whole family names ways in which that family member contributes to the family's *shalom*. These ways are written on each piece and then the family puzzle is assembled. As with the Shalom Sheet, it can be shared at the table with one or two other families, posted in the meeting room, or posted at the door of the family's sleeping quarters.[7]

Shalom Towers: Each family, whether of one member or many, is given an 8″ section of "sonatube." This is heavy cardboard tubing that concrete is poured into to make construction posts. From a resource table of magazines, glue, and scissors, each

---

[6]From "Families Covenanting for Peace"; see below, p. 83.

[7]From "Family Church Camps"; see below, p. 84.

family selects the appropriate supplies necessary to make a collage of pictures on the "sonatube."

Each family is asked to select one picture of *shalom* in action that they wish to highlight and, at the specified time, they share this picture from their collage with the entire group. (Urge the families to select different "family reporters" for different activities). Shalom towers can then be used for centerpieces and taken home to be used (with plastic bags) as planters, wastebaskets, etc.[8]

Shalom Rainbow: Either as a substitute for the leader's Shalom Mural or Banner (see above) or as

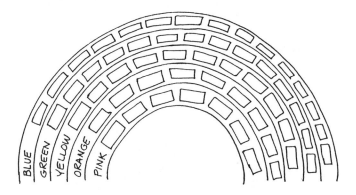

a complement to it, participants are asked to construct a Shalom Rainbow. Using strips of colored construction paper, each family writes out several aspects of *shalom* — one per strip and as specific as possible, for example, family picnics for fun and sharing. They tape them to each color of their rainbow (one color for each line).

This rainbow mural can be expanded throughout the program as participants add more strips of paper or draw pictures around the rainbow. Since the rainbow is a symbol of hope, it is especially appropriate as the framework for God's promise of *shalom.*[9]

Shalom Sayings: Several pieces of newsprint (at least $3' \times 4'$ sections) can be hung on a wall in the main room for participants to write phrases or quotations they feel express what it means to be an agent of *shalom.*   The leader might have one or two already posted and invite participants to add to the list whenever they choose during the program.

[8]From "Family Church Camps"; see below, p. 84.
[9]From "Little Friends for Peace — Peacemaking Education"; see below, p. 82.

The Shakertown Pledge (see Worksheet 23 below) might be included, as might such statements as: "Live simply so that others might simply live" or "There's enough in the world for everyone's need but not for everyone's greed" (Gandhi).

6. GOD'S CALL TO BE AGENTS OF SHALOM

Jumping Mouse: A contemporary parable that draws on Native American folklore and implants a moving image of discipleship is entitled *The Story of Jumping Mouse.*   The Native American legend is retold and illustrated by John Steptoe (Lothrop, Lee and Shepard Books [105 Madison Ave., New York, NY 10016], 1984, $12.50). Jumping Mouse embarks on a risky journey to a far-off land. During the journey, he receives talents and insights from Magic Frog. He gives away his senses (of sight and smell) to other animals that are hurting and in the process discovers the reality of Mark 8:34–38 ("Anyone who wants to save her or his life will lose it; but anyone who loses her or his life for my sake will save it").

Having different readers for each animal, in addition to the narrator as Jumping Mouse, makes an engaging presentation. If the children sit in front, so they can see the pictures each time the narrator turns a page, it helps keep them more engaged.

It takes 15 to 20 minutes to read the story slowly and with expression, showing the pictures. The image of Jumping Mouse can then be used throughout the program.

After comparing Jumping Mouse to Jesus and other agents of *shalom* throughout history, each participant or family is asked to identify at least one way each has been like Jumping Mouse and has given selflessly (for example, a talent, time) for another person. Each person or family is then asked to draw a picture of that moment on the Shalom Mural (see p. 24).

Stories of Discipleship: Other stories of discipleship, from both Scripture and contemporary children's books, can be used. The parable of the Good Samaritan (Luke 10:29–37) can be told and acted out by volunteers. Good children's stories include:

The Legend of the Bluebonnet, by Tomie de Paola (Putnam, 1983). The girl gives up her most valuable possession, her doll, to the rain gods because there is a drought and the only way for rain to occur is for the people to become less selfish.

The Giving Tree, by Shel Silverstein (Harper and Row, 1962). The story of how a tree sacrifices itself for a person, responding to the person's needs.

The King, The Mice and the Cheese, by Nancy Gurney (Beginner Books, 1965). A good book to help young children start their understanding of sharing.

The River That Gave Gifts, by Margo Humphrey (Children's Book Press, 1978). In this Afro-American story, four children in an African village make special gifts for an elder who is going blind.

Toad Is the Uncle of Heaven, retold and illustrated by Jeanne M. Lee (Holt, Rinehart and Winston, 1985). An amusing Vietnamese folktale about how the ugly toad cooperated with other animals to save the earth from drought.

Shalom Hands or Helping Hands: Participants are given two pieces of construction paper (8 1/2″ × 11″) on which they trace their left and right hands and then cut out the drawings. On one side of the left hand, each person writes out ways they have been a "helping hand" or a "*shalom* hand" for others (like Jumping Mouse). On one side of the right hand cut-out, the participant writes out ways this hand has been used to hurt others. These hands are then placed in the family Shalom Box (Worksheet 1), to be used at various other times during the program.

Some sharing within each family, and perhaps also with other families at each table should be encouraged. This sharing should focus particularly on ways family members have been "*shalom* hands" for others. In keeping with the theme of "hands," the group could sing, "We've Got the Whole World in Our Hands." (A variation of this activity can also be used with the "Shalom in the Home" session; see p. 28).

7. CONCLUDING PRAYER

A concluding prayerful song is generally best for engaging all participants. Picking up on the theme of being God's agents of *shalom,* "Peace is flowing like a river, flowing out of you and me..." is quite appropriate. So is *"Shalom Chaverim"* (see Worksheet 38), which can be done with gestures and can be sung in Hebrew as well as in English.

8. FOLLOW-UP

Cabin Name: If participants are staying in cabins, each cabin can be asked to name itself and share that name at breakfast the next morning.

Shalom Banner: Each cabin is asked to create their own Shalom Banner during the remainder of the program, if some of the other group banner and mural options are not being included in the program.

Biblical Shalom: The biblical passages on *shalom* should be given out or pointed out in the packets, if they have not already been used (see Worksheet 4). Participants can be encouraged to pray over them in the hours, days, and weeks ahead.

9. CONCLUDING ANNOUNCEMENTS

Logistical announcements go best at the end of the session, so as not to lengthen the beginning and distract from the content.

- Make sure that child-care workers are ready at least 15 to 30 minutes before the beginning of the next session and that adults are urged to bring their preschoolers to child care 10 to 15 minutes before the session begins.

- List all the tasks for which volunteers will be needed. The list will probably include song leaders, planners for worship, MCs for the talent show, and as many performers as possible. Other responsibilities are teaching participants to make origami paper cranes (see Worksheet 15), reading for stories or slide presentation scripts, and storytelling.

- Inform participants about the various resource tables and newsprint and encourage their own contributions during the program.

- If group project options are going to be offered for participating families to support as part of the session on "Consumerism and Stewardship" (chapter 7) and the closing worship, announce this and encourage participants to identify a project they want the whole group to consider. Newsprint posted on a prominent wall in the meeting or dining room enables participants to write their nominations for all to see and consider before decisions are made.

CHAPTER 5

Shalom in the Home

In a one-day program, "Shalom in the Home" is the best theme with which to begin the day, perhaps incorporating one or two activities from "Families in Search of Shalom" (chapter 4), for example, Shalom Box introductions (p. 22), the Family Puzzle (p. 24), or the Family Shalom Sheet (p. 24), especially since these latter two are quite affirmative.

"Shalom in the Home" is the theme with the most perceivable utility of all the PPJ themes and can be the focus of "series sessions," especially those series with an "evenings" format. Such a format lends itself to having participants practice the techniques suggested in the sessions and report back at subsequent sessions.

Goals

Rather than just talk about affirmation, conflict resolution, and family decision-making techniques, in this session participants give affirmation, deal with conflicts, and hold family meetings. The activities are diverse and engaging in order to energize the group and prevent boredom. Song and humor are included to give the program a lighter tone.

Small group sharing is encouraged to help participants feel their contributions are worthwhile and to generate a sense of community. Whole family time together is balanced with opportunities for similarly situated participants to work together in smaller groups.

This is the session for the leaders to establish their credibility and generate a feeling of trust and openness in the group. If this happens, then subsequent sessions, on generally more threatening themes, go much better.

Components

1. GATHERING SONG OR SHORT GAME

Songs like "Morning Has Broken," "We've Got the Whole World in Our Hands" (with verses focusing on family relationships), "His Banner Over Me Is Love," or another appropriate song focus and energize the group. A short cooperative game (see pp. 32–35 below), especially for participants who arrive early or on time, can do this too.

2. BIBLICAL REFLECTION AND STORY

Colossians 3:20–21 asks children to obey their parents — and parents not to nag their children lest they lose heart. Asking participants if they have ever nagged or been nagged can be done in an enjoyable way. Sharing a story from the leader's own family experience of conflict at home is very helpful, especially if it can provoke laughter as well as help the participants identify with the leaders and be more willing to share personally and honestly.

3. AFFIRMATION

Real Family Jewels: As a way of affirming family members, participants write on $1'' \times 8\frac{1}{2}''$ strips of colored construction paper (at least fifteen strips per participant) special qualities or times together for particular family members (one per strip). Tape or glue these strips as rings or links ("jewels") on a chain. Make the chain long enough so that when connected as a lei it can fit over the participant's head.

Partners or whole families should work on these together. The first time a necklace is made, it may work best if the family focuses on one family member, relative, or close friend not present, someone they would like to affirm at this time.

Participants can complete the task at home, or at another time during the program, so that every family member has one made by the other family members. Ask participants to identify other persons who should receive such "jewels" and when.

Brainstorm with the whole group ways and times this activity can be used effectively.

Brainstorm with the whole group other ways of affirming family members. Either before or after brainstorming affirmation possibilities, it is helpful to state briefly some of the reasons for stressing affirmation. These include creating a positive atmosphere in the home and building self-esteem. Self-esteem and self-confidence are crucial if adults and children are going to dare to be different, to stand up for their values, to take risks, and to care for others.

Family Puzzle: See p. 24.

Shalom Sheets: See p. 24.

Shalom Hands or Helping Hands: See p. 26. As a transition to the conflict resolution component, participants can take one of their construction paper hands and write on one side ways they have used their hands for promoting peace in their family. On the opposite side, participants write ways they have used their hands to hurt other family members.

Lola Mavor's Australian family camp model offers two other affirmation activities (see Study Activities, p. 105). "I Think You're Wonderful" is a delightful song on affirming one another for children ages 4 to 9 as well as adults; it is part of the "Teaching Peace" audiotape recommended below (see p. 91).

4. CONFLICT RESOLUTION

Peace Pie and Trouble Cake: Children ages 6 to 10 and at least one of their parents go to a separate meeting space to do Worksheet 7 (Peace Pie and Trouble Cake). Instructions are on the worksheet (one per family group). Emphasis should be placed on generating additional ingredients for this task. After 10 to 15 minutes of individual family "baking," the leader should solicit some of the additional ingredients each family identified. If space permits and the leader is so inclined, both a "peace pie" and a "trouble cake" can be drawn on large newsprint, with ingredients written on the various slices.

PEACE PIE

TROUBLE CAKE

Case Studies: Distribute Worksheet 8 (Case Studies in Creative Conflict Resolution) to the remaining adults and teens. Ask them to choose the case most appropriate to their current situation and divide the groups into smaller groups around each case study. Have them work silently for several minutes on the questions at the end of Worksheet 8 before beginning their discussion.

Or choose one of the case studies for the whole group — if it is a small group and the same case study is appropriate for all its members. Call for suggestions ("bright ideas") from the whole group after 10–15 minutes of individual family discussion of the case study.

Fighting Fair: *Fighting Fair*, an especially helpful audio-visual for junior high children and their parents, is a 17-minute video about Martin Luther King's nonviolent approach to conflict resolution. It uses episodes from King's life to illustrate principles that are then applied to a conflict between two groups of 11- and 12-year-olds. A chart with six rules for "fighting fair" comes with the curriculum guide that accompanies the video. The whole package can be purchased from the Grace Contrino Adams Peace Education Foundation, P.O. Box 19-1153, Miami Beach, FL 33119. It is an excellent resource for upper elementary, middle, and junior high schools.

Conflict Faces: One way to introduce the conflict resolution theme is to draw beforehand five faces depicting five ways of handling conflict (see the box on p. 30).

Display these faces or scenes in different parts of the room. After a brief explanation of each drawing, ask families to move around the room to each face and, at each face, to talk about a time when a family conflict was handled that way.[1]

Family Conflicts: Using Worksheet 9 (Conflict Resolution Skills), each family focuses on actual conflicts they have recently experienced. Ask family members to list specific kinds of behavior that tip the family climate in one direction or another. Some examples are provided to help get them started.

If they finish before 10 minutes, they may want to consider individually each of the questions on the worksheet. If they do not get to them during the program, the questions might be useful at home as a

----

[1]From "Families Covenanting for Peace"; see below, p. 83.

follow-up or a periodic check-up on how the family is feeling about its conflicts.[2]

Family Feud: This is an intergenerational family peacemaking game. Announce that the room you are in has become a TV studio and the participants will be the studio audience for Family Feud. Set four to five chairs in each of two rows facing each other (enough for competing families). Between the two rows, place a Wheel of Fortune board.

WHEEL OF FORTUNE

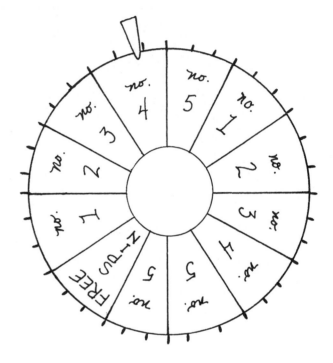

Contestant families (as teams) have one person spin the wheel. The number on the wheel determines the family conflict to which they must offer a solution. The opposing team has a chance to "counter." Each team is given 60 seconds after they spin. Finally, the "studio audience" is asked for their opinion of the team's advice plus any other alternatives. (As an alternative to the Wheel of Fortune, each conflict could be written on a 3″ × 5″ card; contestants pick one of the cards, which is then read aloud to all.)

Samples of "family problems" that might be considered in this game:

----

[2]From "Pass It On"; see below, p. 82.

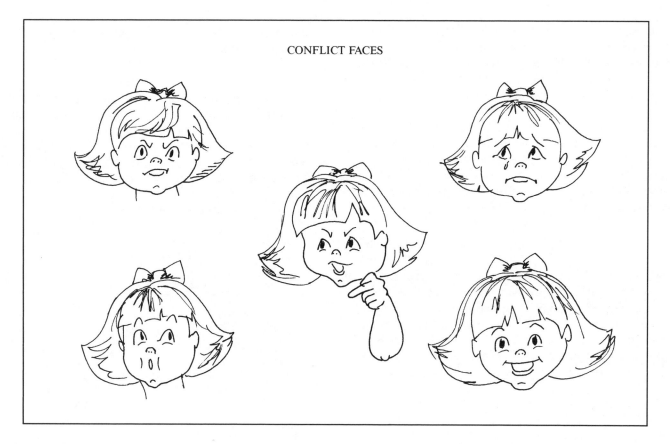

CONFLICT FACES

1. Mother works and gets home two hours after the fifth- and seventh-grade children do. The children have agreed to carry out some chores each afternoon, but every afternoon the seventh grader complains and "dumps on Mom" when she gets home that his younger sister won't do chores. He says "I'm not going to do my part if she doesn't do hers."

2. Mother has a part-time job, which she enjoys and which permits her to be home by 3:00 p.m. Her employer has asked if she would like to become an assistant manager. She would have to work until 5:00 or 5:30 if she had this job. This job would bring in much more money, but the older children would have to take turns coming home immediately after school to assist with the younger children and to begin dinner.

3. The family visits grandparents in a neighboring state three or four times a year. They always stay over on Friday night. Now the oldest child, a 12-year-old girl, has been invited to a slumber party and wants to stay back with the friend and her family.

4. The family has decisions to make regarding purchases with their income tax refund. Some want to join an athletic club and some want to buy a computer. They can't do both.

5. The family has one TV and have heated discussions every evening, after homework is done. Some want to watch the sports channel and others want to watch the movie channel.

6. Both the mother and the father work outside the home. They decide that all the children will put dirty laundry in the laundry room and that the oldest teens will be responsible for the laundry. Two of the children never take in their dirty laundry, yet many mornings they yell because they have no clean clothes.

The goal of this activity is not so much the actual solution to these problems as it is "practicing" the *process.* The facilitator plays "devil's advocate."[3]

---

[3] From Barbara Oehlberg, local PPJN coordinator, Cleveland, Ohio.

Puppet Skits and Replays: Role-play with puppets a Saturday morning "discussion" about the children cleaning their rooms. With an adult playing a child's role and with one of the children playing the father's role, make all the classic mistakes — name calling, comparisons among the children, not listening, yelling, threatening, hitting, crying and stomping out of the room. Ask the group to identify all the mistakes.

Then each family pairs with another and tries to replay the conflict in creative ways. The partner family evaluates the replay and then tries its hand at replaying the situation and is evaluated in turn. Then the group reassembles and each family is asked to identify a family conflict on which they would like to focus in a special way after returning home. They write their decision on an index card and put it in their Shalom Box (see Worksheet 1).

A variation of this is to have each family select its own conflict for demonstrating with puppets. The puppets can be paper bag or sock puppets, simple enough to make on the spot. Families pair off as above, giving one another feedback.[4]

Dealing with Anger: Two songs are especially helpful. Chant and act out "If you're angry..." as a whole group, assembled in a circle outdoors if possible (see box on p. 32). Invite other ways of expressing anger constructively that can be stated in three or four syllables. Sing and act out several.

A second song, "Use a Word" from the *Teaching Peace* audiotape (see p. 91), contrasts words and fists with easy-to-remember lyrics and melody.

5. FAMILY MEETINGS

One way of presenting this component is through the video clips of the McGinnis family meeting on the *Building Shalom Families* video program and the *Phil Donahue* video on PPJ (both available from the Institute for Peace and Justice).

Introductory Story: A story from the leader's own experience with family meetings or the "cable TV episode" from the *Building Shalom Families* video personalizes the topic.

Initial Description of a Family Meeting: Point out several of the "do's" and "don'ts" of family meet-

ings; Worksheet 10 should be distributed to each adult participant.

Video Presentation of "McGinnis Family Meeting": Show the first four episodes (17 minutes) of this video segment (or at least the first two). Follow this by a couple of minutes of group reaction. If the video is not used, an alternative is to elaborate on the "do's" and "don't's" on Worksheet 10 with specific examples. Personal testimonies from families who have family meetings are quite effective, especially if children add their reflections.

Family Covenant: Have each family discuss the possibility of having or improving their family meeting and make some decision on this possibility. The Family Covenant (Worksheet 11) could be used for this.

6. ADULT DISCUSSION

While the children and teens are separated from the group, preferably for some cooperative game for at least 30 minutes, adult participants get a chance to raise questions and insights about the session content, especially the family meeting.

Family Reconciliation Service: See Worksheet 12.

7. NEXT STEPS

If the conflict resolution activities and the family discussion/decision period did not adequately yield individual family decisions about next steps in being peacemakers at home, several creative options can be added at the end of the session. Children should rejoin their parents for these:

Hands: Participants write on the construction paper hand (see pp. 26 and 28) one way they could personally promote peace in their homes; then they share their decisions with other family members before returning the hand to the Shalom Box (Worksheet 1).

Gift Certificate: Each family member makes a gift certificate for one other person, preferably another family member, promising some gift of time, for example, household chore, special walk, reading a book together. If the gift certificate is for an absent person, it could be mailed as a special surprise.[5]

---

[4]From "Pass It On"; see below, p. 82.

[5]From "Youth Camps on Peacemaking"; see below, p. 83.

IF YOU'RE ANGRY...	
Words	**Gestures**
"If you're angry and you know it, stop and think"	*fists pounding up and down; palm out; index finger to head*
"If you're angry and you know it, stop and think"	*[repeat]*
"If you're angry and you know it, it's OK for you to show it"	*fists pounding up and down; open hands extend forward*
"If you're angry and you know it, stop and think"	*fists pounding up and down; palm out; index finger to head*

8. CONCLUDING REFLECTION

There are many inspirational reflections on family living. Two of the most moving are:

- "On Children," from *The Prophet*, by Kahil Gibran.
- "A Prayer for the Family," by Mike Nobel, visually illustrated as a 7-minute segment on the *Building Shalom Families* video program (see p. 149).

Cooperative Games and Family Play Time

Playing together generates the positive feelings that make family conflict resolution more effective. It also heightens the self-esteem of family members who get opportunities to shine.

1. COOPERATIVE PLAY[6]

In most competitive games, the individual task of accomplishing a personal goal is often thwarted by ill luck and the moves of other players, opponents in a struggle to win. In a cooperative game, individual tasks are met through the combined efforts of all to accomplish a group task. The challenge is as great,

---

[6]This section is taken from *Peacemaking: Family Activities for Justice and Peace,* by Jacqueline Haessly, Paulist Press, 1980, pp. 36–39. Reprinted with permission of the author; the book is available directly from the author (see p. 83, no. 4).

and in some instances greater, as when we merely attempt to "bump" people off.

Cooperative games do not eliminate challenge, as is often suggested by those who defend the merits of competition. Rather cooperative games alter the focus of the challenge. I now must pay close attention to my partner or the group, not with a goal of beating her or him, but rather to achieve our mutually agreed upon purpose.

The following criteria may prove helpful in evaluating adult and children's games for qualities of cooperation or competitiveness.

1. When these games are played, are the participants laughing with, not at, each other?

2. Is the laughter contagious?

3. Does the activity allow for full participation by most persons? Or are several persons or large numbers standing around awaiting their turn?

4. Can the activity be modified to include persons with age, skill, physical, or mental limitations? If so, how?

5. Does the activity challenge all persons to work together for a common end?

6. Do good feelings or bad feelings dominate during or at the end of the activity?

We can't all rush out and purchase brand new cooperative games. To do so would be to contribute to the already massive consumerism of our society. We can however encourage our schools and libraries to purchase these games as they do books, to be loaned or even rented to eager users. Such games also make thoughtful gifts by which to remember those occasions of special importance to those we love.

In the meantime, and just as effectively, we can alter the games we already play, thus changing the tone from one of competition to one of cooperation. We do this by changing the purpose. Instead of playing against each other to determine a winner, we play with each other to achieve a common goal. In such

play, the game is won, is finished, when the mutually agreed upon goal is achieved by all members of the group working together toward this end. Puzzles are one excellent example of this type of cooperation. A number of other ways to alter common children's or family games are suggested below.

But what, you ask, do children's games have to do with peacemaking in our global village? We delude ourselves if we think that the attitudes and skills fostered through the play do not effect our children's worldview. Children, exposed through play to the value of cooperation within the family, are enabled to move into their neighborhoods and schools with a new set of skills.

A cooperative spirit thus nurtured enables them and us to take a stance of caring and sharing with others in the play and work activities of our daily lives, as well as in the market places of our towns, cities, and world. In the security of a nurturing family, the values essential to caring and sharing with all our neighbors in our global village find nourishment.

Listed below are some commonly played games for children and adults that readily lend themselves to modification of goals from winning to group sharing and cooperating. These suggestions were developed and tested at home over a number of years and have proven successful. Many of them have also been used in workshops for parents and teach-

ers interested in learning and teaching new ways of play. As you play them and become familiar with the goals, try your creativity and develop together your own way of playing games cooperatively in your family.

Bingo, Lotto, UNICEF Lingo: These and comparable children's games teach essential skills such as matching and word, number, or picture recognition. Play the game in such a way that filling all the squares of all players cards becomes the goal. You'll soon discover that all cards will be filled at about the same time. Even older children can enjoy the fun of the game, as well as the learning experience. Lingo has an added incentive for older children as well as adults, as the game pictures basic foods from many cultures with each food identified in three languages.

Sorry, Trouble, Parcheesi: The object of these games is to move a token around a board from start to home (safety). Tokens of other players are usually displaced in the process. These games can be modified into cooperation games in several ways, ranging from simple to complex. Specific rules should be agreed upon in advance.

- Retain game rules that suggest a specific number, such as 1 or 6, to move from home base, or to move into the place of safety.

- When players land on a space occupied by another token, move the other's token ahead an agreed upon number of spaces.

- Make it a group game where "ownership" of the pieces is shared. Every player may move any token on the board. The object is to see if all tokens can finish by reaching home at about the same time. This process also allows more than the usual four players to participate.

- For greater challenge, make a rule that no player can land on an occupied space. This challenges players to develop excellent problem-solving skills, as they work together to see which moves will enable them to meet any of the goals.

Scrabble: Word and skill games such as Scrabble can be modified by changing the goal from achieving the highest score to working together to achieve a group score of 500, 1000, or 5000 points. This method is particularly effective in families and class-rooms where all persons can be challenged according to their age or skill.

2. UNDERSTANDING PLAY

Susan Morse adds the following games and suggests that participants discuss the six questions below.

Playing against Gravity: Take a table soccer or foot-ball game and lift one end on blocks so that the play-ers work together against gravity rather than working against each other.

Ping Pong: Ping pong and volleyball can be mod-ified by having people rotate from team to team; simply try to keep the ball going as long as possible rather than keeping a comparative score. A large number can play ping pong by rotating around the table, each getting one quick chance to hit the ball before passing the paddle on to the next person.

Discussion Group Brainstorm:

1. Why do you play?

2. How do you feel when you lose?

3. Does losing get in the way of your reasons for playing?

4. What are the positive values in competition?

5. What are the problems with competition and the values in cooperation?

6. How can we get the most positives and least neg-atives in our play?

3. ADDITIONAL GAMES

People Pyramids: Start with four big people on the bottom kneeling shoulder to shoulder. Next, three middle-size people, then two, and finally the littlest person in the group on top.

Night Walk: Blindfold all the participants and tie them together around the waist so they are in a line, single-file. They then have to work together to move from one location to another. This works well as an ice-breaker.

Group Treasure Hunts: These can be lots of fun and can have a cooperative dimension. The treasure could be something every participant can enjoy (for example, several Oreo cookies for each), but it can-not be found until every group (family, cabin, clus-ter of families) completes its hunt and finds a puzzle piece that must be put together with all other groups' puzzle pieces to make the final clue; this sends the whole group on the last step of the search.

Blindfold Trust Walk: The participants pair off. One of each pair puts on a blindfold. Then they walk through the camp for a set time, experiencing sharing and trust. Encourage them to touch trees, buildings, rocks, noticing texture, smells, and sound. Caution them not to guide their blindfolded part-ners into the trees or the lake. *Be firm.* This is not a time to turn the participants loose without supervi-sion. Talk about the experience afterward (see also "Disability Awareness," p. 54).

Apt Adjectives: A person in the circle starts with a self-descriptive adjective that begins with the same letter as that person's first name, for example, Happy Helen, Courageous Christopher, Gorgeous George, Delightful Diane. The next person does the same but must also say the name and adjective of all those who have gone before. This breaks the ice quickly, can become quite hilarious, and helps everyone re-member each other's names.

Egg Toss: Fill small balloons with water (not too much). Everyone chooses a partner and stands three feet apart. On signal, toss the balloon back and forth. Then take one step back. Continue tossing and stepping back until one couple is left with a whole balloon (from *New Games Book,* below).

Rain Making: The leader assembles the group in a circle and, as the leader rotates, motions to each section of the circle to do each of the following and to continue to do so until the leader completes the rotation and indicates a new activity:

- rub hands together (= *gentle rainfall*)

- snap fingers (= *little heavier rainfall*)

- slap thighs (= *heavier yet*)

- stomp feet (= *even heavier*)

The leader then reverses the order to end the rain storm gradually.

Racing Car: Assemble the group in a circle and challenge the group to send its racing car around the track (their circle) as fast as possible. Time the group several times to see if they can better their time with each race. Praising the group for establishing a new world record for a group its size doesn't hurt either. The racing car travels around the track by having each participant "pick up" the car from the person next to him or her — by bending toward that person, picking up that racing car noise, and then pivoting to the next person and passing on the noise.

Herman-Henrietta: Herman-Henrietta is an imaginary blob of clay. Anyone can shape it into anything — anything! The leader begins to pantomime, pulling the magic blob from his or her pocket (or some other hiding place) and sets the tone by getting involved in creating something. To start with, it is helpful to create things that the children or adults can easily identify. It is fun to guess what is being made, but not necessary, as it is essentially a nonverbal game. Then the magical lump is mushed down to its original size (still in pantomime) and passed reverently to the next person. The game continues around the circle.[7]

Among the resources that Haessly and Morse both suggest are:

Cooperative Sports and Games Book, by Terry Orlick, Pantheon, 1978.
New Games Book, ed. Andrew Fluegelman, Doubleday, 1976.
More New Games, ed. Andrew Fluegelman, Doubleday, 1981.

See also *New Games for the Whole Family*, by Dale LeFevre, Putnam Publishing, 1988; also available from the Alternatives Book Service, P.O. Box 429, Ellenwood, GA 30049.

---

[7]From *A Manual on Nonviolence and Children,* Stephanie Judson, compiler and editor; order from Nonviolence and Children Program, Friends Peace Committee, 1515 Cherry St., Philadelphia, PA 19102.

CHAPTER 6

Shalom in the Global Family

Often the "Shalom in the Global Family" session is divided into two sessions of 90-plus minutes each. In a one-day program, they are generally combined as the afternoon complement to the morning session on "Shalom in the Home." Depending on the degree of openness and political readiness of the group, leaders may want to focus only on the "global family" and not do the "Shalom in the Home" session.

Goals

In this session participants are most seriously challenged to expand their vision and range of concern and to open themselves to risk-taking action. Thus, in line with the suggestions in chapter 2, it is especially important to incorporate the four ingredients for nurturing a compassionate and courageous heart (see p. 7, no. 4). Stories present the victims of global violence and injustice personally. Ruth Nelson's witness in the film/video *Mother of the Year* is particularly inspirational (see below p. 44). Prayer and small group sharing are essential.

Whenever this session is the afternoon of a full-day program, particular care for involving children needs to be taken. They tire easily. Two hours is generally the longest that children can last. If more than two hours is desirable for adult participants, then a period of cooperative games and other highly engaging activities should be planned for the children while adults continue with the more serious content. Another possibility, which would keep the whole group together, is a concluding "peace festival" for the final 30–60 minutes (see below p. 76).

Components

1. GATHERING SONG AND REFLECTION

Many songs are appropriate for the global dimension of *shalom.* Two of the most singable are "We're All a Family Under One Sky" and "We've Got the Whole World in Our Hands." A short reflection on one or more of the biblical passages on Worksheet 4, especially John 17:21–23, can begin this session. Biblical reflection is probably best incorporated by including it in several of the session components.

2. OUR ONENESS WITH THE EARTH

Earth Ball: Use inflatable earth balls (available from the Institute for Peace and Justice as well as

from many UNICEF or United Nations Association outlets) or the hug-a-planet cloth earth balls (from XTC Products, Inc., 247 Rockingstone, Larchmont, NY 10538; tel.: 914-833-0200).

An outdoor setting is appropriate for this activity. Divide the group into over-6's, teens, and adults; subdivide any of these groups so that there are no more than 10–15 in any one group. Have participants form circles and think for a moment about ways they have cared for the earth (for example, recycling, gardening, vegetarian eating, photography). Have the earth ball passed around each group. As each participant holds the earth, they each explain how they have cared for the earth.

This activity can be concluded with participants gathering around one person holding the earth ball in the air. While all touch the ball, pray that all may find the compassion and courage to preserve the earth at this crucial moment in earth's history.

Peace Pal: Peace Links has a wonderful 9-inch bunny known as "Peace Pal," who has the whole world in her hands. She can become the narrator of this component or at least the visual symbol that can serve as a reminder of caring for the earth (available for $10 from Peace Links, 747 8th St., S.E., Washington, DC 20002).

World Hunger Simulation: Linked with the dessert portion of the noon meal, this simulation can be adapted in many ways, depending on the time of day and the size of the group.

Distribute baskets of cookies in the following manner:

- 6 percent of the people get two-thirds of *all* the cookies;

- 69 percent get one cookie per person;

- 25 percent get nothing but a few crumbs.

Allow a few minutes for participants to react before making any observations.[1]

A number of PPJ family camps have also used the "100 Hungry People" hunger skit from *Helping Kids Care,* by Camy Condon and James McGinnis (Institute for Peace and Justice and Meyer-Stone Books, 1988).

3. GLOBAL CONNECTIONS

Family Links: This activity focuses on our "global family links." It is effective and engaging, especially if the construction paper links were used for the Real Family Jewels activity in the "Shalom in the Home" session (see above p. 27).

Have each family identify their personal connections with specific individuals or groups in other countries (for example, an exchange student from Ghana ate in our home, a sister-in-law lives in Peru). Write the name and country, one per strip, on the colored construction paper strips ($1'' \times 8 1/2''$). Have each family prepare several and then link the strips with those from other families at the same table, explaining their links to one another. Then link the chains from various tables together, forming one long chain of global connections. Several participants carry this chain around the room while the whole group sings either "We've Got the Whole World in Our Hands" or "We're All a Family Under One Sky." Tape or tack the chain in a prominent place.

Earth Ball Connections: After asking each family to identify all their global connections, invite all those with Asian connections to stand and identify quickly those connections as the earth ball is passed to each person naming a connection. As soon as these connections are named, the whole group sings one verse of "We've Got the Whole World in Our Hands" with the line "We've got the people of Asia in our hands...." This is repeated for each of the continents. Ask for U.S.S.R. connections specifically, especially if U.S.-U.S.S.R. reconciliation is one of the themes of your program.

The Shakertown Pledge: This is an option for the session on "Consumerism and Stewardship" (chapter 7), but it can be used here as well. If it does not fit into the time available for either session, it can be given as a handout for later consideration at home (see Worksheet 23).

Global Product Connections: Do this activity as a total group unless the group is too large. Using a world map or globe, attach one end of a long string of yarn to each of the objects listed below and the other end to the country from which it comes. This exercise helps us realize how much we rely on people of other countries.[2]

- diamonds/gold: South Africa

- bananas: Ecuador

- cocoa: Ghana

- coffee: Brazil

- sugar: Dominican Republic

---

[1] From "Pass It On"; see below, p. 82.

[2] From "Families Covenanting for Peace"; see below, p. 83.

- jute: India

- rubber: Indochina

- shirts/sweaters: Hong Kong/Taiwan

- silver: U.S.A.

- newsprint: Canada

- wool: Argentina

Global Family Collage: Work tables should be already prepared, each having several magazines (for example, *Maryknoll, National Geographic*) with pictures of people from different countries, scissors, and tape.

Participants find pictures that say something meaningful to them, cut them out, and tape them to a large sheet of paper entitled "The Global Family." They write the name of the country below their picture.

If posters of the people of the Soviet Union are used, ask participants to study these after posting their pictures.

Participants return to their seats and in small groups tell why they chose the picture they did and share their reactions to the posters or other pictures on the collage.

4. CRITICAL GLOBAL CONNECTIONS

It is usually not possible to consider more than one or two of the following critical areas of the global family. Which area to consider depends on time, the leader's experience, and the group's interest and degree of readiness. We strongly suggest including "U.S.-U.S.S.R. reconciliation possibilities." Also, areas with Third World handicrafts available present a less threatening global action option.

As a way of extending and enriching this dimension of *shalom,* the menu for the evening meal might be representative of one country or region. The evening program can include assorted artifacts and pictures, an audio-visual, and other cultural items to enhance the experience. Hiroshima and the story *Sadako and the Thousand Paper Cranes* is probably the most engaging of the five options listed below (see p. 40). Seriously consider it as an evening program.

THE PHILIPPINES

The bone pendant and other handicrafts made by Santiago Alonzo in the Philippines and distributed by Jubilee Crafts (300 W. Apsley, Philadelphia, PA 19144) are wonderful gifts.   For Santiago's moving personal story, see the Resource Book for the *Hope Springs from God* intergenerational curriculum (see p. 63) or write Jubilee Crafts. Have their catalogs available, as well as those of other distributors, for example, SERRV Self-Help Handcrafts (P.O. Box 365, New Windsor, MD 21776), SELF-HELP Crafts (P.O. Box L, Akron, PA 17501), and Pueblo-to-People (1616 Montrose #1027, Houston, TX 777006).

Any number of countries could be highlighted in this activity. Having some handicrafts available (usually you can get them on consignment) not only provides a good shopping possibility for participants but can also help them to arrange an alternative holiday bazaar for their own church or community.

U.S.-U.S.S.R. RECONCILIATION POSSIBILITIES

(Canadian groups can adapt this to their own situation.)

On a topic as volatile as this, it is important to anticipate some prevalent objections and allay some initial fears. Biblically, Christians are called to be "ambassadors of reconciliation" as followers of Jesus, who gave his life for the reconciliation of all persons with God and with one another (2 Corinthians 5:18–21). God's great plan for the earth is the reunification of all in Christ (Ephesians 1:10). We are called to confront the powers and principalities of this world that frustrate this plan, that build barriers between peoples (Ephesians 6:10–20).

The political behavior, especially the foreign policies of the two superpowers (the U.S. and the U.S.S.R.), may be among these "powers" we are to call to repentance. We are to be the bridge-builders between our two peoples. Thus, in exploring such bridge-building possibilities, we cannot be naive about the political policies of either country. But as followers of Jesus the reconciler, we must find ways of bridging the gap between our peoples and be "good Samaritans" to one another.

Three excellent short readings on this topic are

- "The Cross and the Cold War," by Ched Myers, in the November 1986 issue of *Sojourners*

- the whole February 1987 issue of *Sojourners* magazine

- *Sorting Out the Soviets*, a 10-page booklet on the twelve most frequently asked questions about the U.S.S.R. (from American Friends Service Committee, 1501 Cherry St., Philadelphia, PA 19102).

Biblical Reflection: Distribute Worksheet 13 to the participants and ask them to read over the biblical passage as well as the captions to the pictures, to study the pictures, and then to share their reactions as a family. Younger participants may need to have the captions explained. Sets of twelve postcards and posters are available through the Fellowship of Reconciliation. These can be displayed as part of the wall decorations in the main meeting room. If this is done, participants can be invited to walk around the room and reflect on the posters.

This whole activity could be done in the presence of a North American and a Russian bear who have become "pen-pals" and are working to build bridges between the people of the U.S. or Canada and the people of the Soviet Union. Donnelly/Colt (Box 188, Hampton, CT 06247; tel.: 303-455-9621) sells two delightful stuffed bears, one brown and one white, for $10 each. These animal representatives could become the narrators of this activity and then serve as a visual reminder of the actions that they suggest. Contact James McGinnis for a description of the two bear characters he has developed while doing this activity as a clown. These are contained in a booklet of stories and activities entitled *Francis and Friends* ($4, postage included, from the Institute for Peace and Justice).

Reconciliation Possibilities: Distribute Worksheet 14 to participants, asking them to read over the sixteen suggestions. Allow some time for comments or questions in the whole group. Then invite each family to decide which of the suggestions they want to do, or at least to consider doing.

Concluding Reflection: Have the whole group read the Soviet schoolgirl's poem (Worksheet 13).

Several excellent audio-visuals can be used if time is available either during the session or at other times.

For adults and older teens:

- *Forbidden Faces* is an 80-frame, 15-minute slide/tape presentation from the Fellowship of Reconciliation, incorporating the postcard visuals in a series of "faces" portraying our common humanity with the people of the U.S.S.R. (purchase price: $72).

- *Discover Our Oneness* is a 15-minute filmstrip/tape presentation from the Presbyterian Peacemaking Taskforce (341 Ponce de Leon Ave., N.E., Atlanta, GA 30365) chronicling a 1984 trip to the U.S.S.R. and effectively countering many of the myths about the U.S.S.R. This is helpful for Christian church groups, particularly Presbyterian churches.

- *What About the Russians?* is a 30-minute video from the Educational Film and Video Project (1529 Josephine St., Berkeley, CA 94703; tel.: 415-849-1649); it presents U.S. military and arms control experts answering the most commonly asked "What about the Russians?" questions.

- *War Without Winners II* is a 30-minute video from the Center of Defense Information (1500 Massachusetts Ave., N.W., Washington, DC 20005; tel.: 202-862-0700); it points out the fallacy of believing either side can fight and win a limited nuclear war, with wonderful people-on-the-street interviews with people in both the U.S. and the U.S.S.R.

For younger children as well as older participants:

- *A Day at School in Moscow* is a 20-minute video tape and guidebook that portrays the life of Soviet school children ($30 from Educators for Social Responsibility, 23 Garden Street, Cambridge, MA 02138; tel.: 617-492-1764).

- *What Soviet Children Are Saying* is a 20-minute video from the Educational Film and Video Project (see above) on Soviet children's reflections on the possibility of nuclear war ($35 to purchase).

NICARAGUA

Nicaragua is a country with whom reconciliation is sorely needed. No matter what participants' attitudes are to the Nicaraguan government, the Nicaraguan people have suffered considerably because of U.S. policy. Solidarity projects as well as political action are ways of reconciliation that all North Americans should consider.

AV Presentation: For a 10-minute look at life in Nicaragua from a child's perspective and at action possibilities for children, show *Amigos de los Niños,* a slide/tape presentation (also on the *Building Shalom Families* video program) from the Institute for Peace and Justice.

Playgrounds, Not Battlegrounds: This solidarity project is described in *Amigos* and *1987 Update,* both from the Institute for Peace and Justice; see James McGinnis, *Solidarity with the People of Nicaragua* (Orbis Books, 1985), for further details and many other solidarity projects.

Educational Aid for Nicaragua: This project of Quest for Peace and the Quixote Center (P.O. Box 5206, Hyattsville, MD 20782; tel.: 301-699-0042) has numerous possibilities for children as well as adults. Write for free brochures on the project, distribute them to participants, and raise the possibility of sending any leftover supplies from the PPJ program to the project.

Godparent Project: One PPJ family camp contributed $120 as part of the offering during the closing worship to sponsor a Nicaraguan child orphaned by war. North American families wishing to "adopt" (financially sponsor) a Nicaraguan orphan have a unique opportunity through a program organized by Sally Pettit at the Ecumenical Refugee Council (ERC) of Milwaukee. Over 250 children (newborns to 6-year olds) at six Nicaraguan orphanages are currently being sponsored by families through ERC.

North American families contributing $10 a month are paired with a specific child, receive pictures and letters about that child, and can contribute recreational and educational supplies. Amounts above $10 a month support a fund for priority medicines for children, a pediatric physical therapist, a doctor, and urgent items like disinfectant, diapers, and other supplies embargoed by the U.S. government.

Checks (payable to "ERC: Godparent Project") and supplies should be sent to the ERC, 2510 N. Frederick, Milwaukee, WI 53211; call Sally at 414-332-5461 for further information.

THE MIDDLE EAST

In the Middle East, where children grow up with little experience of peace, they often have an intuitive understanding of what a peaceful world would be like. For stories, poems, and drawings by children who lived through the Six-Day War, see *A Childhood Under Fire,* by Sifriat Poalim.[3]

Look at Arab and Israeli cultures and how they compare with our own. The food, shelter, clothing, play, dance, schools, religion, and the way of life of Israeli and Arab children are illustrated and discussed in *A Childhood Under Fire.*

Other resources include *I Live In Israel,* by Max Frankel (Behrman House, 1979), and the biblical text Genesis 8:18.

Examples of Israeli and Arab culture include kefiya, yarmulka, and talis; postcards, books, and maps from or about the countries are also useful.

JAPAN: HIROSHIMA AND THE STORY OF SADAKO

At least four ways are available of telling the story of Sadako, one of the victims of the atomic bomb at Hiroshima:

- Eleanor Coerr's book, *Sadako and the Thousand Paper Cranes,* is available from the Fellowship of Reconciliation (P.O. Box 271, Nyack, NY 10960). It is geared to middle-grade readers and includes gentle images of this dying young peacemaker, not the more gruesome pictures of the thousands of burn victims of the bomb.

- A 12-page reader's theater version of the story is available from the Institute for Peace and Justice for $1.00. It has been performed by junior and senior high students at several PPJ family camps. It takes little preparation and is an excellent activity for an evening program that might also include a talent show.

- AV versions of the story are available as slides with a 12-minute written script for readings

---

[3]From "Youth Camps on Peacemaking"; see below, p. 83.

(from the Institute for Peace and Justice) and as a filmstrip/cassette presentation entitled *Creating Peace in Our Lives* (from Twenty-Third Publications, P.O. Box 180, Mystic, CT 06355; tel.: 203-536-2611). The Sadako portion of the Shalom Mural (see p. 24 above) could be appropriately used as the screen for any AV presentation.

- A puppet skit variation on this theme by Camy Condon is contained in *Helping Kids Care* (Institute for Peace and Justice and Meyer-Stone Books, 1988), pp. 19–20.

Paper Cranes: In keeping with the Japanese legend that 1000 paper cranes would grant the maker longevity and as a prayer for peace that other children would not have to suffer as she did, Sadako tried to complete 1000 paper cranes. She died after having made 644. Ever since, children all over the world have been making these cranes and distributing them as symbols of and invitations to other peacemaking activities.

Using the directions below (Worksheet 15) and with one of the participants as instructor, invite each family to make at least two cranes per family — one for the family to keep with its Shalom Box (see Worksheet 1) and at least one other to share with some other person or group as an invitation to join the family in global peacemaking in some way.

Lantern Boats: The Japanese (and others as well) float small boats with a lantern or candle as symbols of those victims of the bombing who jumped into the rivers of Hiroshima trying to escape burning. The group might float one or more such boats in a lake, pond, or river. In a family camp setting, this is often possible. Prayers and songs for peace should accompany this activity. The tolling of a bell can also be done.

Other Action Possibilities: Since PPJ family programs are often conducted during the summer — close to the August 6 and 9 anniversaries of the Hiroshima and Nagasaki bombings — focusing on these observances can be appropriate. At a minimum, petitions calling for a Comprehensive Test Ban Treaty, or other similar disarmament efforts between the U.S. and the U.S.S.R., could be posted on the Shalom Mural for participants to consider signing (see p. 24 above). A list of other action possibilities is available yearly from many peace groups.

Contact denominational peacemaking task forces or Pax Christi USA (348 E. 10th St., Erie, PA 16503; tel.: 814-453-4955).

Cultural Accompaniments: Include a Japanese meal (with vegetables, rice, fish) and an appropriate audio-visual. One effective video is *Karate Kid II,* which could be shown as a late evening option for junior and senior high school youth and for adults. Not only does it present a sensitive view of Japanese culture in a popular medium, but its example of "enemy love" is a moving antidote to all the images of violent resolution of conflicts that bombard youth.

SOUTH AFRICA

As the struggle against apartheid has intensified, so has the repression, even against the children of apartheid. While programmatic resources for children are not as readily available as are resources for some of the other country connections above, this area of violence and justice cannot be ignored.

At a minimum, we suggest including mention of the struggle in prayer. Also consider including part of the *Kwanza* celebration (see Worksheet 29) in a program meal, session on racism, or handout to take home for a family celebration. Jubilee Crafts (300 W. Apsley, Philadelphia, PA 19144) distributes handicrafts from Black artisan cooperatives in South Africa, with a 4-page "Update" describing their work and situation.

5. FAMILY PROJECTS

As an alternative to the leaders' choosing the area of focus, participants can be encouraged to bring literature and visuals to set up a display for a project or group that they are promoting.

These displays can be set up around the main meeting room or a second room. Participants are given time during this session to visit the displays and discuss action possibilities with the various group representatives.

Leaders might add one or more displays of their own or invite nonparticipant representatives from several groups to come for this portion of the program. The "peace festival" described below, p. 76, is another way of incorporating this idea into the PPJ program. This component can be developed more fully in the following ways:

Family Brainstorming: Ask each family or participant to make a list of social actions they have done, especially but not exclusively at the global level.

Large Group Sharing: Using "circles of involvement" on large pieces of newsprint, have participants name actions they are involved in as a family that relate to the various circles: family, church or community, nation, world. Write these on the newsprint as a way of affirming each person and action and reminding others of the many possibilities for next steps.

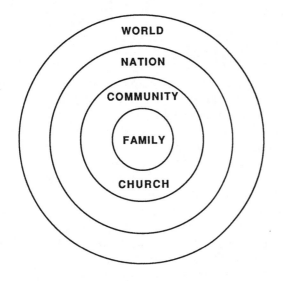

Guidelines for Family Social Action: Distribute Worksheet 16 to adult participants and briefly explain each of the five guidelines, offering one or two examples of each guideline and asking participants to name examples from their own experience.

Decide the Family's Next Step: Each family has a short family meeting to discuss their feelings about and findings from the display visits and other discussions and to decide on their next step as a family in working for *shalom* outside their home. The Family Covenant sheet (Worksheet 11) might be a helpful tool. Whatever tool is used, be sure the decisions are recorded and placed in each family's Shalom Box (Worksheet 1).

Sharing These Decisions: To express a public commitment (and, therefore, accountability) as well as

to provide mutual enrichment and inspiration, each family is asked to write out its decision on a strip of construction paper and tape it to the third panel of the Shalom Mural (see p. 24 above) and state it to the group.[4]

6. GLOBAL SHALOM

The shift from building global linkages to working for world peace is less a shift in topic than in emphasis. Here the concern is confronting the nuclear arms race and working for alternatives to war as a means for resolving international conflict. That this is an appropriate topic for families is becoming clearer each year as adults begin to discover the depth of the fears and sense of despair in so many children — because of the threat of nuclear war. The saying on a T-shirt — front side: "Life is uncertain...," back side: "So eat dessert first!" — reflects the attitude of many young people.

See the AVs listed in no. 7 below as well as the book *Facing the Nuclear Age: Parents and Children Together* from Parents for Peace (P.O. Box 611, Station P, Toronto, Ontario, M5S 2Y4, Canada), 1985.

What Are We Already Doing for Peace?: As a way of affirming what participants have already done and of sharing new action possibilities with one another, ask each family to make a list of what it is doing or has done for peace, using Worksheet 17, "How Are We Global Peacemakers?" The Worksheet might suggest actions or categories that the participants might not think of on their own. It also offers a place for participants to note possible next steps as they listen to others describe the actions they are already doing.

Pantomime for Peace: As a lighter way of engaging this heavier topic, ask for volunteers to come forward and pantomime one of their activities. Have the whole group try to guess what the action is. If it is connected with a current project or campaign that others can join, invite verbal explanations and write the pertinent information on newsprint.

Global Family Bingo: Using Worksheet 18, have the non-adult participants (adults might pair with 6- and 7-year old participants) take their bingo cards around the room, trying to match each of the sixteen

---

[4]From "Family Weekend Celebrations"; see below, p. 83.

activities listed with at least one person who has already done that activity. Leaders can adapt this list, adding or substituting items. The name of the person who has done the particular activity is written in each square until the whole card is full.

If prizes are given (for example, a postcard of Soviet people from the *Forbidden Faces* series), each family should receive one (everyone wins, not just the one who finishes first). While children are doing this activity, adults are encouraged to read the resources on global peacemaking that are available around the room.

7. DEALING WITH CHILDREN'S NUCLEAR FEARS

Several AV's are excellent:

- *Buster and Me,* a 25-minute video cassette, available for purchase from Impact Productions (1725B Seabright, Santa Cruz, CA 95062; tel.: 408-427-2627; $55) and as a video rental from PPJN regional AV centers and the Institute for Peace and Justice, is excellent for 6- to 11-year-olds. Using three muppets for children and two adult characters, this cartoon-type show for elementary aged children and for adults presents children's fears of nuclear war and how adults should help them. It moves from fear to action and ends with Buster asking viewers how they can help him work for peace.

- *In the Nuclear Shadow: What the Children Can Tell Us,* a 25-minute video cassette (and 16 mm film) also from Impact Productions, presents the same insights as *Buster and Me* but through interview clips with twenty-seven children ranging in age from 6 to 18 years. Highly emotional, it is excellent for parents and teachers and teens but not for younger children.

- *Bombs Will Make the Rainbow Break,* a 17-minute film from Films Incorporated (1213 Wilmette Ave., Wilmette, IL 60091; tel.: 800-323-4222), is geared to junior high youth, describing the Children's Campaign for Nuclear Disarmament.

No matter which of these AV's is used with different age groups, a parent (at least one per family) should watch the video with their children so that discussion can take place right away. Generally, because the *Mother of the Year* film/video is so good

for adults, we use only *Buster and Me* during the session so that as many parents as possible can see *Mother* (see below no. 8). Teens can usually see *In the Nuclear Shadow* without their parents as long as an adult is present to help them process the video afterwards.

Following *Buster and Me,* while adults are viewing and discussing their own audio-visuals, the children can:

- share with a parent their feelings about what they saw.

- brainstorm on how to respond to Buster's final words to the viewers: "What can I do for peace? It's a cinch I can't do it by myself. I need you to help me."

- formulate petitions on newsprint (as Buster suggests in the video); decide to whom to send them (most groups choose the president of their country and the president of the Soviet Union); decide who will read them to the adults and invite adults to sign them, when both groups reassemble toward the end of the session.

- draw posters or pictures for peace that can be placed on the Peace Poster and Peace Picture panels connected with the Shalom Mural (see p. 24).

- play with the various "peace toys" that they brought to the program.

- read the *We Can Do It* ("ABC" book on twenty-six children's peacemaking ideas, one for each letter of the alphabet; available for $2 from either the Institute for Peace and Justice or the publisher, Namchi United Enterprises, P.O. Box 33852, Station D, Vancouver, B.C., Canada V6J 4L6; tel.: 604-733-4886). If adults or teens are available, they can assist younger readers in going through the book. Children might also be encouraged to read the book at a later time with either a parent or their adult partner for the program.

- learn to make paper cranes (see Worksheet 15) if making the cranes is not to be included elsewhere in the program — and if time is available (at least 20 minutes).

- sing "Everyone 'Neath Their Vine and Fig Tree" (see the box on p. 45). This is an enjoyable adaptation of the *shalom* promise in Isaiah 2:4 that involves bodily movement. The children can learn it and then teach it to the adults when they reassemble during the talent show or at some other time during the program.

8. ADULT RISK-TAKING ACTION FOR PEACE

Mother of the Year: Of all the audio-visuals available on global peacemaking, by far the most effective with the most audiences is *Mother of the Year.* This 30-minute film/video by John de Graaf (contact him at KCTS-TV, 4045 Brooklyn Ave., N.E., Seattle, WA 98105, about purchase prices) is available as a film rental from Augsburg Publishing Co. (417 S. 4th Street, Minneapolis, MN 55415; tel.: 800-328-4648; $10) and as a 1/2″ VHS video rental ($10) from the Institute for Peace and Justice and the PPJN regional AV centers.

It describes the life of Ruth Nelson, an 80-year-old grandmother and life-long peace activist, who was named U.S. "Mother of the Year" in 1973. While the film highlights her act of civil disobedience in confronting the Trident submarine, it is much more the story of how to encourage risk-taking action on any issue and how to pass on values in a family. Intensely patriotic as well as courageous, Ruth presents a gentle yet compelling challenge to people of all ages to be prophets for peace and the poor.

Participants should be encouraged to open themselves up to what God is asking of them at this moment in their lives and not to feel guilty because they do not feel ready to copy Ruth's example. Each of us is called to be prophetic in different ways and with different people. After showing the film, process it as follows:

- Immediately after the video, ask participants to get in touch with their feelings during a moment of silence.

- Read Jeremiah 1:4–6 and 17–19 and ask participants to reflect silently for a minute on the question: "To whom is God sending you...."

- Invite participants to share their reflections in pairs.

- If time permits, invite comments, questions, or decisions from participants to the whole group.

For Teens: If teens are not viewing *In the Nuclear Shadow* or *Mother of the Year* or helping with the "over-6's" watching *Buster and Me,* they can be engaged in one of the following activities:

- viewing *Top Gun;* in addition to the full-length video of the popular 1986 film, the PPJN has a 30-minute video of excerpts plus a discussion guide prepared by David McLintock, a regional PPJN coordinator and former "top gun" U.S. Navy fighter pilot.

- viewing *Every Heart Beats True,* a 20-minute filmstrip about Christian perspectives on military service, a moving reflection on the pacifist option for teens, from Packard Manse Project, Box 450, Stoughton, MA 02072.

- examining military recruiting ads in teen publications. Contact the PPJN for the August–September 1987 issue of the PPJN Newsletter, a special issue on militarism and U.S. youth.

EVERYONE 'NEATH THEIR VINE AND FIG TREE

Everyone 'neath their vine and fig tree
shall live in peace and unafraid

[repeated]

And into plowshares turn their swords;
nations shall make war no more

[repeated]

Simple body movements depict the words:

"'neath their vine": hand over the head
shaking leaves
"shall live in peace": hands lowered and
holding the hand of the person
next to you
"plowshares": hands digging into the
ground
"turn their swords": hands coming up in
front of the body and forming two
fists, one on top of the other,
simulating holding a sword
"make war no more": hands crossed
horizontally in front of body
sweeping outward to show "no more"

---

9. CONCLUDING PRAYER AND SONG

"The Lord said, 'Go.'" The commissioning character of the following prayer is appropriate for this session, especially in conjunction with the passage from Jeremiah 1. If possible, have the participants sing "Here I Am, Lord" by the St. Louis Jesuits, as their personal response to God's call.

THE LORD SAID, "GO"

And the Lord said, "Go!"
   and I said, "Who, me?"
   and God said, "Yes, you!"
   and I said, "But I'm not ready yet
   and there is company coming,
   and I can't leave my kids;
   you know there's no one to take my place."
And God said, "You're stalling."

Again the Lord said, "Go!"
   and I said, "But I don't want to,"
   and God said,
   "I didn't ask if you wanted to."
   And I said,
   "Listen, I'm not the kind of person
   to get involved in controversy.
   Besides, my family won't like it,
   and what will the neighbors think!"
And God said, "Baloney!"

And yet a third time the Lord said, "Go!"
   and I said, "Do I have to?"
   and God said, "Do you love me?"
   and I said, "Look, I'm scared...
   People are going to hate me...
   and cut me into little pieces...
   I can't take it all by myself."
And God said, "Where do you think I'll be?"

And the Lord said, "Go!"
   and I sighed,
   "Here I am, send me!"[5]

---

[5] By Lois Hodrick from Oakland, Calif., a Disciple of Christ missioner in Zaire, in *Maryknoll* magazine, November 1984.

CHAPTER 7

Consumerism and Stewardship

The "Consumerism and Stewardship" session is generally perceived as helpful and immediately attractive to a wide range of adults, who are often quite concerned about the effects on children of TV, peer pressure, and other sources of consumerism or materialism. Action possibilities, especially in terms of lifestyle changes, are readily available at all levels of risk or sacrifice.

On a weekend program, this session fits well in the Sunday morning slot, especially if followed by a worship service. The offering in the service can be related to individual and group projects of the preceding session. This session also integrates well with the "global family" theme and especially our oneness with the earth itself (see pp. 36–37). Our oneness with the earth and with present and future generations of our global family requires a stewardship mentality.

Goals

Both inspirational and practical dimensions are important for promoting a greater commitment to work for personal lifestyle changes as well as changes in the policies of economic, political, and religious institutions. The activities are also engaging and often fun; the key to personal lifestyle changes is to find *joyful* alternatives to a materialistic lifestyle.

Components

1. FAMILY WALK

Before or after breakfast or perhaps right before the session begins (especially if it is scheduled for morning), ask each family to take a 15- to 30-minute reflective walk, observing and admiring the beauty of God's gifts of creation. Symbols of that beauty can be gathered for a table or altar display in the meeting room or worship area. Silence should prevail during the walk. Afterward family members gather in a circle and each person shares a short reflection or single word that expresses what the experience meant for that person. A brief prayer of praise and thanksgiving might conclude the family sharing.

2. GATHERING SONG AND REFLECTION

There are any number of morning hymns of praise for God's abundant love and gifts of creation. Also appropriate is the Quaker hymn "'Tis a Gift to Be Simple" (see Worksheet 19). The biblical reflection on stewardship might use selections from the Sermon on the Mount (Matthew 5–7) or Peter 4:9–11. This should be brief. At this time the term "stewardship" should be introduced to the group. One way of learning and remembering its meaning is to repeat several times in a chanting style, holding the earth ball:

STEWARDSHIP MEANS

Sparing and sharing as two ways of caring
for the earth and all of God's people.

For groups wanting more background information on the reasons for a simpler lifestyle, see Worksheet 19.

3. VALUES DILEMMA

The following story is told on the *Building Shalom Families* video program (see p. 149) and illustrates a dilemma faced by many middle-class families:

For his tenth birthday, Tom asks his parents for a new bike costing $110 at a local department

46

store. His two best friends recently got new bikes and he is tired of always having used things. "It's my *tenth* birthday besides," he tells his parents. "I should get something special." His parents are reluctant to say yes, knowing they can get him a good used bike for less than $50. They feel it would be wrong for them to spend $110 for one present. But Tom insists he wants a new bike. What should they do?

Ask each family to take three minutes to come up with some "bright ideas" for dealing with the dilemma and then solicit some of these suggestions in the whole group. There are no "right" answers. If you are interested in how the actual dilemma was resolved, play the *Building Shalom Families* video. The resolution took a month and involved Tom's discovering that initial ideas for raising $60 (to match his parents' $50 contribution) did not work out. He found a good used bike, but added some new parts for a final assembly that his friends thought was "awesome."

4. WHAT ARE WE DOING?

What Can We Do?: Distribute Worksheet 20 to each family and ask them to write out what they're already doing with regard to stewardship in each of the five categories. Be sure to stress that they work only on the "Already Doing" column, not on what they *might* do. That is for later. Families might compare lists with others at their table, if time permits.

Solicit their practices and write each one on newsprint or a blackboard, two or three minutes for each category, considered one at a time. Encourage participants to write down in the "Possible Next Steps" column ideas they hear that they want to consider. An engaging way of sharing ideas is to combine pantomime with verbal descriptions, that is, have the first two or three examples for each category be acted out in pantomime, with participants guessing the activity; this is followed by several other examples shared orally. Be sure to solicit examples that incorporate "sharing" as well as "sparing" and that involve the whole family, not just individual members.

101 Ways: As an alternative to Worksheet 20 or as a supplement at the end of that activity, distribute Worksheet 21, which lists 101 ways of "living

green." This means promoting respect for the earth and for human diversity and encouraging involvement in changing social structures. Ask participants to mark those items they are already doing, perhaps distinguishing those they do regularly from those they do only occasionally. Then ask them to identify those items they would like to do or do more of. These too can be divided into things they would like

to do in the next month, the next year, the next five years. It's best not to overwhelm people by suggesting that they should be doing dozens of new things at once.

Savings and Sharing: In individual family units once again, write down thirteen ways your family can save money. Prioritize. Then create a family bank. Have on hand several discarded containers, such as soup cans, margarine containers, bleach bottles, fabric softener bottles. Be sure to have enough so that each family has one container. Create a bank out of your container. Families may wish to illustrate or write some of their thirteen money-saving ideas somewhere on the container-turned-bank.

As families, they decide on how to use the money saved — a mission project, a family outing, a special family purchase that all agree on. The bank can then be decorated with pictures of the people with whom some of the savings will be shared.

As an alternative, get a "world bank" (a small globe bank) from the Holy Childhood Association,

1720 Massachusetts Ave., N.W., Washington, DC 20036, or from local dime stores.[1]

Shakertown Pledge: Distribute Worksheet 23 and read aloud the pledge in the left-hand column. Families are asked to brainstorm about ways of implementing each of the nine points, putting each way in its appropriate column.

For an audio-visual presentation on the Shakertown Pledge, use a 15-minute filmstrip entitled *Bread, Justice and Global Interdependence,* by James McGinnis (available from the Institute for Peace and Justice; $15 rental).

Have–Need Checklist: Distribute Worksheet 24 to each family and ask them to answer the questions. Then ask them to discuss their responses and decide what changes they might like to consider making as a family.

Ten Objects Exercise: This activity (Worksheet 25) can be fun for families at home. Duplicate a copy for each family.

5. GROUP PROJECTS

Examine the various projects nominated by participants and written on newsprint (see p. 26). Try to reach a quick consensus on one or two projects as options for financial support as well as other supportive measures (for example, letters to political leaders, victims, or advocates involved in the project; personal involvement through volunteer time).

6. FAMILY NEXT STEPS

Ask each family to make decisions on both their own lifestyle changes and on how they want to relate to the group project options.

7. DEALING WITH CONSUMER PRESSURES

Seeing Through Commercials: The over-6's, and the adults who want to, view *Seeing Through Commercials,* a 17-minute 16mm film from Barr Films (P.O. Box 5677, Pasadena, CA 91107; $300 purchase, $30 rental).

For elementary-aged children as well as adults, the film shows how TV commercials manipulate children through deceptive techniques. After the film, children can be asked to respond to the film narrator's final question about identifying the various tricks used in the final commercial.

Critical Viewing: Teens and adults view *The Six Billion Dollar Sell,* a 15-minute color film from the New York State Consumer Protection Board, 256 Washington St., Mt. Vernon, NY 10553. The discussion of this film and *Seeing Through Commercials,* above, can include the following questions:

* Have you ever really wanted something you saw advertised on TV (candy, doll, toy car, vegematic)?

* Have you ever been disappointed after you got something advertised on TV (for example, the toy broke quickly, it was smaller than you expected it to be, or it was not as exciting as you thought it would be)?

* Does anybody know any commercial jingles? Why do advertisers use jingles?

* What can we do to keep from being taken in by commercials?

A Commercial Circus: Discuss how TV, radio, magazines, and advertisements encourage us to value material goods as the most important things in our lives. Have the children act out commercials they remember. Then have them think of things they enjoy that do not cost anything, such as a sunset, petting a cat, playing with a friend, swimming in the lake. Ask them to make up commercials to advertise these and perform the commercials for the rest of the group.[2]

Family Commercials: Several families are responsible for making a commercial that tries either to sell a good and useful product or a spoof that tries to trick us into buying something. Use the following starters:

Ground rules:

* Everybody in the group must get to appear in the commercial.

* The commercial can be no longer than two minutes in length.

---

[1] From "Families Covenanting for Peace"; see below, p. 83.

[2] From "Youth Camps on Peacemaking"; see below, p. 83.

Questions to consider:

- How can we make the product look attractive?

- What can the narrator say to encourage people to buy it?

- What sound effects might be helpful?

- What do you want the audience to believe about the product?

Videos and Values: For teens and adults, the PPJN has a 15-minute video, *Videos and Values,* made up of several 1986 and 1987 rock videos that illustrate societal values that are either consistent with or counter to Christian values, including several on consumerism. A discussion guide accompanies the video.

Magazine Ads: Participants, particularly teens, browse through teen magazines with a critical eye for advertisements. Then they fill out a simple questionnaire:

- How much space is devoted to ads?

- What's the purpose of the ads for the magazine? For you?

- What's the pitch?

- How is it directed toward (1) women? (2) men? (3) children? (4) minorities? (5) people in general?

- Are the images humanizing (*shalom* inducing) or dehumanizing?

- What is stewardship?

- What does stewardship mean to an affluent person or society?

- What does it mean for those who don't have the basic necessities?

- How can we be better stewards — by consuming less? recycling? conserving energy? eating lower on the food chain? working against pollution? working for a clean environment and renewable resources?[3]

Peer Discussion: Divide into groups of teens, over-6's, and adults with preschool, elementary school, teen, or grown children. Participants discuss how to deal with consumerism and its pressure from peers, from relatives, and from the media on themselves or the children they care for.

8. JOYFUL ALTERNATIVES

As a part of either a long first session on consumerism and stewardship or a second session on the same theme, generate some joyful alternatives to consumerism. For example, focus on the next major holiday or gift-giving occasion; then alternative ideas can be put into practice right away, for example, Halloween, Thanksgiving, Christmas, Valentine's Day, Easter, weddings. Birthdays are a good focus any time of year. The discussion should focus on this question:

> What are some alternative ways to celebrate (less materialistic, more person-centered than thing-centered, ecologically sound, inexpensive, globally conscious)?

If Christmas is the focus, an excellent AV is *Have Yourself a Merry Little Christmas,* a 17-minute filmstrip from Alternatives (P.O. Box 429, Ellenwood, GA 30049). For teens and adults, it describes the commercialism of Christmas and presents a wide variety of joyful, creative, people-centered alternatives.

The discussion can take place on three levels: first, within each family; then at the same table; finally, as a whole group, with the leader soliciting "bright ideas" with the light bulb microphone.

9. CONCLUDING REFLECTION

Slides of the earth or of specific manifestations of the beauty of God's creation are projected on a screen as participants read together the reflection of Chief Seattle, printed on Worksheet 20. This reflection is also visually illustrated as part of the *Building Shalom Families* video program.

---

[3]From "Youth Camps on Peacemaking"; see below, p. 83.

CHAPTER 8

Celebrating Diversity and Human Possibilities

Often there is not enough time, especially in a two-day program, to include the topics of racism and sexism. We approach these topics in terms of their family connections:

- how to develop healthy racial attitudes in our children;

- how to break down sex-role stereotypes at home and promote our children's full human potential;

- how to work together as families to combat the racism and sexism in our society.

Because of the importance of these themes, we try to incorporate them as much as possible into any PPJ program, even if separate whole sessions on each theme are not feasible. Sometimes they are combined into a single session. Other times they are incorporated into other sessions. Examples include:

- using the story of Jumping Mouse, a Native American folk tale (see above p. 25);

- using Chief Seattle's reflection with the stewardship session (see Worksheet 20);

- using the Kwanza celebration during the program (see Worksheet 29);

- having the video *Free to Be You and Me* as part of the children's program or available during open AV time (see p. 53);

- having a display of good multicultural and anti-sexist children's books;

- using inclusive (nonsexist) language in all presentations, songs, and prayers;

- modelling nonsexist ways of doing program tasks like food preparation, clean-up, and child care.

Goals

Adult participants are encouraged to reflect on their own upbringing in terms of racial and sex-role attitudes.

All participants are helped to see the subtlety and pervasiveness of racial and sex-role stereotypes, how they consciously or unconsciously perpetuate some of these stereotypes, and then how to counteract them.

Practical strategies for change focus on the home environment, local institutions like school and church, and larger social institutions that families often relate to, like the media and entertainment and recreation industries.

Components

1. GATHERING SONG AND REFLECTION

"We've Got the Whole World in Our Hands" and "We're All a Family Under One Sky" can both be adapted to include different racial groups and peoples of all ages, sexes, and handicaps. Biblical passages for silent reflection and small group or family discussion include Matthew 7:12, Ephesians 2:19–20, and especially 1 Corinthians 12:12–13. This text can be combined with a series of slides or a collage of pictures (see below). The *Building Shalom Families* video program includes a visual reflection on this text.

Global Family Collage: If this was not done in the "Shalom in the Global Family" session (chapter 6, p. 38), it would fit well here. Have participants go through magazines for appropriate pictures of people of different racial groups. This task could well be expanded to include men and women in a variety of roles, positive images of older persons, and persons with disabilities.

The Good Samaritan: Read the parable of the Good Samaritan (Luke 10:25–37) and encourage a discussion of "Who is my neighbor?" List many different kinds of people, for example, old ladies in nursing homes, Russians, drunks, a big kid who lives down the street, teachers, Africans, best friends, and decide who are our neighbors. The parable can also be acted out.

Identify prejudice. Discuss what a prejudice is. Give some examples. Describe the prejudice of the people who passed by the Samaritan. Ask participants to try to identify one of their own prejudices.[1]

2. DISCOVERING WHO WE ARE

As a prelude to discussion of racial or sex-role stereotypes, it is important to have each person discover something about his or her own background and experience with regard to the themes of this session. This can be done in several ways:

Personal Experience of Stereotypes: Ask participants of all ages to identify ways they have been stereotyped themselves (teens and over-6's should respond enthusiastically to an opportunity to say how adults stereotype them, and vice versa!). Older participants, short persons, heavy persons, persons with a disability, and many others have a wealth of personal (generally painful) experiences to share. Invite these persons to share how they felt and how they would like to be treated.

Racial Background Sheet: This worksheet is a good tool for adults (possibly teens) to fill out and discuss in small groups (see Worksheet 26).

Drawing Indians: Participants draw what comes to mind when they hear the word "Indian." This is a good prelude for over-6's before viewing the filmstrip *Unlearning Indian Stereotypes* (see below).

Word Associations: Participants of all ages respond to words like "Indian," "Black," "blind," "cripple," "homosexual," "babe," "boy." Saying the first thing that comes to mind can unveil stereotypes we all carry around, generally without being aware of them.

---

[1]From "Youth Camps on Peacemaking"; see below, p. 83.

3. RACIAL STEREOTYPES

A number of excellent audio-visuals are available, many from the Council on Interracial Books for Children. Among the best for an intergenerational program is *Unlearning Indian Stereotypes.* This 15-minute filmstrip has Native American children

telling viewers how they are stereotyped and how they feel about the injustices done to Native Americans throughout U.S. history. In the film there are implicit strategies for viewers to change their own attitude and behavior as well as the policies of political and economic institutions. The children say things that are hard for many non-Indians to hear and they express strong feelings.

It is important to remind viewers that we need to hear such things, even if they make us uncomfortable. And it is crucial to help viewers realize that, even if they are not personally responsible for any of the injustices, they benefit from them. Once we become aware of such injustices and of what we can do to challenge them, then we have a responsibility to act. If we fail to act, *then* we become guilty. Dealing with responses of guilt, defensiveness, and "blaming the victim" requires an alert and sensitive leader. The filmstrip is best handled as follows:

- have some kind of preliminary personal inventory (see no. 2 above, "Discovering Who We Are");

- encourage openness in viewers, pointing out the observations noted above;

- after the filmstrip, have viewers respond either in pairs or as a family to the question "How did you feel as you watched the filmstrip?";

- have a more focused discussion at individual tables before the whole group discussion; include some or all of the following questions:

- How did the children in the filmstrip feel?

- Why do you think they felt this way?

- How did you feel as they shared their thoughts and feelings?

- Are there ways we perpetuate any of the stereotypes?

- What can we do to counter these stereotypes?

- separate over-6's from older participants to read a children's book that presents a positive view of Native Americans, preferably a book by a Native American author (see the bibliography below, especially pp. 92–94);

- have adults and teens continue their discussion later (it has to be short initially in order not to lose the children's attention).

The Secret of Goodasme: If the racism and sexism topics are combined into a single session, an excellent filmstrip combines the two: *The Secret of Goodasme,* a 17-minute filmstrip from the Council on Interracial Books for Children (1841 Broadway, New York, NY 10023; tel.: 212-757-5339). For middle-grade youth and up, it presents the realities of racial and sex-role stereotypes through interactions among three North American youth (a White female and Black and Cherokee males) and two visitors from the planet Goodasme.

Other Filmstrips: If Native Americans are not the most appropriate stereotyped racial group for your group to consider, other Council filmstrips are available: *Unlearning Chicano and Puerto Rican Stereotypes* and *Unlearning Asian American Stereotypes.*

Black History: An entertaining and insightful 16mm film on stereotypes of Black Americans is *Black History: Lost, Stolen or Strayed.* Narrated by Bill Cosby, this 60-minute film is available in many public library film centers and can be shown in 30-minute segments.

Children's Books: If an audio-visual presentation is not feasible, examining children's books for racial (and other) stereotypes can be an engaging alternative for participants of all ages.

Positive Images: Examining magazines, TV shows, children's toys, and other items for a lack of positive (or any) images of different racial groups can be an insightful activity. Question 6 on the "Checklist for My Home" (Worksheet 27) is good for each family to discuss and then use more systematically upon returning home; TV readily engages people of all ages.

Childcare Shapes the Future: Anti-Racist Strategies: This is a two-part filmstrip: the first examines racial stereotypes unconsciously perpetuated in most child care and home environments; the second identifies ten specific strategies for change. Available from the Council on Interracial Books for Children.

Wesley: As another option particularly appropriate for teens, read the story of Wesley and discuss the questions attached (see Worksheet 28).

4. WHAT CAN WE DO ABOUT RACISM?

If the discussion of the audio-visuals or books used in Component 3 did not focus explicitly on what participants can do about the stereotypes presented, this probably should be done before moving on to the more general strategies suggested by Worksheet 27.

Checklist for My Home: Each family fills out Worksheet 27, identifying those items that they feel most able to address at this time and specifying what they will do.

Bibliography: Distribute the bibliography of children's books (see below, pp. 89–94) to each family. Encourage them to use it for their family reading and to share it with their school, church, and public libraries.

Rewrite Stereotyped Stories: Take children's books, stories, or fairy tales that use stereotypes and rewrite them in nonstereotypic ways.[2]

Kwanza and Other Multicultural Celebrations: Distribute the Kwanza description (Worksheet 29) and encourage families to consider incorporating aspects of the celebration into their own December 26–January 1 celebration. To model this suggestion, incorporate some aspect into the PPJ program itself,

---

[2]From "Little Friends for Peace — Peacemaking Education"; see below, p. 82.

for example, one of the program meals could be the Kwanza meal described in the final paragraph.

The principles of Kwanza can be linked with the various aspects of *shalom* considered in each of the program sessions, for example, Umoja as "unity" and Ujima as "working together as the good of all" parallel the unity of *shalom* most prominently illustrated in "Shalom in the Home" (chapter 5) and "Shalom in the Global Family" (chapter 6).

What Can We Do About Racism?:   Worksheet 35 is a one-page listing of family actions to counter-

act racism and Worksheet 36 is a similar listing of school and church actions. These can be duplicated for participants and serve as an important resource for leaders who want to become more sensitive and knowledgeable on this issue.

5. SEX-ROLE STEREOTYPES

As noted at the beginning of this chapter, this theme often has to be combined with racism. If so, *The Secret of Goodasme* is generally the best audio-visual. One or two of the "What can we do?" activities below is generally all that time permits. The various other activities can be suggested for use at home.

Biblical Reflection: Jesus' attitude toward and treatment of women challenged the cultural practices of the time. Many episodes could be shared, including Luke 21:1–4, 7:36–50 (faith of widows and outcast

women), and 24:10, 22–25 (women as first witnesses of the resurrection).

Childcare Shapes the Future: If *The Secret of Goodasme* filmstrip is not used, then we suggest either or both parts of the two-part filmstrip *Childcare Shapes the Future: Anti-Sexist Strategies* (see above, p. 52). While applying to young children, this filmstrip is really geared to adults. Consequently, it might be best to combine this adult activity with the following for over-6's and teens.

Free to Be You and Me: This film/video is entertaining for viewers of all ages, but it is over-6's and adults who enjoy it the most. We usually show the first 20 minutes to both adults and children and ask them to discuss several of the episodes right after their showing: What do you think about boys playing with dolls (from "William Wants a Doll"), about boys who cry (from the song "It's All Right to Cry"), about mommies who are umpires or daddies who bake (from "Parents Are People")? Then the over-6's view the remainder of the video while adults view and discuss further the audio-visual chosen in the preceding activity.

Magazine Advertisements: Another teen option (which can also include adults) is to examine teen magazines for sexist (and other stereotypic) ads. A helpful progression of questions includes the following:

- What did you see in the ad?
- What does it mean?
- How do you feel about it?
- What can you do about it?

6. WHAT CAN WE DO ABOUT SEXISM?

Family Task Chart: Distribute Worksheet 30 and have each family complete it as described on the Worksheet.

Gender Binds: Participants identify two or three things they would like to do as a girl or boy, woman or man that they do not or cannot do because others think it should only be done by members of the opposite sex. Compare lists within each family and with other families at each table. Decide how each person can take a step out of the bind and support others taking similar steps.[3]

Family Vignettes: Distribute Worksheet 31 to each participant. Have over-6's and their parents read and discuss the "Bobby" vignette, while teens and their parents read and discuss the "Saundra" vignette.

TV Monitor Sheet: Distribute Worksheet 32 and encourage families to do the activity together when they return home. Asking for comments from the whole group on several of the questions as soon as the worksheet is distributed increases the likelihood that families will use it later on their own.

7. CONCLUDING REFLECTION

Read the following passage on Sojourner Truth. Pause for a few minutes of silent reflection.

In the last century, there was a woman named Sojourner Truth. She was born a slave. She escaped from her master as an adult and spent most of her life fighting to free all slaves as well as fighting for the rights of women. This is her famous reply to a man's statement that women were inferior to men and could not manage without men's directions:

> *"What's all this here talking about? That man over there say that woman needs to be helped into carriages, and lifted over ditches, and to have the best place everywhere. Nobody ever helps me into carriages, or over mud puddles, or gives me any best place, and ain't I a woman? Look at me! I have plowed, and planted, and gathered into barns, and no man could head me — and ain't I a woman? I could work as much and eat as much as a man (when I could get it), and bear the lash as well — and ain't I a woman! I have borne five children and seen them most all sold off into slavery, and when I cried out with a mother's grief, none but Jesus heard — and ain't I a woman?"*

"There is no such thing as . . . male or female; for you are all one person in Christ Jesus"
                                        (Galatians 3:28, NEB*).*

One appropriate sung response is the Christian hymn "We Are One in the Spirit" (also known as "They'll Know We Are Christians by Our Love"). To make this hymn as inclusive as possible, substitute "each one's dignity" for "each man's dignity" and "they'll know we are faithful" for "they'll know we are Christian. . . ." See the prayer book *More Than Words* (Meyer-Stone, 1988) for many other song and prayer options.

8. DEALING WITH OTHER DIFFERENCES

As mentioned above, there are many other groups who are stereotyped in our society and thereby have their own full human potential jeopardized. The experiences and feelings of these persons can be shared as in the first part of the racism session (see above, "Discovering Who We Are," p. 51). If it has not been done, then such sharing can be added to the session "Sex-Role Stereotypes" above. In addition, leaders might consider the following options:

Disability Awareness: Distribute Worksheet 33 or use a copy of the Easter Seal poster. Families discuss the four questions on the sheet.

Simulated experiences can follow or precede the discussion of persons with disabilities. For example, each participant chooses a handicap to role play for a specific length of time, perhaps through a meal. A person might pick blindness, for example: a blindfold is worn and a friend guides the person during the allotted time. The two might change places halfway through. Another person might decide to use only one arm, the other gently tied to the body. Simulate being hard of hearing by wearing safe earplugs.

At the end of the specified time period, it is important to gather and talk about the experience. How did it feel to be helpless and need to depend on others for certain things? What did you miss? What ways did you compensate for the handicap? For those who were blind, did their hearing become more acute? Does the experience change the way you will think about and relate to handicapped persons in the future?

This can be a very powerful experience. Listen carefully to the feelings of the group as you help them process this experience.[4]

---

[3]From "Little Friends for Peace — Peacemaking Education"; see below, p. 82.

[4]From "Youth Camps on Peacemaking"; see below, p. 83.

Homophobia: It is important to realize that the "Bobby" vignette (see Worksheet 31) generally raises the whole issue of homosexuality. This is a difficult issue for many people to deal with. There is a lot of "homophobia" (fear of homosexuality) in our society. As with the other groups of stereotyped persons, so too here probably the most insightful way of beginning to deal with this issue is to listen carefully and openly to the experiences and feelings of gay and lesbian people. If this is not possible or desirable within the program sessions themselves, perhaps such opportunities can be provided or encouraged outside the program.

How a family responds to a gay member as well as how parents educate children to understand and respect homosexual people in society are important concerns. One resource that we recommend is *Homosexuality and Families: A Resource Packet for Parents and Local Church Leaders.* The packet contains an assortment of leaflets and brochures intended for use by families with gay members and by church leaders who are planning ministries with such families. It was compiled by Leon Smith for the United Methodist Church and is available from Discipleship Resources, Box 840, Nashville, TN 37202.

CHAPTER 9

Worship Suggestions

As emphasized in chapter 5, prayer and worship are an integral part of any PPJ program. Participants are invited to an ongoing conversion of heart more than to learning a series of techniques or performing a series of actions. The inner core of solidarity needs to be nurtured if participants are going to be faithful over the long haul to compassionate and courageous acts of solidarity.

Therefore, each session incorporates an element of prayer and reflection, at least at the beginning and end. In addition, many family experiences build in a time for morning prayer before break-

fast and evening prayer after dinner or as part of an evening program or campfire. Combining song, group prayers, moments of silent reflection, and spontaneous prayer is important.

Also, as stressed in chapter 5, it is important to be as inclusive as possible in the language, imagery, and faith traditions out of which our prayer arises. Again, *Peacemaking Day by Day* (Pax Christi USA, 348 E. 10th St., Erie, PA 16503) and *More Than Words* (Meyer-Stone Books, 1988) are wonderful resources for such inclusive prayers and worship services.

Frequently Used Prayers

In addition to the prayers and reflections suggested for specific sessions in this program, there are several prayers that are especially appropriate and that can be repeated several times during a program.

The Peace Prayer of St. Francis:

Lord, make me an instrument of thy peace;
where there is hatred, let me sow love;
where there is injury, pardon;
where there is doubt, faith;
where there is despair, hope;
where there is darkness, light;
and where there is sadness, joy.

O Divine Master,
grant that I may not so much seek
to be consoled as to console;
to be understood as to understand;
to be loved as to love;
for it is in giving that we receive,
it is in pardoning that we are pardoned,
and it is in dying that we are born to eternal life.

The World Peace Prayer from the Fellowship of Reconciliation:

Lead me from death to life,
from falsehood to truth;
lead me from despair to hope,
from fear to trust;
lead me from hate to love,
from war to peace.
Let peace fill our heart, our world, our universe.

Closing Communion Service

CALLED, EMPOWERED,
AND SENT FORTH BY THE SPIRIT

We strongly recommend a Sunday morning Communion service for any weekend program or as part of the final session in any weekly or monthly program series. The drawing together of the program experiences and themes, the bonding of program participants, the lifting up of participant decisions, and the uniting with our God, the earth, and the peoples of our world that can happen in a Communion service such as outlined below can be the most transformative experience of the entire program.

Worship that emerges from the people and experiences of a program are generally more meaningful and participatory than those created beforehand by the program planners or leaders. But it is often difficult and quite time-consuming to start from scratch on a Saturday night when most participants are exhausted. Thus we recommend that one program planner and one program leader work with several participant volunteers (solicited at the first session) in designing the Communion service. The program planner and leader might have specific readings, songs, and other components in mind ahead of time that can be used if they are consistent with the way the program was actually experienced.

The following Communion service was created during a family camp weekend. Because it was created as a way of experiencing more deeply the specific themes and activities described in this guidebook, it will probably have many components that are appropriate for any PPJ family program conducted according to this guidebook. Use as much of the following as you and your group find meaningful. But also use your own creativity and the movements of the Spirit of God within your own program.

1. CALL TO WORSHIP

One of the program planners shares a brief opening reflection on the meaning of the experience as the planners had conceived it months before and how it came to bear the fruit that it did.

The song "Spirit of the Living God, Fall Afresh on Me," which can be accompanied by bodily movements, or another Spirit-related song, introduces the theme, "Called, Empowered, and Sent by the Spirit."

2. RECONCILIATION RITE

The worship leader recalls Jesus' first appearance to his disciples after his resurrection (John 20:19–23). We, like them, often hide behind locked doors for fear of being nailed as Jesus was nailed. We, like them, need to hear Jesus' words of acceptance, forgiveness, and commissioning. Instead of chiding us for our failures to follow him to the cross, he simply says, "Peace." He accepts us right where we are.

Then he sends us his Spirit so that, empowered by that Spirit, we can say "yes" to his sending us forth just as God sent him forth. Realizing the acceptance and forgiveness of our Lord, we are free to look at specific areas of our lives and mission where we need reconciliation.

First, we seek reconciliation within our families. Each family is asked to huddle together. Each person identifies a specific behavior or attitude for which he or she wants forgiveness or names one way he or she can make *shalom* more a reality within the home. This sharing might be enriched by the questions in the Family Reconciliation Service (Worksheet 12). The sharing should conclude with some kind of expression of love, for example, a group hug.

Second, we seek reconciliation with those people whom we have long regarded as "enemy." Those peoples that had a special place in the program are the logical groups on which to focus at this point. Prominent in this guidebook are the peoples of the Soviet Union and the Japanese, particularly the people of Hiroshima and Nagasaki.

The People of the Soviet Union: For a focus on the people of the Soviet Union, the following was very meaningful:

- The group rises and moves to a portion of the main meeting room where the posters of the people of the Soviet Union are hung around the poem by a Soviet schoolgirl printed large on newsprint (see Worksheet 13). After a brief comment by the leader on Jesus' command to love our enemies, the group recites the poem.

- This is followed immediately by the recitation of a litany prayed every Sunday in the Russian Orthodox church. Praying in the words of another people is to bond with them. To accept their prayers for us is to experience their care and desire for reconciliation. Praying together with them is to experience our mutual reconciliation. The litany can be duplicated and distributed to each participant or, at least, the response printed on the wall. Having a copy of the litany may encourage participants to pray it after the program as well (see Worksheet 37).

The People of Japan: Reconciliation with the people of Japan can be expressed as follows: project a visual from the *Sadako* slides on the Shalom Mural blank space (see p. 24). Recall Sadako's words printed on the mural: "I will write 'peace' on your wings and you will fly all over the world." Invite participants to share briefly the names of the person to whom they plan to give their paper crane. A

camp or church bell can be rung as a sign of mourning. If the candle lanterns were used the evening before and were burned (see above p. 41), the ashes can be incorporated into this reconciliation rite.

The Earth: Reconciliation with the earth is best expressed outdoors. With the leader holding an earth ball, participants are asked to identify for themselves ways they have misused the earth or used their hands to harm or neglect the earth (for example, a tree, flower, the ground). Then they are asked to pronounce a silent blessing for Mother Earth and to pledge their renewed efforts always to be a blessing, not a curse, for the earth. Invoking the Great Spirit and recalling Chief Seattle's words from the prayerful conclusion to the session on "Consumerism and Stewardship" (see Worksheet 20), the leader concludes this portion of the reconciliation rite.

3. HYMN OF PRAISE

While still outdoors, a designated reader recites one of the Psalms that sings of the splendor of God's creation and the everlastingness of God's love. An "alleluia" response is sung.

4. READINGS AND RESPONSES

Isaiah 32:15–20:   This is a beautiful prophetic passage linking true peace and security with justice and integrity, proclaiming the ultimate harmonization of all the earth and its peoples, and acknowledging that this realization of *shalom* will be the work of the Spirit once again poured out over the earth.

An appropriate response to this reading is this prayer:

> Come, Holy Spirit,
> fill the hearts of your faithful
> and enkindle in us the fire of your love.
> Send forth your Spirit, Lord,
> and we will be recreated
> and you will renew the face of the earth.

This could be spoken, chanted, or sung more than once, to impress its meaning more fully on participants. Since most people do not know this prayer, post it on newsprint in front of the group.

Isaiah 2:3–8:   This is another familiar prophetic expression of God's promise of *shalom,* with emphasis on peace among nations. An appropriate sung response, especially if it was used during the program, is "Everyone 'Neath Their Vine and Fig Tree" (see above, p. 45) or "I Ain't Gonna Study War No More."

Cloud of Witnesses: As a transition to the third biblical reflection, the leader can share the "cloud of witnesses" theme in Hebrews 10–11, where Paul recalls many of the great witnesses of faith in the Hebrew Scriptures. These witnesses and the Hebrew prophets, like Isaiah and Jeremiah, are God's early dreamers. Today we have similar dreamers, prophets, witnesses. The leader invites participants to name some of these dreamers who have been very much with the group through the program. As each dreamer is named — for example, Ruth Nelson, Sadako, Gandhi, Dorothy Day — his or her name is written in bold print on the Shalom Mural in the lefthand column for "peacemakers" (see p. 24).

I Still Have a Dream: An inspirational sermon is Martin Luther King's "I Still Have a Dream." This is printed below (see Worksheet 39) and can be read against a backdrop of a picture or slide of Dr. King. Far more effective, however, is to play this sermon from the video *Trumpet of Conscience*, a 1985 one-hour TV documentary of his life. The Institute for Peace and Justice has a single copy, which can be borrowed if there is no other source (for example, a local TV network affiliate).

5. RESPONSE TO THE READINGS AND SERMON: OFFERING

On the table or altar are placed containers for each of the group project options decided on by the group during the preceding session on "Consumerism and Stewardship" (see p. 48). With these are also placed other symbols special to the program, for example, an earth ball (see above p. 36), candles, a loaf of bread, the Real Family Jewels necklaces (see above p. 27). Family representatives are invited to put their family's offering in the container. Other family representatives present a strip of construction paper on which is written the family's decision about their next step as agents of God's promise of *shalom*. These can be placed on the right-hand column of the Shalom Mural.

6. KISS OF PEACE (PASSING THE PEACE)

Singing and dancing *"Shalom Chaverim"* (see Worksheet 38) is a wonderfully engaging way to share greetings or blessings of peace with one another.

If there is a transition from the main meeting room, where this "litany of the Word" has been celebrated, to a chapel for the Communion service, the exchanges of peace can take place as participants move to the sanctuary. One of the Communion ministers takes the loaf of bread, symbol of our oneness as God's global family, and leads the procession.

7. GATHERING AROUND THE ALTAR IN THE SANCTUARY

Exchanges of peace can be completed, if necessary.

The symbol of the Cross should be noted — that all the symbols of *shalom* that adorned the opening table or altar will become reality only because Jesus paid the price for peace — his own blood poured out for us, and only if we, as followers of Jesus, are willing to pay a price as well.

The leader then reminds the group that by sending his Spirit Jesus empowers us to follow him.

8. COMMUNION

The gifts of bread and wine and the symbols and commitments of the program participants are blessed and offered to God.

The Lord's Prayer is recited or sung together.

Communicants are reminded that just as Jesus manifested himself to the disciples on the road to Emmaus in the breaking of the bread, so too he makes himself present to us through the Eucharist.

Four Communion ministers each take a quarter of the one loaf to one part of the chapel or sanctuary. There they break off a piece of the loaf, hand it to another person, and pronounce a brief blessing on that person (for example, "May this Bread of Life be a source of fuller life for you" or "May the Jesus who gave his life for all of us give you the courage to follow in his footsteps").

Any number of Communion hymns emphasizing our oneness in the Body of Christ are appropriate; remember to make them as inclusive as possible.

9. COMMISSIONING

If they were not used as part of the closing reflection in the session on "Shalom in the Global Family" (p. 45), then the reflection "The Lord Said, 'Go,'" Jeremiah 1:4–8, and the song "Here I Am, Lord" by the St. Louis Jesuits make an inspirational commissioning component.

If they were used, then some other appropriate commissioning text can be substituted, perhaps incorporating parts of John 15 and 16 and a hymn reflecting our being called, empowered, and sent forth by the Spirit of God, for example, "Be Not Afraid" by the St. Louis Jesuits.

10. FINAL BLESSING

The worship leader concludes the service with a final blessing, inviting participants to "go forth to serve God and God's people."

CHAPTER 10

Where Do We Go from Here?

As noted in chapter 2, we remain faithful to compassionate and courageous action in part when we experience the support and challenge of a small community of faith. Nurturing this sense of "in it with others," of not being alone, needs to happen through all aspects of the program. And it needs to be the main thrust of any final "where do we go from here" session.

Any temptation to drop this session so that weekend participants can get an early start home should be resisted. Sharing and covenanting with other participants is essential. Determining follow-up mechanisms and beginning the planning for follow-up activities while everyone is together is considerably easier than waiting until later when people are less able and less willing to reassemble for such planning.

Personal/Family Covenanting

1. SHARING COMMITMENTS

Each individual or family should be encouraged to pair with one other individual or family, to share the decisions they have made throughout the program, especially at the end, and then to plan how they can support one another in carrying out these decisions.

At a minimum, partners should consider a pause for daily prayer for each other. Further helpful steps include setting a time for checking in with each other to see how each is doing. This might be a one-time meeting or phone call, or it can become a regular activity (weekly or monthly). Getting together for a meal or other activity as well can enrich the experience and nurture the relationship. For families, this get-together might be the beginning of a "family support group" (see below, pp. 64–71, for models).

Participants from the same area or church should be encouraged to meet together either at breakfast or lunch the last day of a multi-day program, if not during the final session, to identify their specific needs, interests, and availability for follow-up experiences. This sharing can be facilitated by having each participant or family fill out a follow-up Interest Form (Worksheet 34).

2. DEEPENING A COVENANT

The creators of the "Pass It On" program include the following follow-up exercise as part of the conclusion of their one-day program model. While it deals specifically with the threat of nuclear war, its applicability to all the issues of this PPJ program is readily apparent. It can be a beautifully bonding experience.

COMPASSION IN A NUCLEAR WORLD

We live in an age characterized by widespread hunger, poverty, homelessness, to a greater extent than we in our smaller paths really recognize. The separation and brokenness of humanity are intense. Violence pervades our age from all directions: individual violence, institutional violence, revolutionary violence. These problems are not new, though their scale and cost, in terms of human lives, is unprecedented.

Something, however, is new about our age. That, of course, is the scale of our destructive capacity as a species. Our very survival as a species is now imperilled by the fruits of some of our highest mental and intellectual achievements, with our motive being to defend and secure us from one another.

Given this, how can we discuss loving, as Jesus has loved us, in a global context, without addressing this overriding question of our day?

How do we, who are Christians, in this nuclear age, deal with this? How do we respect our Creator's world? How do we overcome the forces of death? What does Jesus mean when he says to us, "Follow me," and goes to the cross? What do we have to do to pass on the gift of life to our children?

This subject is often seen as controversial. Yet we all share a common concern for the future. We all hope that we won't destroy ourselves in defending ourselves. What could be more tragic for our Creator who gave us so much, and even himself, so we might live?

In a recent study, psychiatrists found that adolescents expressed considerable anger that, although a threat so serious as the destruction of all of us and

life on our planet exists, most adults are going on in their day-to-day business as though nothing were wrong — and, furthermore, that the adults don't even want to talk about it. The youth said they see adults treating their anxiety about the future as a taboo, and they deeply resented and were frightened by the apparent lack of interest and concern by parents and other adults.

When one class was asked about their expectations for the future, all but one responded that there would be a nuclear war. The one person who did not think so said that he was sure it would not happen because his parents and their friends were working hard to prevent it.

Our Christian theology bases our life on the compassion of Christ. Our calling is to be compassionate, seeing ourselves connected, belonging to our neighbors. In the reality of the world's brokenness and separation, we are to work for restoration and recon-

ciliation. We are not alone in this work, for there is a spiritual current already existing, flowing like an underground river through us and society. We do not need to force it or manipulate it, but we can help it flow out to the surface, into the light of day, with currents mingling, gathering power and momentum.

In the face of the distress and tensions that barrage us, we defensively contract, psychically and physically. To be better freed to flow with the compassion of the Spirit, let us take a moment to relax, to tune in to the deep current of being. Let your body find a comfortable position and relax, deeply relax, in every part of your body. Allow a feeling of relaxation to flow from the top of your head, through your ears and forehead, relaxing your eyelids, nose, mouth and tongue, your neck and shoulders, arms and hands, your chest and stomach, your back and sides, your hips and legs, knees, ankles and feet. Feel the air of your breath, breathing deeply, letting the air flow through your body like a blessing for every part, bringing aliveness to every cell. Feel your breath in and out, cleansing and opening. This breathing connects you with so many living beings who are breathing like you, in and out.

Now let yourself flex and stretch certain muscles. Slowly rotate your head, easing your neck. Shrug and rotate your shoulders, releasing the burdens and tensions they carry. Flex your legs, ankles, feet, and allow them to release tension and relax more deeply. Enjoy this period of breathing and relaxing. Gradually open your eyes and come back to the rooms in your mind.

Now find the person nearest you, and form a pair, sitting face to face. I'm going to ask you to discuss a couple of things with this partner. First, share your names. Then each will state something you love about this world, something that makes you glad to be alive in God's world. [Leader does this first.]

Now share with your partner something from the past week that caused you pain or sadness for our world — some personal incident, news item, dream, or story. [Leader does this now, first, as a model.]

Now I am going to ask you to take turns answering this exercise. It is a series of unfinished exercises. Partner A will be the one to go first. Let the one willing to go first indicate this to the other. Partner A will repeat the unfinished sentence, then complete it. Partner B will say nothing in return, nothing at all — and will listen as attentively and supportively as possible. After all the sentences are finished, you switch roles.

1. *I think the chances of nuclear war are getting...*

2. *When I think of the world we are going to leave for our children, it looks like...*

3. *One of my worst fears for the future is...*

4. *The feelings about all this that I carry with me are...*

5. *When I try to share these feelings with other people...*

6. *The ways that I avoid expressing these feelings are...*

7. *Some ways I can help other people deal with their feelings of pain and fear for our world are...*

Now, Partner A, thank Partner B for his or her support and presence, with Partner B still not saying anything at all in return.

Now Partner B will repeat the unfinished sentence and complete it. Partner A will say nothing in return, keeping absolute silence as you listen, just listen, as supportively and attentively as possible. [Repeat the seven unfinished sentences, and the thank-you process, with Partner A remaining silent.]

As this exercise is finished, become aware of your body and its responses as you have talked about these things. Close your eyes and let your breathing show you where there is tension or release. Tune in to show how your body responds to these feelings.

As you open your eyes, you will see your partner, with whom you have just shared. Study your partner's hands. They are uniquely different from all other human hands. Take them in yours, feel the life in them.... Notice their strength.... Notice their vulnerability, these instruments of expression, of feeling, of giving, touching, soothing, comforting, healing; of breaking, hurting, crushing; of creating, building, shaping.... All that this hand has done, exploring, learning... to tie shoelaces, to write... all that it has in common with other humans around the world... all that is unique.

Now turn your eyes to each other's faces. Stay silent. Take a couple of deep breaths. Look into each other's eyes. If you feel discomfort, or an urge to laugh or look away, just note that embarrassment with patience and gentleness toward yourself, and come back, when you can, to your partner's eyes. This is a unique human being, whose presence is a gift to you.

As you look into this person's eyes, let yourself become aware of the powers that are there,... the gifts and strengths and potentialities that are in this being.... Behind these eyes are reservoirs of ingenuity and endurance, of wit and wisdom. There are gifts there, of which this person is still unaware. Consider what these untapped powers can do for the healing of our planet and for our common life.... As you consider that, let yourself become aware of what you want for this person,... for him or her to be free of fear,... of hatred,... of sorrow, of anything that would hurt him or her and cause suffering.... Experience this loving kindness for this other person....

Now, as you look into those eyes, let yourself become aware of the pain that is there. Sadnesses have accumulated in that life's journey.... There are failures, losses, griefs, disappointments beyond the telling.... Let yourself open to them, open to the pain of this person, the hurts that this person may never have been able to share with another person.

As you look into those eyes, open to the thought of how good it would be to work in a common cause with this person, gaining new appreciation of his or her powers and abilities and joys.

Now let your awareness drop, deep within yourself, deep, below the level of words or acts or thoughts,... to the deep web of relationships that underlies and interweaves all experiencing.... It is the web of life in which you have taken being and in which you are supported.... You cannot fall from this connectedness. You belong. You are not alone. Ever.[1]

Follow-Up Program Options

In addition to the programs described in chapter 13 on resources, there are several other options:

1. ADDITIONAL SESSIONS FROM THIS PROGRAM

As a Part II experience, some or all of the current program participants might want to reassemble for a one-time session, a series of three or four sessions, or a longer series of gatherings (weekly or monthly) to consider themes or aspects of themes not adequately covered in their initial program.

---

[1] From "Pass It On"; see below, p. 82.

2. BUILDING SHALOM FAMILIES

Adults might want to meet without their children for some of these sessions, using the PPJ video program. *Building Shalom Families* includes many of the activities described in this guide and adds the McGinnises' own input on the various themes. The video is appropriate for small group use in participants' homes as well as for larger group use in a church setting (see p. 149).

3. HOPE SPRINGS FROM GOD

This 1987 intergenerational program developed by James McGinnis for JED, CE:SA (Joint Education Development, Christian Education: Shared Approaches) offers intergenerational groups two six-session program options on hope — one in relationship to the arms race and world peace and the other in relationship to local and global poverty. Both enable groups to go much more deeply into the "global family" and "global peacemaking" themes of session 3 in *Building Shalom Families.*

Hope is the biblical theme developed in each of the six sessions. The kit includes a planning guide and activity leaflets outlining the activity options for each session in detail, a 50-page resource book for participants, and three filmstrips. The kit is available from the Institute for Peace and Justice as well as JED, CE:SA and its participating U.S. and Canadian denominations.

4. BOOK DISCUSSION GROUPS

Adults often find follow-up sessions more satisfying when there is a specific resource to discuss.

In addition to the video presentation in *Building Shalom Families* and the audio presentation in the five-cassette series *Parenting for Peace and Justice* by the McGinnises (both available from the Institute for Peace and Justice), there are several good written resources. These are listed on p. 85. In addition, the Parenting for Peace and Justice Network Newsletter offers an excellent bimonthly thematic option for groups. Each issue focuses on a specific theme. The Newsletter covers a wide range of topics, some not included in this guide. See "PPJN Membership" below for more detail, and p. 85 for a listing of back issues available for individual or group use.

5. LEADERSHIP TRAINING WORKSHOP

Whether or not leadership training is incorporated into your intergenerational program, some of the adult participants might be interested in a more concentrated and in-depth leadership experience.

Each year the PPJN offers several special leadership training workshops for program leaders desiring greater understanding, competency, and commitment to implementing the PPJ values and themes in their own lives as well as to sharing these with others. While participation in a leadership training workshop is not a requirement for leading *Building Shalom Families* or any of the other PPJ program models, it has proven highly beneficial.

Contact the PPJN for a list of scheduled workshops. Better yet, become a member of the PPJN and receive this information on a regular basis, along with the many other services for program leaders.

Family Follow-Up Possibilities

1. WRITTEN AND AV RESOURCES

All the resources described above and in the adult and children's bibliographies in chapter 13 can be used by individuals and families.

2. PPJN MEMBERSHIP AND NEWSLETTER

Begun in 1981, the Parenting for Peace and Justice Network (PPJN) is currently coordinated by the McGinnises, with an interfaith board representing sixteen national religious denominations and regional PPJ coordinators representing local PPJ coordinators and teams in 150 U.S. and Canadian cities and communities. Through the PPJN, more than 8000 families are being linked locally in family support groups, nationally through the PPJN newsletter, and globally through "pairings" with families and groups in other parts of the world.

SERVICES

PPJ Newsletter: Members receive the newsletter six times a year. Each issue focuses on a specific theme: multicultural celebrations, blended families and single parenting, racism, sexism, global connections, disabilities, family conflict resolution, teens, global peacemaking, and economic justice have been presented over the past two years. Each issue offers specific family actions, resources for children of all ages, at-home activities, as well as a calendar of PPJ workshops and assorted other PPJN activities and events.

Discounts on PPJ Resources: Members can purchase at a 15 percent discount. Quantities are also available on a consignment basis for sale at PPJ presentations and programs.

Leadership Mailings: In addition to the PPJN Newsletter, program leaders contributing $20 or more to the PPJN receive several additional mailings offering strategies and resources for local outreach and for PPJ presentations and programs, new worksheets, and family action projects.

Leadership Training and Family Enrichment workshops: The McGinnises, some regional and local PPJ coordinators, and other program leaders are available to conduct both kinds of workshops. Formats include one- to three-day workshops, family camps and retreats, and continuing education seminars through universities and seminaries.

Local and Family Support Groups: The local PPJ coordinator or team in your area can help organize PPJ programs, give PPJ presentations, put families in touch with others interested in PPJ themes, and help form and nurture family support groups. Contact the national office for the name of your closest local coordinator.

Regional AV Centers: Some twenty centers in the U.S. and Canada have the PPJ audio-visuals available for rental to PPJN members, sometimes for only the cost of postage. Contact the PPJN office for a listing.

MEMBERSHIP OPTIONS

Individual or Family Membership: Individuals or families generally contribute between $15 and $25 (some more, others less — according to ability to pay). They receive the PPJN Newsletter and other services identified above. Program leaders contributing a minimum $20 membership also receive the special leadership mailings.

Church or Group Membership: Individual congregations, family support groups, and other community groups have two membership options. The $50 minimum membership entitles the entire group to five copies of each issue of the PPJN Newsletter ($10 for each additional copy), the 15 percent discount on the purchase of all PPJ resources, and the special leadership mailings. The $100 minimum membership entitles the group to ten copies of each issue of the PPJN Newsletter, the other services above, and one copy of the guidebook and the *Families in Search of Shalom* filmstrip.

A special introductory church packet is available for $6 from the PPJN. It includes six pamphlets: *Families Acting for Peace, Families Acting for Economic Justice, Advent Activities for the Family, Lenten Activities for the Family, Family Support Group Models,* and *PPJ Program Options and Strategies for Congregations/Parishes.*

Family Support Groups

One of the goals of the PPJN has always been to link families in their local area to generate support, challenge, insights, and possibilities for more effective and sustained action that only a support group can provide. Based on the experience of twenty or so such groups, we offer the following guidelines and models for starting a PPJ family support group in your own area.

1. GUIDELINES

1. Quality versus quantity: even if only one or two others are interested, begin. Most groups have expanded over time. On the other hand, such groups tend to be less effective and satisfying if they go beyond twelve to fifteen adults.

2. Personal invitations are always more effective than mailings. Share an article, tape, or chapter in a book on PPJ with others as a way of introducing PPJ to interested persons.

3. Generally it is better to ask people to commit themselves to a shorter time span (for example, three, six, or twelve months), after which the group can evaluate itself and decide if and how it wants to continue. Long-term commitments from the outset tend to scare many people.

4. It is preferable to let the topics emerge from the group itself rather than tying the group down to someone else's outline. At the same time, however,

it is helpful, especially at first, to have an outside resource to discuss (see suggestions, p. 85).

5. Family support groups that include the children for occasional whole family events (for example, picnics, family camp, group letter-writing, public demonstrations) seem to be more satisfying and enduring than adult-only discussion groups.

2. STRATEGIES

1. Invite a couple of friends or members of your church or a community group to join you, preferably at your house, to discuss a PPJ theme and the possibility of forming a family support group. A positive response is more likely if those invited have been part of a recent PPJ presentation or program.

2. Ask your local PPJ coordinator (contact the PPJN if you do not know who this is) to invite all the people on his or her PPJ mailing list to a presen-

tation on some specific PPJ theme (generally more likely to draw people than a general introductory PPJ presentation) and on the possibility of forming one or more family support groups, depending on the numbers and geographic spread of those interested. If only a couple of people come, each of them can invite one other person or family for a second meeting. This should also be focused on a specific PPJ theme; again all people on the mailing list can be invited.

3. Invite an already existing adult or parent support group (for example, Marriage Encounter follow-up group, a PET or STEP group, a church study or prayer group, a RENEW group, a food or child-care coop group) to take on PPJ themes as part of

their study/action focus. One church-based book club that met monthly in Ohio chose the PPJ book as their focus for six months and found themselves moving toward a family support group.

4. Most groups begin as discussion groups, many using the PPJ book or tapes, one chapter or tape per session, and gradually add other dimensions — political action, family fun events, prayer or worship.

5. "The Family Cluster" is an excellent model for PPJ family support groups. A "family cluster" is defined by Dr. Margaret Sawin in *Family Enrichment with Family Clusters* as "a group of four or five complete family units which contract to meet together periodically over an extend period of time for shared educational experiences related to their living in relationship with the family. A cluster provides mutual support, training in skills which facilitate the family living in relationship, and celebration of their life and beliefs together."

The program objectives of PPJ are entirely consistent with this process. In her new book, *Hope for Families,* Dr. Sawin gives people who have experienced the family cluster model in a variety of settings the opportunity to tell their stories and reflect on their successes and failures. Here is a possible reply to those who attend introductory sessions of PPJ and ask, "Fine, but where do we go from here?": Form a cluster with friends using the PPJ objectives and content and the family cluster model as the process. (Both these books are available from Family Clustering, Inc., P.O. Box 18074, Rochester, NY 14618.)

Models

We include here reports from five family support groups.

1. FAMILY VALUES SUPPORT GROUP, COVINGTON, KENTUCKY: JIM AND SUSAN VOGT

The support group we formed was called a "Family Values Support Group." The overall aim of this model is to help families identify the values they are trying to live by and to provide a structure within which these values can be discussed. The name "Family Values Support Group" was chosen because (1) we felt people in our area would not respond as readily to a group labeled Parenting for Peace and Justice — the words "peace and justice" might be turn-offs; (2) we thought there may be some family values or issues other than those addressed by PPJ that families would want to discuss.

The several leaders who had convened the group did share openly at the first meeting that PPJ formed for them an important part of the framework for our gathering together.

This model was developed on the assumption that whole families, both parents and children, would be present and participate in each session. At least two other approaches are possible:

- Alternate participation by adults with participation of whole families. In other words, look at a particular value first with adults only, then with whole families at the next session.

- Have the sessions for adults only, with periodic gatherings to include the children.

Families were asked to commit themselves to a monthly session for a period of six months. This model envisions that all the planning for the group will take place during the gathering and not require additional meetings. The initial gathering would probably have to focus on identifying the issues and values that are of most interest to the participants. Working within the PPJ framework, we suggested the following possibilities:

- Family conflicts: how can we settle them more peacefully?

- TV: are we a more or less peaceful family because of it?

- Our family and the world: how does it affect us, how can we affect it?

- Materialism and consumerism: how can they be avoided?

Six or seven families seem to make the best-sized group. This depends, however, on the number of children involved. It's very helpful to have a balance of age range with the children so that no child is without at least one peer. It might be necessary to limit the number of families with only preschoolers since the participation of those children would be minimal.

Each session ran from 7:00 to 9:30 and we found a weekend night to be best. The sessions included:

- some fun (for example, singing, cooperative games);

- input by the leaders on the topic of the evening;

- discussion in response to the topic, either in small groups, individual family units, or age groups;

- snack time;

- a brief planning session to address details of the next meeting as well as future topics or concerns. (This was often chaotic since the younger children were looking for their parents by then!)

The provision of on-site child care for preschool children is helpful. The children in our group were allowed to move to the child-care area whenever they "had enough" of the adult session. Child care was provided by a service club from a local high school.

There were some final considerations:

- It's important to take enough time to get to know one another when the support group first gathers.

- It's important that many of the adult participants have a chance to prepare and lead one of the sessions. In our group, most people who led a session felt that they got a lot out of that session. This responsibility also increases their sense of ownership of the group. Some participants, however, may not have the skills, experience, or confidence to lead a session, and this should be respected.

- A facility of adequate size and an environment suitable for the children, with some resources for play, was very important for a positive child-care experience.

- People liked the minimal amount of planning involved.

- Meeting only six times is probably not enough.

2. FAMILY SUPPORT GROUP,
   ASHLAND, OREGON:
   JERRY AND PAT ELLSWORTH

Pat and I and the kids attended a PPJ family camp in the summer of 1983. During the course of the fall we put together a three-part PPJ intergenerational workshop for our parish and other interested members of the community. The workshop was held on three Sunday afternoons in the Lent of 1984. Each workshop was about two hours long ending with a potluck dinner. We covered the same topics that are covered in the PPJ program guide. About forty people attended the workshops.

At the end of the workshop, we invited interested persons to get together to form a support group to follow up on the topics covered in the workshops. About six families expressed interest and we have been meeting monthly ever since. During that time, we have had snow parties, new games parties, swimming parties (we got rained out!), family VCR movie times, etc. Each time we got together for a Sunday afternoon, we had time for fun for the whole families, a time when the kids were separate from the adults so the adults could carry on a discussion (the kids would often see a movie), and a potluck meal. The topic of discussion among the adults had for many months been a chapter-by-chapter discussion of *Parenting for Peace and Justice.*

We are trying to keep a PPJ support group alive to provide a model of hope for our children and source of nourishment for ourselves. We would like our kids to see active, concerned, significant adults working to be peacemakers. In this way they can learn those peacemaking skills that will sustain them in a very competitive, aggressive world. When in "Show and Tell" at school our kids share the response to a letter to a senator or representative or president, we are indeed hopeful.

Now that the book discussion has finished, we feel the need to reach out to the community. We will be getting together monthly to do some sort of service project: for example, yard cleaning for the elderly, soup kitchen work, helping the local St. Vincent de Paul group. As our children grow, we hope to do evenings of letter-writing. To keep the experience positive, we hope to maintain the work-fun-meal approach at our get-togethers.

Our group is involved with Peace House, a center for activism, in planning a fall peace conference, Unite for Peace. The conference will include presentations by Dr. Benjamin Spock, Holly Near, and others. Our PPJ group will do two workshops: "Families and Creative Response to Conflict" and "Living Simply in a World of Limits." Pat will also be working with the local Educators for Social Responsibility coordinator to put together a conflict resolution workshop for children. Jerry will be working with

ESR members on a workshop for teachers. The PPJ group is also arranging child care for the conference in conjunction with the local parish youth groups.

In the meantime, the group will do some food collection for a foodbank. This activity may become a regular service. Also, we want to keep alive the "joyful alternative" aspect in our get-togethers so that our children will look forward to participating.

The make-up of the support group has changed since the beginning. Only about two families that were part of the original workshop are still part of

the support group. It seems hard to get a commitment from people who are already spread very thin. We still miss a level of intimacy that we have had in other circumstances of shared faith experiences, shared worldview, shared value system. Maybe part of our mission is to keep searching and working toward creating such community.

We certainly don't evaluate our group according to the number of participants. If that were the case, we would have given up long ago! Sometimes we have three families, sometimes six. Evaluation and sustenance is based on the glimmer of hope and encouragement we give to each other.

3. PARENTING FOR PEACE AND JUSTICE
   IN THE HEART OF TEXAS,
   WACO, TEXAS: REV. TRISH HOLLAND

Parenting for Peace and Justice in the Heart of Texas family support group began in response to an anticipated workshop with Jim and Kathy McGinnis, scheduled by the Peacemaking Committee of Grace Presbytery for February 1985, in Dallas, Texas. I had initiated and coordinated support groups for parents of infants and toddlers, for folks interested in simpler lifestyles and alternative celebrations, and I was eager to use the McGinnis book *Parenting for*

Peace and Justice in our church and in our own family.

Knowing that we need all the encouragement we can get in any counter-culture effort to overcome racism, sexism, materialism, militarism, and violence, I wanted to be able to take a group from the Waco area to Dallas for the McGinnis workshop — with the understanding from the beginning that we would return and organize to support and encourage each other.

The first step was to recruit an ecumenical, interracial planning team of nine to twelve women and men from seven congregations (Presbyterian, Roman Catholic, Methodist, Southern Baptist, and Lutheran).

The value of an ecumenical group cannot be overemphasized. It not only bears witness to what God is continually about — breaking down dividing walls — but it offers encouragement and strength to the handful of peace and justice activists scattered in various congregations. It affirms the good news that we are not alone! One member said, "Wouldn't it be wonderful if we were all in the same congregation!" Another replied, "Yes, it would be fun, but how much better to be scattered like leaven in the dough in many congregations."

We noted an increase in our courage to speak up on peace and justice issues in our own congregations and to encourage use of peace and justice oriented curricula in church and school classes, on retreats, in women's programs, in newsletters.

Due to time and budget-year factors, funding was requested and received only from a local congregation, Presbytery, and national office of the Presbyterian Church (USA). I'm sure support and funds could have been found through other denominational channels as well, had time permitted. During the year, the group did meet in several different church buildings, which we felt increased our understanding and mutual respect.

By the time the planning team met in early January 1985, the McGinnis event had been postponed until May, so the project was redesigned to begin with two all-family events as a way of introducing PPJ to the community. These were planned for Friday evenings in March and April. Both began with a shared meal and included group-building activities, presentation of a PPJ film or video, cooperative games, and concluding worship.

The first meal was provided by the Waco Peace Alliance, as we felt it important for the event to be free and not have even a minimal amount keep anyone away. We had "agape sandwiches" — four long loaves of bread specially baked at a local supermarket and sliced horizontally with trays of sandwich makings on each table.

The first "cooperative event" of the evening was for everyone at the table to construct a common sandwich, making any necessary negotiations. This was delightful to do and to watch. The large loaf was then sliced and enjoyed. Around 120 folks from thirty-five families showed up for this. Both events received newspaper and television publicity as well as notice in church bulletins and newsletters.

The second event began with a potluck supper. Exercises in expressing anger and managing conflict were led by a local family counselor who was a member of the planning team, and we showed the section of the video on the McGinnis family meeting. At the end of the meeting, families were asked to indicate their interest in a continuing contract family support group.

In May, twenty-two people from six families were able to attend the McGinnis workshop in Dallas. In June, we held a family picnic, and the group made plans for the fall. In August, four members of the group, working through the Waco Peace Alliance, helped design and sponsor a Hiroshima Day family picnic at Indian Springs Park on the banks of the Brazos River, which runs through downtown Waco. T-shirts were printed "Hiroshima no more." Slides were made from the beautiful illustrations in the children's book *Hiroshima No Pica,* and the text of the book was read as the slides were shown. Families were provided materials and instructions for making small boats, which were launched in the Brazos River at the end of the picnic. The picnic also received television and newspaper coverage.

In September, eight families met for an "adults only" supper to share our experiences of what had been working for our families during the summer, to hear clearly one another's hopes and needs for the fall meetings, and to commit ourselves to the group. Leadership was divided among the group, with two or three parents assuming responsibility for planning each meeting.

Each meeting included a shared potluck meal, cooperative games, time for sharing family experience, presentation of the topic, and closing worship. We found that Friday nights were a very rushed time for everyone, and it was impossible to begin the meal at the agreed on time. The December meeting was scheduled for 10:00 to 1:00 on Saturday morning, and we found this to be much more relaxed and pleasant.

Due to rushed schedules and family illness, the final event of the project — an all-family retreat — was not held until the end of February; only six families were able to participate and not every member of those families. Due to freezing weather, the camp setting in the woods was changed at the last minute to a church fellowship hall, and only three of the six families spent the night.

This was a delightful experience nonetheless. Friday evening was spent sharing a meal and playing games, with each family leading the group in their favorite. We performed Camy Condon's participatory puppet show "Sticks and Stones and the Dragon" (included in *Helping Kids Care,* by Camy Condon and James McGinnis, Institute for Peace and Justice and Meyer-Stone Books, 1988); the stairway made a marvelous mountain for the confrontations with the dragon. We closed the evening with a worship service.

In the evaluation session the next morning, the adults met for a couple of hours. The consensus was a desire to continue meetings, but we had a real struggle with over-full schedules. Several members had been part of and wanted to continue to support the Waco Peace Alliance efforts. It was agreed that our group would support the Waco Peace Alliance. We will offer:

- peace activities during child care for Waco Peace Alliance meetings, so that more parents in the area can become active;

- at least two PPJ programs for the Alliance during the year;

- one PPJ public witness event through the Alliance;

- a family retreat once a year for PPJ families;

- a meal and games before the Alliance meetings for those who wish and who have the time;

- material on PPJ themes for the Alliance monthly newsletter.

We are excited about this plan to spread the word about PPJ, to continue to be encouraged and strengthened by the group in our own efforts, to strengthen the WACO Peace Alliance, and to spread the word to its mailing list of about 250 families.

4. FAMILY LIVING FOR PEACE AND JUSTICE, TALLAHASSEE, FLORIDA: ROSS AND SUSAN FLANAGAN

When this group first came together, we had many dreams and hopes. What follows are excerpts from the brochures and letters that we sent out to prospective members.

WE ARE PLANNING A NEW APPROACH AND WOULD LIKE YOUR HELP! *Parenting for peace and justice is a goal for many of us. Unfortunately, we often lack the time and the support necessary for acquiring the needed skills. We are looking for twenty families to be part of a year-long experiment in family living. We promise not to take you away from parenting to learn about parenting!*

We will meet in a large group once a month (with families). All other activities will be in the home or in groups of two or three families. Our goal is that the skills we acquire in family living will be transferable to the school setting, the church, the community, and the world at large. We have excellent people working on a curriculum specifically designed for this project. COME GROW WITH US AS FAMILIES AND PEACEMAKERS!

It is our intent to meet together for a year. The values that we will be working with are lifelong values that need time, study, and support to be made lasting.

This is an experimental program, and we need all the help we can get. We would like your help in writing the curriculum as we go along, in sharing ideas for activities, and in giving regular feedback on what works and what needs changing.

We will focus on a different theme each month. There is a developmental sequence to these themes. If you have skills in a particular area, please feel free to share. We may need to adjust for summer vacations, but here is a basic outline:

- February — Covenant:
  We covenant to be a family and to grow in peacemaking skills.

- March — Communication:
  Step one in learning how to live together.

- April — Connectedness and Cooperation:
  We need one another.

- May — Risk, Trust, and Change:
  Builds on skills of the three previous months.

- June — Lateral Resourcing:
  Reaching out and about for sources.

- July — Rules and Negotiation:
  Rules as guidelines and aids.

- August — Conflict and Crisis:
  What do we do when we fight?

- September — Stop, Look and Listen:
  Let's take a look at the world outside our family.

- October — Advocacy:
  How do we take all that we have learned and work for change?

- November — Futurizing:
  Where can we make a difference?

- December — The Prince of Peace:
  Deepening of Spiritual Roots that are grounded in an attitude of peace.

- January — Evaluation and Celebration.

Just think, this could be the start of our very own Family Peace Academy! Thanks for taking the risk of growing something new.

This family support group in Florida, which originally included sixteen families, has gone through some changes recently. An evaluation by the group's leaders found that even though the "experiment" worked extremely well, finding people who had the time to commit themselves to an ongoing support group was the challenge. Because the focus of the group was to help each family minister to itself, many of the families did not see the need to gather together.

The future plans include the formation of a smaller group of families that would come together regularly to share and participate in peace and justice activities for the adults and children. Although they have found it has been difficult to find families with similar values, they feel very hopeful about the future.

5. PARENTING SUPPORT GROUP,
   ST. LOUIS, MISSOURI:
   JIM AND NANETTE FORD

We were "veterans" of other kinds of community support groups. Although these groups were helpful in their own way, we as parents and as individuals were not being "fed" enough. A level of intimacy was lacking, and until we got to know each other better we felt we would not be able to truly support each other. So we gathered with the hope of forming a support group for us as individuals, parents, and families. We were small, but determined to make our new group work.

It was obvious from the beginning that if we were going to create anything meaningful, we would have to invest a certain amount of committed time. We all agreed that if we met less than every other week we would not have enough time invested to become closer to each other. We believed that our group was going to be more than a discussion group for peace and justice themes in the family. Ours was to be a sharing group, where we could talk about the past two weeks, the high points and the low points.

Our group consists of three families: six adults and eight children ranging in age from 16 months to 16 years. At least once a month we plan some type of activity that the kids will enjoy, such as family meals together, picnics, or apple-picking adventures. We worship together when schedules permit and participate in service projects together in the St. Louis area. We support each other's involvement in peace and justice work as individuals and as families.

But the core of our parenting group is the time spent together as parents, couples, and individuals trying to lead a simple lifestyle rooted in peace and justice values. When we gather in each other's homes, we spend the first part of the evening sharing the "important events" of the past two weeks. These include issues related to work, relatives, the growing pains of marriage, and the challenge of raising toddlers and teens.

Because of our deep commitment and caring for each other, this is not just discussion time, but an opportunity to share personal feelings and emotions. Sometimes this takes an hour, sometimes the whole evening. We next try to include some type of input that can be discussed or experienced.

In the past two and a half years, we have dealt with racism, sexism (especially in the church), war tax resistance, personality types (we all took the Myers-Briggs Personality Inventory), disciplining children as well as self-discipline, and creation spirituality. We are open to each other's needs, so flexibility is very much in order. We conclude our gatherings with prayer.

For the past two years, we have made an annual

retreat together with all the members of our families. It's quite an experience in communal living! The retreats were held outside the city with recreational facilities (fishing, swimming) available for us and the children. We chose the faith experience model for each retreat format (see the PPJN Newsletter, no. 17, Summer 1985, for a detailed description of the format of the Faith Experience). It is very important to us that our children's experience of their parents' "parenting group" be a positive one. Thus, the retreats and all family gatherings are meant to be fun and worthwhile. As the children get older, we hope to incorporate them into the adult activities of the group.

Our parenting support group is like going to church. It is something we plan to do always. We evaluate periodically, but know that this group is a priority in our lives. We will always make room and time for each other. The future will probably see many changes, but the basic goal will remain the same: to support each other in the daily search and living out of parenting for peace and justice.

CHAPTER 11

Meals and Other Lighter Elements

Meals: Importance and Guidelines

Food makes a significant difference in determining the success of an intergenerational program, for several reasons. First, children are far more willing to come and to participate if there is food they like. Second, meals offer wonderful opportunities to model the values implicit in the PPJ themes as well as to enrich the experience of these themes. Thus, the following guidelines are basic:

- **Simplicity.** Too much food creates waste. Fancy or expensive foods also demonstrate poor stewardship. Less rather than more, especially for meat and sweets, is a good general rule.

- **Diversity.** Foods from a variety of cultural traditions can be fun as well as instructive. Stretching participants' range of "acceptable" foods is a plus for most families.

- **Options.** Participants' tastes can be at least partially accommodated by providing simple options — for example, salad bar set-ups are universally appreciated; several different fruit options often help; building one's own sandwich, with several bread and sandwich options, works well. A vegetarian option whenever meat is served not only encourages more vegetarian eating but also accommodates those participants who are vegetarians.

- **Nutrition.** Combining nutrition with taste is sometimes a challenge, especially with children. Nutritious snacks are important to model.

- **Participation.** Potluck meals and snacks that require all participants to bring something not only reduces costs but also is fun and allows participants yet another way of introducing themselves or sharing themselves with the group. Use the criteria above in invitations to participants: for example, "each family bring a favorite snack that is inexpensive and is nutritious and that the children will enjoy."

Special Meals

1. SOLIDARITY AND FASTING

In keeping with the themes of "Shalom in the Global Family" (chapter 6) and "Consumerism and Stewardship" (chapter 7), offer at least one opportunity during the program for participants to eat sacrificially. This can be done in several ways, with options built in. It might be good to share some of the "Reflection on Sacrificial Eating" (below) with the group before, during, or immediately after the experience.

Individual Fast: Participants are invited to fast at any of the meals and encouraged to share any monetary savings with some group fighting hunger or with one of the "group project options" identified during the "stewardship" session (see above p. 48) or as part of the closing worship.

Group Fast: The whole group is invited to fast at a particular meal, with water or juice and a little bread or fruit or soup available for those who should eat at least a minimal amount. Here there is a definite savings (the cooks know ahead of time to prepare very little) that can be shared with the hungry in some way.

Solidarity Meal: The previous example can be called a "solidarity meal" if eaten in conscious solidarity with those who hunger involuntarily. To increase this awareness, the minimal menu should in-

72

clude foods in the diets of the poor, for example, beans, bread, rice, or potatoes.

Third World Banquet: See p. 37 above for directions for these simulations in which food is distributed to the group according to the percentage of world food distribution. The more this activity involves an

actual meal rather than snacks between meals when participants are not as hungry, the more emotion the activity generates and therefore the more debriefing time is required.

REFLECTION ON SACRIFICIAL EATING[1]

Fasting has a significant role to play in deepening our relationship to God as well as deepening our commitment to peace and justice, our willingness to sacrifice and take risks for peace and justice, and our sense of solidarity with others.

Fast days should be special days of prayer, of prayer not just in periods set aside for prayerful reflection on the Scriptures, but primarily in tiny moments of wanting to eat during the day. These moments become opportunities and invitations to prayer — to speak with Jesus, to be more fully aware of his presence, to beg for peace, to be reminded that God's will for the world is truly *shalom.* When our fast days are regular — at least weekly — this sense of prayerfulness seems to carry over to other days as well. Some combine their fast days with silence, to more consciously focus on the presence of God.

The overwhelming sense of evil manifested in the arms race and the suffering in Central America, Ethiopia, and elsewhere, brings us to our knees, figuratively and literally. This sense of evil can drive

[1] From James McGinnis, *Solidarity with the People of Nicaragua,* Orbis Books, 1985.

us on to work harder for peace and justice, but it should also drive us back to God. After we have done what we can — writing Congress, giving talks, writing books or articles, mobilizing local groups, setting up "urgent action networks," vigiling and demonstrating, resisting war taxes — we are faced with the realization that all that is still not enough. God, we depend on you. Raise up ever more courageous instruments of your peace. Work your miracles through others. Touch the hearts of decision-makers. Give courage to those victimized by the evils we are resisting. Give us greater courage, hope, and insight into your will and our role.

Jim Wallis, in the November 1983 issue of *Sojourners* magazine, reflects on the "cost of discipleship" and challenges us with Jesus' questions about whether we have "counted the cost" of following him (see Luke 14:25–33). Are we really willing to suffer or are we just "hanging around" the gospel? We are not sure how really willing we are to suffer for peace and justice, but we know that the tiny acts of self-denial involved in fasting can be a prepara-

tion for greater demands made by sacrificial love. Most of us do not jump from 0 to 10 in one leap. We move one step at a time. The pruning process (John 15:1–7) that God has in mind for each of us — calling us to be ever more willing to let go and follow Jesus — involves many moments of self-denial. Fasting can be an important part of this process, preparing us for the greater demands of sacrificial love.

A tiny "no" of self-denial can also be a tiny "yes" of solidarity. We can experience many moments of solidarity on fast days, as we bring to mind the lives of those victimized by the evils we are resisting — friends in Nicaragua, other victims of injustice we have met or read about, those persecuted for their convictions, peacemakers working hard for change. It might be especially helpful to write one such person each day we fast, to communicate that sense of solidarity and thus encourage that person to remain faithful and strong. The more we bring to consciousness and prayer the lives of persons for whom or with whom we are resisting, the more deeply drawn into resistance and fidelity we are likely to find ourselves.

The U.S. Catholic bishops recommend that fasting "be accompanied by works of charity and service toward our neighbors." Fast days are opportunities for fuller presence to those around us, if we do not allow our work schedule to dominate our day. Special little acts of service — doing an extra task for someone we live with, a phone call to a hurting friend or relative, time for a co-worker at the office — makes the solidarity of fasting more genuine. Those closest to us should also be the beneficiaries of our fasting.

To be more serious about our solidarity projects and to sustain our prophetic efforts for justice and peace, we need to be engaged at the deepest levels of our being. Service and simplifying our lifestyle, as well as prayer and fasting, all have a way of opening us up at these levels, making it possible for God to work more fully in our lives and the world through us.

2. COOPERATIVE EATING

Both food preparation and the meal itself can be a community-building activity, especially when everyone participates. There are several ways for this to happen as part of every meal as well as special "cooperative meals."

- Rotate responsibility among all participants for setting up before and cleaning up after each meal; put fresh flowers at each table; put surprise tokens under one plate at each table — the lucky person gets a special dessert.

- Have some meals prepared by participants, who can be organized into special groups, for example, a teen group, a grandparents group, a fathers group, a Hispanic group.

- Encourage participants to eat with different people at each meal or encourage specific groups to eat together at times to build a sense of community among them, especially at the beginning (to get to know one another better) and at the end (to discuss follow-up support possibilities). The groupings can be based on age, geographic location, denomination, or family situation (for example, single parents, grandparents, nonparent adults).

- Have potlucks for meals and snacks. If the program includes prepared meals by a separate cooking staff, participants can at least bring the snacks (see the guidelines above p. 72).

- Make a "cooperative sandwich." Each family brings ingredients for the giant sandwich, with the huge loaf of bread provided by the planners.

3. GLOBAL FAMILY MEALS

As recommended in the session on "Shalom in the Global Family" (chapter 6), that theme can be enhanced by a cultural experience of one or more peoples or countries that includes a meal as well as music, dancing, pictures, and other items representative of that culture or country. Planners can arrange this ahead of time, knowing which culture or countries would integrate best with the program events. They can also allow other possibilities to emerge, depending on what cultures and countries are represented by the participants themselves. But it works best if these participants know ahead of time and can thus bring foods, music, and artifacts. Some suggestions for food, visuals, and projects relating to specific cultures and countries are found elsewhere in this guidebook: for Nicaragua, see p. 40; for Japan, see p. 40; for the Soviet Union, see p. 38; for Black Africa, see Kwanza, p. 52.

4. PLACEMATS

An engaging addition are placemats printed with hunger data, games, action suggestions, or information on a culture or country. "Shalom Placemats" are available from Shalom Publications and Creative Ministries, 7225 Berkridge Dr., Hazelwood, MO 63042; tel.: 314-521-6051.

Other Lighter Elements

Fun or play in intergenerational programs is critical. Especially with themes as "heavy" as the ones in this program, it is absolutely essential to build in as many lighter elements as possible. This is particularly true if participating children are to be satisfied. There are many possibilities:

1. GATHERING SONGS AND GAMES

This has been stressed in each session. Encourage participants to arrive five minutes early for each session, promising them a game or song as their reward.

As stressed repeatedly, singing is not only fun, it's prayerful, energizing, and gives a variety of people a chance to shine. Encourage more than one person to serve as song leader during the program. Encourage participants ahead of time to bring their musical instruments and multiple copies of any song they especially like that would fit well with the themes of this program. One wonderful source of peace related songs is *Children's Songs for a Friendly Planet,* by Evelyn Weiss (115 songs; $6 from the Riverside Church Disarmament Program, 590 Riverside Drive, New York, NY 10027).

See pp. 32–35 for cooperative games.

2. CAMPFIRES AND TALENT SHOWS

Campfires and talent shows offer participants additional opportunities to sing, to be creative and humorous, and thereby to be affirmed and to bond more closely. Talent shows are important for other reasons and should be included, if at all possible, on the second night of a program. This gives participants at least some time to prepare but comes early enough to loosen up a group, to give it another way to know one another, and to provide experiences that often can be pointed to in subsequent sessions (for example, the lyrics of a song might fit well with a later session and the leader can recall these lyrics and affirm the singers).

Talent shows give everyone chances to perform in public, an important ingredient in schools organized in India along the principles of Gandhian nonviolence. Gandhi felt it was essential for people of all ages to learn how to stand up in public, to get over the self-consciousness that inhibits public behavior, and to learn to be creative on their feet. Talent shows provide just such an opportunity.

Finding campfire leaders and talent show masters of ceremony should be a first-night task. Posting a piece of newsprint where individuals and families sign up (name and type of activity and projected length of time to perform) not only helps the MCs to organize the show but also encourages reluctant participants to volunteer.

3. OUTDOOR ACTIVITIES

Depending on the location of the program and the amount of time available, the outdoor dimension of the program can be enhanced considerably. Special consideration should be given to the following possibilities:

Nature Experiences: Besides the scheduled time for a family nature walk (see above p. 46), participants should be encouraged to relate to the beauty of God's creation as often as possible. Holding morning or evening prayer sessions outdoors helps. So do sunrise or sunset meditative gatherings. Providing trail guides or recommendations encourages this as well.

Outdoor Play, Games, Sports: As much as possible, hold the cooperative games outside. Similarly, encourage child-care workers and leaders of separate sessions for the over-6's to use the outdoors whenever possible. Encourage group volleyball, soccer, or other sport activities that participants of all ages can enjoy.

Outward Bound: If the facility is fortunate enough to have physical challenges available — for example, pole-climbing, rope-walking — these tend to build group cohesion quickly and give participants opportunities to test their limits, develop skills and self-confidence, and be affirmed.

4. INDOOR ALTERNATIVES

Every planning team should be ready for indoor fun in case the weather makes outdoor activities impossible. Because some facilities are less conducive than others to outdoor activities and because some participants may be more comfortable indoors, depending on their health or age, it is good to have a balance of both indoor and outdoor fun. Besides a talent show and indoor cooperative games, there are several other enjoyable options:

Cooperative Crafts: Susan Temple constructed Worksheet 22, combining several of the craft activities suggested in this guidebook with several of her own and used them as a lunchtime activity in her one-day programs. Often young children get restless during the second half of a one-hour or longer lunch break and need some kind of focused activity. Providing tables with appropriate supplies for the various options listed on Worksheet 22 offers a creative alternative to generalized chaos if weather prohibits outdoor activities.[2]

Peace Festival: Either as part of the session on "Shalom in the Global Family" (chapter 6) or as a separate activity altogether, each family could be invited to set up a booth that offers other participants a specific possibility for doing or promoting peace in some way. *Families need to know ahead of time that this is an option* so they can bring whatever materials are necessary. As organized by one PPJ program leader, her "peace festival" included the following:

- *Hands Working for Peace:* draw your hands and put your names inside.

- *Peace Post Office:* write a letter to the president or mayor or other government leader, thanking them for their work and expressing your views or solutions to a problem.

- *Peace Tree:* make a paper peace crane and put it on the tree.

- *Peace Mural:* cut pictures of peaceful places, things, and people and attach them to the poster.

- *Our Global Neighbors:* display artifacts or pictures from different countries.

- *Compañeros–Friends in Nicaragua:* tape record a message to friends in a village in Nicaragua.

- *Peace Links:* draw and write a message to children in Nicaragua on a long piece of paper.

- *Peace Button:* design your own button.

- *Peace Toys:* use toys for peaceful play.

- *Filmstrip: Creating Peace in Our Lives* (see p. 41), or any of the others recommended in this guide.

- *Pin the Dollar on the Cow:* raise money to buy a cow in Nicaragua; give out milk and graham crackers (alternatively, use tape and nickels).

Local peace and justice groups can be invited to set up their own booths. To respect the diversity of participants, have groups reflecting a variety of issues and approaches to working for peace and justice, for example, a balance of local and global concerns, issues that concern different economic classes and races, approaches to peace to which pacifists and nonpacifists alike can relate. This kind of sensitivity toward participants needs to be reflected by leaders throughout the program, especially during the content sessions. In terms of the "peace festival," this concern can best be met by having the booths created and staffed, as much as possible, by participants themselves.[3]

Family Carnival: This requires no advance notice or preparation by participants but does require the planners to have a variety of materials on hand. Each family or cabin is invited to prepare a booth or game for the family carnival, using no more than three or four of the materials available on a center table (or passed out to each booth group by the leader).

Materials should include, for example, balloons, tooth picks, paper clips, rubber bands, paper cups, ping pong balls, coffee stirrers, popsicle sticks, string, index cards, strips of construction paper, glue. Simple yet creative booths can be constructed in 20 to 30 minutes. The dining room is often a good place for this activity, with each table serving as a separate booth. Having construction paper and marking pens available allows each booth to have a sign naming itself. Each booth team should be large enough for members to rotate staffing the booth, so that the nonstaffers can be playing the other games and visiting the other booths.

Videos: A variety of videos, plus a VCR, is usually helpful and appreciated. Program leaders can be provided opportunities to see videos not able to be included in the program itself. People interested in specific issue areas, wanting more content than is possible during the formal sessions, can be provided that additional content through videos and follow-up discussion. Participants can be invited ahead of

---

[2]From "Nurturing Families in a World of Conflict"; see below, p. 84.

[3]From "Little Friends for Peace — Peacemaking Education"; see below, p. 82.

time to bring such videos. Most important, it is good to have several entertaining as well as instructive videos for all age groups as well as some for specific age groups, especially the teens. In addition to those already recommended above — *Amazing Grace and Chuck*, *Karate Kid II*, and *Free to Be You and Me* — see the video recommendations on p. 95.

5. INFORMAL SOCIAL TIME FOR AGE GROUPS

Particularly if the program is conducted in a live-in situation, informal social time should be built into the program. Since this is especially appreciated by adults and teens, probably the best time is after the evening program when younger children have been put to bed.

As a program develops, if it becomes clear that some participants have specific concerns that cannot be adequately addressed during the content sessions, they can be encouraged to address these concerns during such time or at a particular meal.

Often some of the best sharing and learning takes place late in the evening (for "night persons") when other cares or concerns can be let go. For many teens this is "prime time" for friendship building and other sharing, so program planners should be prepared to capitalize on this.

CHAPTER 12

Child Care

Guidelines for organizing good child-care programs are elaborated on p. 10 (no. 5). Despite the logistical challenge that a child-care program always provides, many families will not be able to participate at all or to participate effectively without a child-care option. And program leaders generally have a difficult time meeting the needs of over-6's, teens, and adults if they have to attend to under 6's as well. The key to a good child-care experience at these programs is to have an adequate and competent staff for the number and ages of the children (which means preregistration requests for ages and numbers of children and any special needs they may have). It likewise means a planned program paralleling the main program, in a facility with adequate space for loud play, quiet time, and naps. Good snacks help too.

The PPJ program leaders with the most experience with effective child-care programs for 2- to 5-year olds are Cathy Lieb Reames, Joanne Crandall-Bear, and Candy Pulliman of Sacramento, Calif. The two program descriptions below are theirs. The first, part of the "Pass It On" program recommended on p. 82, is a carefully planned one-day program paralleling a large adult/teen peace celebration that also included parallel programs for 6- to 8-year olds and 9- to 12-year olds. Descriptions of these additional programs are available either from Cathy or the PPJN office.

The sample publicity letter used by the "Pass It On" program team reflects the need for advanced information on child-care needs, as well as for a pricing structure that encourages whole-family participation. It is included here as a model that can be adapted by other planning teams.

Program for 3–5 Year-Olds

9:00 a.m.: SET UP CLASSROOM

Teacher's aides and facilitators meet to go over the days' schedule and get acquainted. Children arrive and receive different colored paper doll name tags, which are stapled to their clothes. The children can begin activities set up in the room.

9:00–9:15: OPENING CIRCLE

Open with simple prayer, sharing names, days' activities, and bathroom procedures. Song with guitar: "Everyone 'Neath Their Vine and Fig Tree" (see above p. 45).

9:15–10:00: INSIDE ACTIVITIES

Group Notebook and Newsletter: A notebook is in the room to record things the children say or do that reflect their understanding of the issues we are exploring. (These will be used later for a newsletter, an idea of one of the primary grade children.)

Shalom Boxes: Each child brings or is given a box. They glue pictures representing *shalom* on their boxes. We talk about feelings (what makes me happy, sad, etc.), and help the children understand the concept of *shalom* through pictures of their everyday experience. Since there will not be time to cover the whole box, this activity can be continued at home with the family (see Worksheet 1).

Playdough: Using playdough at tables, children and adults interact cooperatively in small groups.

Crayon Mural: Using newsprint paper and crayons, children experience cooperation and small group interaction as they draw pictures about peace, family, and our world.

Book Corner: Through pictures and stories, children explore feelings, fantasies, peace, and equality.

Ethnic Dress-up Corner: A mirror, clothes, hats, and basket are available for the children to become aware of the clothes of other people as one expression of culture.

String Paper Dolls: To help children experience a notion of all people of the world, paper dolls are cut out of construction paper in the following proportions:

For every 30:

- 17 Yellow (Asia)
- 8 White (4 European; 2 Russian; 2 North American)
- 3 Black (African)
- 2 Brown (Latin American)

The dolls are strung with nylon thread.

10:00–10:30: SONGS, SNACKS, AND OUTSIDE PLAY

Songs: "Everyone 'Neath Their Vine and Fig Tree" (see above p. 45); "My Friends."

Caterpillar over the Mountain: The children line up on hands and knees, holding on to the person's feet in front of them — GO! With a large group make several caterpillars (from *The Cooperative Sports and Game Book*, by Terry Orlick, Pantheon, 1978).

10:30–11:15: FREE PLAY AND ACTIVITIES

Tracing and Coloring Bodies: Children trace each other on butcher paper or newsprint, then color at least the eyes and hair with the appropriate color. Talk about ways we are the same and the ways we are different: body parts, height, hair color and length, eye color. The key concepts here are affirmation and celebration of differences (Christians could refer to Galatians 3:28 — God sees no divisions; we are one).

Interviews: "Interview" children on a tape recorder, talking about their traced bodies, the banner on the wall ("Give Children Dreams, Not Nuclear Nightmares" — bomb turns into butterfly) and their favorite things. Play the interview back to the child or to the whole group.

11:15–11:30: OUTSIDE PLAY

Kangaroo Hop: A variation on tag. If someone gets tagged, he or she is lucky. The lucky person becomes a kangaroo and hops around, trying to tag someone else. As soon as the next person is tagged, that person joins the first person in hopping around and tagging others. In the end, everyone is a lucky, hopping kangaroo! (from *A Manual for Nonviolence and Children*, by Stephanie Judson, from the Friends' Peace Committee, 1515 Cherry St., Philadelphia, PA 19102).

11:30–11:50: PUPPET SHOW

Create your own puppet show on conflict resolution or use one of those described in *Helping Kids Care*, by Camy Condon and James McGinnis. Toddlers welcome.

11:50–12:15 p.m.: BEFORE LUNCH CIRCLE

Song: "Everyone 'Neath Their Vine and Fig Tree" (p. 45).

Bangalee: This is a children's book on pollution and littering (from Serendipity Books). Talk about ways to take care of the world: water, land, people, animals. Relate to the upcoming lunch: food, waste, litter.

12:15–1:15:   LUNCH

Parents get their children.

1:15–2:15:   REST/NAP TIME

Read some of the books from the book corner; play a tape of ethnic music.

2:15–3:00:   OUTSIDE PLAY

Yoga for Children and a Snack: To introduce the children to some new methods of relaxation and calm, have them imitate animals and nature through some simple asanas: The Frog, The Rooster, The Palm Tree, The Bird, The Lion, The Cobra. Relax in the sponge position: flat on back — be like a cloud floating in the sky, listen to the sounds. See "Yoga for Children," by Janet Sarkett, in *Mothering* magazine, Winter 1983, and *Meditating with Children: New Age Meditations for Children,* by Deborah Rozman, University of the Trees Press (P.O. Box 644, Boulder Creek, CA 95006), 1975.

Touch Nose: Children pair off sitting or standing. The leader calls out a body part and the children touch another on that part (the nose, for example). The adult picks different parts of the body to be touched (from *A Manual on Nonviolence and Children*).

3:00–4:30:   FREE PLAY INSIDE OR OUTSIDE

Mobiles: The children assemble mobiles of pictures of different families, as a way of introducing them to the similarities and differences of families around the world.   Materials should include straws, brad clips, nylon thread construction paper, *National Geographic Magazines,* hooks or tape.

Throwing Balloons: To celebrate "free to be you and me," the children throw balloons to the music you play.

Wrap-up: The children sing "Everyone 'Neath Their Vine and Fig Tree" (p. 45), then finish the stringing of paper dolls (see above), clean up, and

form a closing circle in which hugs are passed around.

4:30–5:00:   INTERFAITH WORSHIP SERVICE

After the service the children return to their classroom where their parents will pick them up.

Program for 2 1/2–3 Year Olds

8:00 a.m.:   LEADER ARRIVES AND
                        BEGINS SETTING UP

8:15:   ASSISTANTS ARRIVE

8:30:   FREE PLAY WITH TABLE TOYS
                  AS CHILDREN ARRIVE

9:00:   INTRODUCE THE ART PROJECT

- Sponge painting using sponge people and houses
- Themes: families; communities

9:30:   CHOICE OF INDOOR OR OUTDOOR PLAY

10:00:   WASH HANDS AND SNACK

10:30:   CIRCLE TIME

- Story
- Songs, prayers, and fingerplays
- Themes: sharing; helping; caring

11:00:   FREE PLAY

11:45:   STORYBOOK TIME

12:00:   MAKE AND EAT "FACE SANDWICHES"

12:30:   QUIET REST TIME — RELAXING MUSIC

1:00:   ACTIVITY CHOICES

- Shaving cream art with warm water
- Water table
- Playdough
- More sponge painting

- Preparing instant pudding for snack

- Outside play

2:30: AFTERNOON ACTIVITY CIRCLE

- Songs, rhythm band, finger play

- Themes: sharing; helping; caring

3:00: SNACK, CLEAN UP, AND CLOSING

"Goodbye Hug" game from *Cooperative Games for Children and Adults.*

Sample Publicity Letter

Dear Parents:

Today in Church School, your child received a brochure and color-it-yourself poster announcing "Pass It On," a day-long mini-retreat to be held here at Fremont Church on January 12, 1985. Children and youth of all ages are encouraged to attend with their families.

"Pass It On" is intended to provide an opportunity for families to explore together concrete ways of "living out" Jesus Christ's call for us to love as we have been loved. In the course of the day, your family will work together on such skills as affirmation, conflict resolution, decision-making, cooperation, sharing and forgiveness. These skills will be explored in the context of our immediate families and in the context of our belonging to a global family.

A special concurrent program for children ages 3 and younger has been developed. It will explore the retreat themes through activities oriented to their needs. We are privileged to have Sharon Kennedy, a Fremont Nursery School teacher, and Traci Freeman, a familiar face in the Sunday morning Toddler Program to lead the programs for ages 3 and younger.

Preregistration is a must, and enrollment is limited, so I encourage you to register early. A discount on the registration fee is offered to those registered by December 15. The fee, which includes all materials, child care, and lunch, is $10 for adults, $4 for each child, to a maximum of $20 for each family registered before December 15 and $24 for each family registered thereafter. Scholarships are available. To register, complete the form on the brochure, detach, and return to the church office.

I hope your family will be able to take advantage of this opportunity for a day of learning, growth and fun. I look forward to seeing many of you there.

Sincerely,

CHAPTER 13

Resources

The Additional Family Shalom Programs that follow here are those from which several of the activities listed in the program session chapters are taken. Footnotes in the text indicate the program that was the source for that activity. Names and addresses are provided here for those programs that have leaders or copies of their program available for workshops.

Most audio-visual and some written resources especially appropriate for the activities presented in previous chapters are described in those chapters themselves. The bibliographies that follow here are primarily written resources that provide further reading for adults and children of various ages. They are organized according to the themes of the program. In many cases, the appropriate age level is noted. The listing of recent videos on the various PPJ themes offers both adults and older children an excellent source for discussion and mutual growth.

Both the adult's and the children's bibliographies are meant to be duplicated for program participants. The first section in the adult bibliography (p. 85) presents those Parenting for Peace and Justice resources most appropriate for group study, discussion, and action.

Additional Family Shalom Programs

1. PASS IT ON

"Pass It On" was developed and presented at Fremont Presbyterian Church (5770 Carlson Drive, Sacramento, CA 95819; tel.: 916-452-7132) by Donna Buland, Patti Dusel, Reverend Dexter Mc-Namara, and John Williams, director of Christian education. The goals of this one-day program — or "mini retreat" as its developers describe it — are:

- to develop awareness, tools, and skills for building cooperative relationships and resolving conflicts constructively within our immediate families;

- to examine the impact of our day-to-day choices on our global family, and to explore concrete ways in which we can express and reflect God's compassion in our world;

- to discover ways that we, as parents and adults, can nurture compassionate behavior in our children and help them develop skills for solving problems nonviolently.

2. LITTLE FRIENDS FOR PEACE — PEACEMAKING EDUCATION

Five programs, a 58-page curriculum and new book, consultant services for schools, and leadership training are all available. The five programs are:

- *Creating Peace in the Family:*
  one to six two-hour workshops for whole families;

- *Parenting/Teaching for Peace and Justice:*
  workshops of different length for parents and teachers;

- *Little Friends for Peace Daycamp:*
  five to twelve three-hour sessions for children ages 4–12;

- *Discovering My Gifts:*
  four two-hour sessions for adults and teens;

- *Building Strong Families:*
  six two-hour sessions for whole families.

Contact Mary Joan Park, 4405 29th St., Mt. Rainier, MD 20712; 301-699-0042.

3. CHRISTIAN FAMILY PEACE WEEKENDS

The Sharon Core Community, an Ontario-based team, has conducted dozens of weekend programs designed for families of all varieties. Each weekend combines fun and celebration with prayer centered around themes. These are presented and reinforced through drama, music, speakers, creativity, reflection, and workshop sessions. Contact Dwyer Sullivan, 80 Sackville St., Toronto, Ontario, M5A 3E5, Canada; tel.: 416-863-6702. For a full description, see below pp. 96–102.

4. FAMILY PEACEMAKING WORKSHOP

Jacqueline Haessly has been conducting peacemaking workshops for teachers, parents, and whole families throughout the United States and Canada for fifteen years. Her book *Peacemaking: Family Activities for Justice and Peace* has helped thousands of families create peacemaking in their homes through the development of skills of affirmation, respect for diversity, cooperation, conflict resolution, and living peacefully with others in our global family. Contact her at Peacemaking Associates, 2437 N. Grant Blvd., Milwaukee, WI 53210; tel.: 414-445-9736.

5. EVENTS ON COOPERATION AND COMPETITION

Susan Morse and her Columbia, Mo., PPJN team have been conducting family events for several years. These have been primarily on conflict resolution and cooperative games, but also on racism, sexism, and stewardship. Contact her at 1616 University Ave., Columbia, MO 65201; tel.: 314-449-5688.

6. FAMILIES COVENANTING FOR PEACE

This is the title of a five-part family series conducted for six families who covenanted together to become an ongoing family support group. The series is led by Susan Stater on five consecutive Sundays from 5 to 7 p.m. Her five-session model was revised for inclusion in a larger series of eighteen peace and justice workshop sessions (for various groups) written by Susan and published by KQ Associates. Contact her at 2300 Clay St., Cedar Falls, IA 50613; tel.: 319-277-3539.

7. YOUTH CAMPS ON PEACEMAKING

This is a curriculum on peacemaking designed by Jean Cooley and Susan Barnard for a Presbyterian youth camp in Roanoke, Va., and used with five groups of 9- to 15-year-olds. The daily themes progressed from personal peacemaking, to Jesus as a peacemaker, to conflicts between U.S. cultural values and Christian values, to peacemaking and our neighbors (prejudice, "the enemy," and the "good Samaritan"), and ending with a peace-day celebration. Unique features of this program include extensive effort to live the themes throughout all aspects of the camp experience, with a special emphasis on service and cooperation. Contact Jean at 743 Clearwater Ave., N.W., Roanoke, VA 24019; tel.: 703-362-0639.

8. FAMILY WEEKEND CELEBRATIONS

Jim and Susan Vogt have conducted a variety of family weekends, generally including all the PPJ themes, with special emphasis on the peacemaking in the home and the consumerism and stewardship themes. Contact them at 523 E. Southern Ave., Covington, KY 41015; tel.: 606-291-6197 (see also above, p. 65).

9. ABC'S OF CONFLICT RESOLUTION

Kathy Beckwith's program on the "ABC's" of family conflict resolution expands the range of activities presented in the "Shalom in the Home" session (chapter 5). The activities are geared primarily to younger children and parents and are creative and engaging. Contact her at 3555 S.E. Locks Road, Dayton, OR 97114.

10. FAMILY CHURCH CAMPS

Betty and Bob Sweet have conducted a variety of
family church camps for a number of years in the
New England area. These camps include many of
the PPJ themes but are always tailored to the needs
of the group. While the Sweets do not have a published program, they are available as program leaders. Contact them at 175 Barney St., Rumford, RI
02916.

11. NURTURING FAMILIES
   IN A WORLD OF CONFLICT

Susan Temple chaired a team that designed this
wonderful one-day program on peacemaking in the
home (morning) and global peacemaking (afternoon). Her 19-page "Facilitator's Guide" provides
clear instructions and even the wording of introductions to activities used during the day. Her publicity
materials are outstanding. Most helpful is the 60-
page "Family Booklet," which contains all the worksheets used during the day, some of which are completed at home afterwards; a 13-page bibliography
of adult and children's books; several good short articles; cooperative games and craft descriptions; six
hand puppets and a family puzzle; a family covenant
envelope; and song sheets. Contact her at 731 Peach
Place, Davis, CA 95616; tel.: 916-758-4408.

12. AN APPROACH TO FAMILY CAMPING:
   THE EXTENDED AND CHURCH FAMILIES

With her husband, Rev. Dr. Ian Mavor, Mrs. Lola
Mavor has developed a range of marriage and family life programs. Their approach to family camping has been, in her words, "to take seriously the
rich images that are part of the word 'family' and
to make that a focus on the programs." Generally
held on weekends, these programs broaden the sense
of family to include the notion of "church family,"
which is increasingly a concern of religious educators doing family programming. For a fuller description of the program see below pp. 103–106

Adult Bibliography

Books for Group Study, Discussion, and Action

Robert and Janet Aldridge, *Children and Non-Violence,* Hope Press, 1987. Inspiration as well as practical examples from long-time peace activists and parents of ten grown children.

Jacqueline Haessly, *Peacemaking: Family Activities for Justice and Peace,* Paulist Press, 1980. Available from Peacemaking Associates, 2437 N. Grant Blvd., Milwaukee, WI 53210.

Inquiry books from the Christian Family Movement in North America. The 1985 book addresses a variety of social issues, while the 1987 book focuses on economic justice issues. The "inquiry" method combines the biblical reflection with an "observe-judge-act" approach, one topic per meeting. Contact CFM, P.O. 272, Ames, IA 50010; tel.: 515-232-7432.

David McConkey, *A Family Global Action Handbook,* available from the Marquist Project, #200, 107 7th St., Brandon, Manitoba, R7A 3S5, Canada; tel.: 202-727-5675.

James and Kathleen McGinnis, *Parenting for Peace and Justice,* Orbis Books, 1981. Their original book addressing all the PPJ themes for families with children of all ages; includes practical examples (failures as well as successes) and biblical reflection.

Kathleen McGinnis & Barbara Oehlberg, *Starting Out Right: Nurturing Young Children as Peacemakers,* Institute for Peace and Justice and Meyer-Stone Books, 1988. Practical application of all the PPJ themes to families with preschoolers.

Michael True, *Homemade Social Justice,* Fides/Claretian Books (221 W. Madison, Chicago, IL 60606), 1982. Family application of many PPJ issues, especially "global peacemakers," by a father of teens and peace activist/educator.

Thematic PPJN Newsletter Issues for Group Study

For single copies of any of these issues, send $1.00 per issue and a self-addressed stamped envelope; for five or more copies of the same issue, send 50 cents per copy plus $1.00 for mailing, to: PPJN Newsletter, Institute for Peace and Justice, 4144 Lindell Blvd., St. Louis, MO 63108.

Value Conflicts between Spouses, Summer 1984. Explores a timeless theme: what do you do when spouses do not share the same values, especially with regard to peace and justice values and concerns?

Handicapism, May–June 1986. Examines disabilities: loving one's disabled child, parenting the learning disabled, extended family reactions to a child with a disability.

Family Stress, July–August 1986. Deals with stress and burn-out: finding time for the family in the midst of social action commitments, stress and the healthy family, a "special family check-up" on coping with stress.

Promoting Peace Education in Schools, October 1986. Focuses on schools: how parents can more effectively encourage their children's schools to incorporate many of the PPJ themes, with checklists for schools and a strategy for starting a peace education program.

Alternative Christmas Suggestions, November–December 1986. Presents a wealth of alternative suggestions for Christmas and other holidays, with a special page on alternatives to violent toys and reflection on holiday stress and the needs of children.

Family Communication, April 1987. Focuses on family communication — about sex, war, and other difficult issues, with suggestions for communicating politely.

TV and War Toys, June 1987. Has this dual focus: concrete suggestions for "taming the tube" and alternatives to war toys, with extensive reflection on the effects of war toys on children.

Militarism and Parenting, August 1987. Examines ways militarism reaches our children, especially through the media; preparing teens for a decision about military service; videos and other resources for countering militarism; helping youth make conscientious decisions on any difficult issue.

Families in Search of Shalom (Chapter 4)

Bananas, *Let's Talk About Peace, Let's Talk About Nuclear War,* 6501 Telegraph Ave., Oakland, CA 94609. Curriculum for elementary age students.

Walter Brueggemann, *Living Toward a Vision: Biblical Reflections on Shalom,* United Church Press, 1976. Probably the best comprehensive background reading for leader and participants.

Children's Defense Fund, *In Celebration of Children: An Interfaith Religious Action Kit,* Children's Defense Fund (122 C Street, N.W., Washington, DC 20001). For preschool–teens; ideas for celebration and worship in the family and with congregations, biblical references, sample prayers, ideas for banner making and other activities, comparative statistics on children and military expenditures, case studies, action possibilities, bibliography of other CDF publications; the workbook format is handy for Sunday-school planning.

Lois Dorn, *Peace In the Family: A Workbook of Ideas and Actions,* Random House, 1983. Suggestions based on Dorn's experience running peace workshops.

J. Lome Peachey, *How to Teach Peace to Children,* Herald Press, 1981. 32-page pamphlet.

Eileen Tway, ed., *Reading Ladders for Human Relations,* American Council on Education. A specialized annotated book list and teaching aid for helping children, from preschool through high school, develop sensitivity in human relations through books of good literary quality.

Thomas D. Yawkey and Kenneth C. Jones, *Caring: Activities to Teach the Young to Care for Others,* Prentice-Hall, 1982. A guide for parents and teachers to help young children develop a sense of altruism; several hundred suggested projects and activities.

*Shalom in the Home and
Cooperative Games (Chapter 5)*

Animal Town Game Company (P.O. Box 2002, Santa Barbara, CA 93120). Write for their catalog of interesting noncompetitive games.

Jean Illsey Clarke, *Self-Esteem: A Family Affair,* Winston, 1978. A leader's guide is also available.

Elizabeth Crary, *Kids Can Cooperate,* Parenting Press, 1983. Parents and children can benefit from the practical activities in this book, all focused on how to encourage children to cooperate.

Elizabeth Crary, *Without Spanking or Spoiling: A Practical Approach to Toddler and Preschool Guidance,* Parenting Press, 1979. Leader's guide also available.

Rudolf Dreikers, *Family Council,* Henry Regnery Co., 1974. Presents an elaborate and effective description of family meetings and the moral basis for this dimension of family life.

Adele Faber and Elain Mazlish, *How to Talk So Kids Will Listen and Listen So Kids Will Talk,* Avon, 1980. Actual samples of family dialogue, warm and humorous.

Fighting Fair, The Grace Contrino Abrams Peace Education Foundation. A provocative 18-minute film showing a coach help a group of angry kids resolve a conflict on the basketball court. Vivid scenes of Martin Luther King, Jr., and the civil rights movement used as a backdrop to help the young people understand the dynamics of nonviolence; a comprehensive teacher's guide, with six complete lessons and reproducible student pages, involves students in brainstorming, role playing, problem solving, and decision making.

Andrew Fluegelman, ed., *More New Games & Playful Ideas,* Dolphin Books/Doubleday, 1981. Collection of games, old and new, that expresses a philosophy of appreciating self and others. Some require skill and strategy, others are pure fun, most require little equipment to play. With an emphasis on participation and cooperation, these games provide creative alternatives for recess, birthday parties, church picnics, or gatherings of any kind.

Earl H. Gaulke, *You Can Have a Family Where Everybody Wins: Christian Perspectives on Parent Effectiveness Training,* Concordia, 1975. Takes the basic principles of "parent effectiveness training," and shows how they parallel many of the principles of the New Testament; provides practical examples. A Christian version of Thomas Gordon's *Parent Effectiveness Training,* Peter H. Wyden, Inc., 1970.

Stephanie Judson, *A Manual on Nonviolence and Children,* Nonviolence and Children Program (Friends' Peace Committee, 1515 Cherry St., Philadelphia, PA 19102), 1977. A wealth of games, techniques, observations, and insights on developing nonviolence in children.

Elizabeth Loescher, *How to Avoid World War III at Home,* Cornerstone (920 Emerson St., Denver, CO 80218), 1986. Concrete suggestions about how to handle conflict in the family.

Bill and Dolores Michaelis, *Learning Through Non-Competitive Activities and Play,* Learning Handbooks, 1977.

Terry Orlick, *The Cooperative Sports and Games Book,* Random House, 1978.

Terry Orlick, *The Second Cooperative Sports and Games Book,* Random House, 1982.

Priscilla Prutzman, et al., *The Friendly Classroom for a Small Planet,* Children's Creative Response to Conflict Program (Box 271, Nyack, NY 10960), 1978. This workbook for elementary teachers and parents contains affirmative exercises, practice activities for teaching creative problem solving, and conflict resolution ideas.

Jeffrey Sobel, *Everybody Wins: 393 Non-Competitive Games for Young Children,* Walker and Co., 1984.

Dudley Weeks, *Conflict Partnership,* Trans-World Productions, 1984. Perhaps the best concentrated focus on interpersonal conflict resolution techniques, with application to intergroup conflicts as well.

Matt Weinstein and Joel Goodman, *Playfair: Everybody's Guide to Non-Competitive Play,* Impact Publishers (P.O. Box 1094, San Luis Obispo, CA 93406), 1980.

Marie Winn, *The Plug-In Drug: Television, Children and the Family,* Viking, 1977.

Shalom in the Global Family (Chapter 6)

Kate Cloud, Ellie Deegan, Alice Evans, Hayat Imam, Barbara Signer, *Watermelons Not War! A Support Book for Parenting in the Nuclear Age,* New Society Publishers (4722 Baltimore Avenue, Philadelphia, PA 19143), 1986.

James and Kathleen McGinnis, *Families Acting for Peace,* Institute for Peace and Justice, 1988. A 6-page pamphlet of peacemaking suggestions at home as well as in the global family; good for bulk distribution for an initial experience of family peacemaking.

Parenting in the Nuclear Age, *What Shall We Tell the Children?* PINA (6501 Telegraph Avenue, Oakland, CA 94609). Pamphlet. Sections include Confronting Our Own Despair, Talking with Kids of Various Ages, Things for Kids to Do, Gaining Strength from Each Other, Frequent Questions and Answers, Finding Consolation and Renewal.

Parents for Peace, *Facing the Nuclear Age: Parents and Children Together,* Parents for Peace (P.O. Box 611, Station P, Toronto, Ontario, M5S 2Y4, Canada), 1985. How to deal with children's nuclear fears; includes a variety of peace action suggestions for different age groups and an extensive resource list.

William Van Ornum and Mary Wicker Van Ornum, *Talking to Children About Nuclear War,* Crossroad/Continuum, 1984

Consumerism and Stewardship (Chapter 7)

Jeanne and Robert Bendick, *Consumer's Catalog of Economy and Ecology,* Jane Addams Peace Association, 1972.

Joseph Bharat Cornell, *Sharing Nature with Children,* Anada, 1979.

William E. Gibson, *A Covenant Group for Life-Style Assessment,* United Presbyterian Program Agency, 1978. A helpful guide for a study/action group dealing with the issues of simplicity and stewardship; includes scriptural and prayerful reflection as well as practical suggestions. Available from Discipleship Resources, Box 840, Nashville, TN 37202.

Winnie Honeywell and James McGinnis, *A Question of Balance: Families and Economic Justice,* Institute for Peace and Justice, 1987. A 16-page booklet of reflection and family action suggestions regarding lifestyle change, direct service, and social change.

Doris Janzen Longacre, *Living More With Less,* Herald Press, 1980. Both beautiful and practical; part 1 examines the basic principles that underlie the specific suggestions for lifestyle change in part 2; using stories of dozens of families, the author offers a lifetime of possibilities for simplifying with regard to money, clothes, home and homekeeping, transportation, celebrations, recreation, meals, and strengthening each other. Available from Discipleship Resources, Box 840, Nashville, TN 37202.

Milo Shannon Thornberry, *Alternative Celebrations Catalog,* Pilgrim Press, 1982. A resource catalog of things to do for celebrations that are "vehicles for nurturing the human spirit"; lots of suggestions for meaningful observations; emphasis on voluntary simplicity and social awareness.

Doris Lee Shettel, *Life-Style Change for Children,* United Presbyterian Program Agency, 1981. An exciting resource to use with children as well as intergenerational groups; full of activities that could be used in a variety of settings.

Celebrating Diversity and Human Possibilities (Chapter 8)

Racism

Council on Interracial Books for Children, *Bulletin,* vol. 2, nos. 3 and 4 (1980): "Children, Race and Racism: How Race Awareness Develops." This special issue deals with positive attitudes about self and others, how to help children deal with racist name-calling, how race awareness develops. A thought-provoking resource for parents of all social groups. A subscription to the Bulletin (CIBC, 1841 Broadway, New York, NY 10023) is $10/year for individuals and $15/year for institutions.

Council on Interracial Books for Children, *Bulletin,* vol. 14, nos. 7 and 8 (1983): "Countering Bias in Early Childhood Education." This issue deals with racism, sexism, and handicapism as they relate to young children. An invaluable resource.

Mary Ellen Goodman, *Race Awareness in Young Children,* Collier Books, 1964. A cultural anthropologist's study of how racial attitudes begin to form in 4-year-olds; it still ranks as one of the most important research studies in the area and is excellent background reading for parents.

Judy Katz, *White Awareness: Handbook for Anti-Racist*

Training, University of Oklahoma Press, 1978. Contains useful activities for adult groups learning about racism.

Louis L. Knowles and Kenneth Prewitt, eds., *Institutional Racism in America,* Prentice-Hall, 1969. A classic that provides an explanation of the key aspect of racism — its institutional dimension.

Herbert Kohl, *Growing with Your Children,* Little, Brown, 1978. A parenting book that deals with the issue of White children and racism. Kohl's basic premise is that "children first learn racism consciously or unconsciously from their parents." He gives specific suggestions about how to create healthy racial attitudes.

James and Kathleen McGinnis, et al., *Educating for Peace and Justice,* Institute for Peace and Justice, 1985. Vol. 1 includes units on Multicultural Education and Racism. This manual is oriented toward teachers but has many suggestions that are immediately adaptable to the home.

Lois Stalvey, *The Education of a Wasp,* Bantam Books, 1971. A personal view of a White person coming to the realization of the realities of racism.

Lois Stalvey, *Getting Ready,* Bantam Books, 1974. A penetrating look at racism in a big city school system and how a family deals with it.

Sexism

Carrie Carmichael, *Non-Sexist Childraising,* Beacon Press, 1977. Has more relevance for parents of younger children, although all could benefit from the thought-provoking issues raised, ranging from participatory childbirth to sexism in schools.

Letty Cottin Pogrebin, *Growing Up Free: Raising Your Child in the '80s,* McGraw-Hill, 1980. "Must" background reading for teachers and parents, with a wealth of insights about how to deal with sex-role stereotyping in everyday life.

Ageism/Handicapism

Ellen Barnes, Carol Berrigan, and Douglas Biklen, *What's the Difference? Teaching Positive Attitudes Toward People with Disabilities,* Human Policy Press (P.O. Box 127, University Station, Syracuse, NY 13210), 1978. A book of classroom activities that suggests over ninety ways for teachers to help students develop greater understanding of their disabled peers.

Council on Interracial Books for Children, *Bulletin,* vol. 8, nos. 6 and 7 (1977): a special issue on "handicapism" that is filled with data, teaching suggestions, and helpful resources; vol. 7, no. 6 (1976): a similar special issue on ageism. Both volumes are "must" readings, even though they are over ten years old (CIBC, 1841 Broadway, New York, NY 10023).

Bernard Ikeler, *Parenting Your Disabled Child,* Westminster Press, 1986. The author shares personally and in concrete ways insights that are meaningful both to parents of disabled children and to others.

Richard O. Ulin, *Teaching and Learning About Aging,* NEA, 1982. Gives information on various aspects of the aging process and recent developments in curriculum dealing with aging.

Children's Bibliography

Peace, Nonviolence, Social Change
(Chapters 5 and 6)

N. Babbit, *The Search for Delicious,* Farrar, 1969. Shows how rumors can lead to violence and war. Older elementary.

Marion Bauer, *Rain of Fire,* Clarion Books, 1983. An anti-war story about two brothers and their feelings about World War II and Hiroshima. 1984 Jane Addams Peace Association Award Book. Grades 5 and up.

Elizabeth Hershberger Bauman, *Coals of Fire,* Herald Press, 1954. Seventeen short stories of people who returned good for evil.

Bernard Benson, *The Peace Book,* Bantam, 1980. What if...a little boy used Gandhi's techniques of dialogue, creative resistance, and focusing attention on survival in dealing with the governments of the superpowers? A new fairy tale. Grades 3–5.

Joy Wilt Berry, *Let's Talk About Fighting,* Children's Press, 1984. Explores how quarrels and fights develop and alternatives to fighting.

Eleanor Coerr, *Sadako and the Thousand Paper Cranes,* Fellowship of Reconciliation, Box 217, Nyack, NY 10960. A gentle presentation of Sadako Sasaki, the 11-year-old victim of the bombing at Hiroshima. Middle grades.

David R. Collins, *Dorothy Day: Catholic Worker,* St. Anthony Messenger Press, 1981. Part of the Young People's Library of Famous American Catholics, this book tells the story of a life courageously committed to a cause, in spite of doubts and mistakes, humiliations, and arrests. Ages 9–13.

Robert Cooney and Helen Michalowski, *The Power of the People: Active Non-violence in the United States,* Peace Press, 1986. A well-researched chronology with many photos and illustrations documenting organized struggle against war by peace leaders and organizations. An unusual and helpful book. Older children.

Russell E. Erickson, *A Toad for Tuesday,* Lothrop, 1974. Held captive to be eaten by an owl, the offering of friendship by the toad changes an enemy to a friend. Ages 8–12.

Elizabeth Goudge, *The Little White Horse,* Scholastic, 1978. Maria sets herself to resolve a long-standing quarrel, originally caused by her ancestors, among the residents of Moonacre Manor; helped by her human and animal friends and sustained by Marmaduke Scarlet's veal pie, she eventually gets people unstuck from their old grievances. Grades 2–5.

Eloise Greenfield, *Rosa Parks,* Thomas J. Crowell Company, 1973. *Rosa Parks* sensitively depicts the indigni-

ties endured by Black people in our recent past and the quiet courage of "the Mother of the Civil Rights Movement" in bravely claiming her rights. Ages 5–11.

Nancy Gurney, *The King, the Mice and the Cheese,* Beginner Books, 1965. This is a great book to help young children start their understanding of sharing.

Jacqueline Haessly, ed., *Peacemaking Activities for Children,* Books 1 and 2. Each book contains selected activities from the first four years of publication of *Peacemaking for Children* magazine, an informative, activity centered magazine for children, ages 6–14. Available from Peace Talks Publications, 2437 N. Grant Blvd., Milwaukee, WI 53210; tel.: 414-445-9736.

John Hershey, *Hiroshima,* Bantam, 1946. Famous account of six people who survived the attack.

Elizabeth S. Hill, *Evan's Corner,* Holt, Rinehart and Winston, 1967. Evan's mother helps him establish a place of his own in their crowded apartment, and also to understand his little brother's need. Ages 5–8.

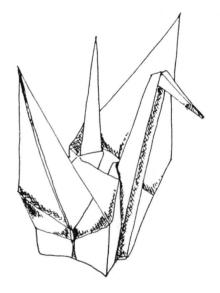

Ann Holm, *North to Freedom,* Harcourt, Brace and Jovanovich, 1963. Twelve-year-old David is given a chance to escape a prison camp in Eastern Europe. He slowly begins to trust people and finds his own identity in the way of peace.

J. Houston, *White Archer: An Eskimo Legend,* Harcourt, 1970. An Eskimo boy is intent on revenging his parents' deaths; he learns the futility of "an eye for an eye." Older elementary.

Irene Hunt, *Across Five Aprils,* Follett, 1964. For the Creighton family living in Civil War times there seemed to be no alternative to war, but always war is set in proper perspective; we see clearly that no one ever wins a war. Ages 9 and up.

Nigel Hunter, illustrated by Richard Hook, *Martin Luther King, Jr.,* Bookwright Press, 1986. Beautiful illustrations and photographs enliven this biography of King.

Gerald G. Jampolsky, ed., *Children as Teachers of Peace,* Celestial Arts, 1982. "This book was written for adults by kids! Because the simplest thoughts are sometimes the best. For peace is the goal of everyone not just you and me" (Lance Lawson, age 11). Pictures, letters, poems, thoughts, definitions, wishes by American children.

Jan Johnson, illus. by Kathryn E. Shoemaker, *Brother Francis,* Winston Press, 1977. An appealing biography of one of the great peace-heroes — Francis of Assisi.

Jane Langton, *The Fragile Flag,* Harper and Row, 1984. The story of children who organize grassroots nonviolent resistance to the nuclear arms race. Grades 5 and up.

Munro Leaf, *The Story of Ferdinand,* Viking Press, 1936. A classic for young readers. Ferdinand the bull enjoys sitting under a tree and smelling flowers; he does not like to fight.

Cornelia Lehn, illustrated by Robert W. Regier, *The Sun and the Wind,* Faith and Life Press, 1983. A beautifully illustrated fable with the sun proving to the wind that love is stronger than force. For young children.

Cornelia Lehn, *Peace Be With You,* Faith and Life Press, 1980. Fifty-nine stories of peace heroes, from the first century to the present. There is humor and sadness; global aspects and next-door neighbor-type vignettes; stories about young people and tales about the elderly; happy and sad endings. Each story is short enough to capture the attention of a young child, yet is written maturely enough for an older person to appreciate.

Seymour Leichman, *The Boy Who Could Sing Pictures,* Doubleday, 1968. The king is at war and doesn't realize the damage it is doing to his people until the boy sings to him...the sadness he sees.

Madeleine L'Engle, *A Wrinkle in Time.* Farrar, Straus, Giroux, 1962. Newberry award-winning fantasy about children who challenge wrong and destroy evil with the power of their desire to love others. Intermediate–advanced.

Eda LeShan, illustrated by Lisl Weil, *What Makes Me Feel This Way? Growing Up with Human Emotions,* Collier Books, 1972. On recognizing emotions, identifying their causes, and some ways to manage them. Grades K–5.

Leo Lionni, *The Alphabet Tree,* Pantheon, 1968. With the help of the word-bug, the letters of the alphabet deal with their fears of the wind and storm by grouping themselves into words, for safety. The words are: "Peace on earth and goodwill toward all men." Ages 3–8.

Anita Lobel, *Potatoes, Potatoes,* Harper and Row, 1967. The story of a woman who refuses to take part in war. Her two sons join opposite armies; they come home with their hungry armies to eat potatoes. Points out the futility of war and the hardships it creates. Grades K–3.

Toshi Maruki, *Hiroshima No Pika,* Lothrop, Lee and Shepard, 1982. A poignant story of the effects of the bombing of Hiroshima, especially on one family. Grades 2–6.

Milton Meltzer, *Ain't Gonna Study War No More,* Harper and Row, 1985. This history of civil disobedience is an extraordinary service to the cause of peace. It illuminates the theories, thoughts, and deeds of generations of heroes who bravely rejected violence or participation in wars they considered unjust. Grades 8–adult.

Edith Patterson Meyer, illustrated by Billie Jean Osborne, *In Search of Peace: The Winners of the Nobel Peace Prize, 1901–1975,* Abingdon. Stories of Alfred Nobel, the originator of the Nobel Peace Prize, and fifty-eight recipients. Intermediate level.

Melinda Moore and Laurie Olsen, *Our Future at Stake: A Teenager's Guide to Stopping the Nuclear Arms Race,* New Society Publishers, 1984. Informative, beautifully illustrated and photographed resource for education and action. Includes personal statements by teenagers themselves. Handy glossary and chronology for teenagers seeking to understand the nuclear arms race. Grades 7 and up.

Ruth Nulton Moore, *Peace Treaty,* Herald Press, 1977. Peter Andreas was the son of Moravian missionaries killed by the French Indians on the Pennsylvania frontier in the 1750s and is later befriended by a Delaware Indian boy. Ages 10–13.

Dorothy Morrison, Roma Dehi, Ronald M. Bazar, illustrated by Nola Johnston, *We Can Do It,* Namchi United Enterprises (P.O. Box 33852, Station D, Vancouver, B.C., Canada V6J 4L6), 1985. This upbeat alphabet book describes all kinds of concrete actions people can take to work for world peace.

Jorg Muller and Jorg Steiner, *The Sea People,* Schocken, 1982. An English translation of the original 1981 German edition. An unusual picture book about two neighboring islands. When people of the large island attempt to dominate the people of the small, they must instead learn a new way to live if they are to continue. Intermediate.

Tomie de Paola, *The Hunter and the Animals,* Holiday House, 1981. A wordless story in stylized detail about a forest of peaceful animals who help their enemy the hunter. The hunter breaks his gun as an indication that he will no longer try to kill. For young children.

Gayle Petersen and Ying Kelley, ed., *A Chance to Live: Children's Poems for Peace in a Nuclear Age,* Mindbelly Press, 1983.

Sarah Pirtle, *An Outbreak of Peace,* New Society Publishers, 1987. Ages 12 and up.

C. Pomerantz, *The Princess and the Admiral,* Addison-Wesley, 1974. The tiny kingdom is about to celebrate one hundred years of peace when warships appear. What happens is not a war — and the celebration does occur after all!

Kjell Ringi, *The Stranger*, Random House, 1968. The reactions of a village to a stranger who is so tall his face can't be seen, but who becomes friends with the villagers. Useful for discussing differences between people, enemies, stereotypes, aggression, war, peace and communication. Preschool–grade 3.

Dr. Seuss, *The Butter Battle Book*, Random House, 1984. Makes a powerful statement about the military mentality, exposing the foolishness of the arms race. Ages 5 and up.

Marjorie Wienman Sharmat, *Walter the Wolf*, Scholastic Book Service (Firefly Paperback), 1975. Peer pressure goads practically perfect Walter to give up the violin for lucrative violence, but in the end he says: "I have big fangs. I did not choose them, but I can choose not to use them!"

Stanford Summers, *Wacky and His Fuddlejig*, 484 W. 43rd, Apt. 24-0, New York, NY 10036. Dedicated to the children of the Third World, the story concerns one of Santa's helpers who finds himself out of step with his co-workers in the military toy department. Finally, he decides to quit, preferring to spend his time creating a toy that will appeal to a child's imagination.

Florence Temko, *Folk Crafts for World Friendship*, U.S. Committee for UNICEF, 1976. All sorts of good things that older elementary children can do at home or the family do together.

Evelyn Weiss, ed., *Children's Songs for a Friendly Planet*, Riverside Church Disarmament Program (590 Riverside Dr., New York, NY 10027). A compilation of 115 songs for peace and global understanding from many times and places. Includes international folk songs ("Kum Ba Yah"), spirituals ("Go Down, Moses"), songs of the past peace movements ("If I Had a Hammer"), songs about heroes and heroines (M. L. King and Harriet Tubman), newly composed songs ("Milestones," "There Is Always Something You Can Do"). The songs are annotated and there is an introduction by Priscilla Prutzman on "Building Friendship in the Classroom."

Joy Wilt, *Handling Your Disagreements: A Children's Book About Differences of Opinion*, Word, 1980. Young intermediate.

Winston Press, *Christian Heroes* (series): *Tom Dooley; Dorothy Day; Harriet Finds a Way; Clara Barton; Brother Francis; The Boyhood of Pope John XXIII; Mary Bethune and her Somedays; Thomas Merton.*

William Wondriska, *All the Animals Were Angry*, Holt, 1970. A dove tells the quarreling animals that she loves them all. Ages 3–8.

William Wondriska, *John, John Twilliger*, Holt, Rinehart and Winston, 1966. The book's message is that dictators are human and reachable as JJ makes friends with the dictatorial mayor and the town changes drastically. Also his *The Tomato Patch*, 1964.

Elizabeth Yates, *Amos Fortune Free Man*, Dutton, 1950. With her characteristic quiet goodness, Elizabeth Yates tells the story of how Amos Fortune finds freedom and works to bring the same fortune to the Black people whose lives he touches. A Newberry Award winner. Ages 10–12.

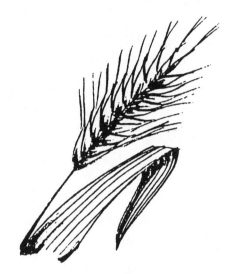

Sofia Zaramboulke, *Irene*, Tee Loftin Publishers, 1979. From Educators for Social Responsibility. A beautifully illustrated fable about peace, including a play for young children. Ages 5–10.

Jacob Zim, *My Shalom, My Peace*, McGraw-Hill, Sabra Books, 1975. A moving collection of paintings and poems on the theme of peace by Arab and Jewish children. All ages.

Charlotte Zolotow, *The Hating Book*, Harper and Row, 1969. Two friends fight but end their "hating" to become friends again.

Media

Red Grammer, *Teaching Peace*, Smiling Atcha Music (939 Orchard Street, Peekskill, NY 10566). Twelve songs on world peace written for ages 4 to 9. Tape.

Stewardship and Consumerism (Chapter 7)

Barbara Cooney, *Miss Rumphius*, Viking, 1982. A personal story about a family tradition of doing "something to make the world more beautiful." Young children.

Greenspeech: The Manifesto of an Indian Chief, Prism Press. "Forced to sell ancestral lands to the American government in 1854, Chief Seattle of the Dwamish tribe responded with a passionate speech, proclaiming his reverence for the earth and all its creatures and attacking those who plunder its resources." Advanced.

Ezra Jack Keats, *Clementina's Cactus,* Viking, 1982. Wordless picture book about a small girl and her father who live in the desert and their anticipation and joy at seeing beautiful blossoms grow from a cactus. Their appreciation of natural riches complements their own very simple way of living. For all ages, although the illustrations are not the style children usually choose for themselves.

Joy Wilt, *A Consumer's Guide for Kids,* Word, Inc.

Celebrating Diversity and Human Possibilities (racial, sex-role, age and disability stereotypes, Chapter 8)

Arnold Adoff, illustrated by Emily McCully, *Black Is Brown Is Tan,* Harper and Row, 1973. Beautifully introduces children to a biracial family; poetic text and lovely pictures. Includes extended family. Ages 4–8.

Linda Atkinson, *In Kindling Flame: The Story of Hannah Senesh, 1921–1944,* Lothrop, Lee and Shepard, 1985. This is an inspiring story of Hannah Senesh, a Jewish poet and resistance fighter during the Nazi era. Grades 6 and up.

Mary Atkinson, *Maria Teresa,* Lollipop Power, 1979. A Spanish-speaking girl moves. It's difficult getting used to her new non-Spanish environment. Her puppet sheep helps her make new friends. Young children.

Charles Blood and Martin Link, *The Goat in the Rug,* Parents Magazine Press, 1976. This is a delightful, fanciful tale told by a goat. It is an interesting way to explain an element of Navajo culture, the art of weaving, to young children.

Robert Burch, *Ida Early Comes Over the Mountain,* Viking, 1980. Things become more lively for a rural Georgia family when Ida comes as housekeeper. Her strange appearance and tall tales make this a warmly comic novel. Grades 3–7.

Vera and Bill Cleaver, *Hazel Rye,* Lippincott, 1983. Hazel is an unusual character, who at 11 would like to quit school, drive a taxi, and make $300 a week. She has to repeat sixth grade, and her teacher calls her fascinating, although she can barely read or write. Grades 5–7.

Lucille Clifton, illustrated by Thomas De Grazia, *My Friend Jacob,* Harper and Row, 1980. This is a wonderful story about a truly mutual friendship between a young Black child and a White teenager who is mentally retarded.

Caroline B. Cooney, *I'm Not Your Other Half,* Pacer Books (Putnam), 1984. The story of an adolescent girl's struggles to balance her own needs and interests with beginning relationships with boyfriends. The central character crosses traditional sex role barriers in a variety of ways. Grades 7–up.

Helen Coutant, illustrated by Vo-Dinh, *First Snow,* Alfred A. Knopf, 1974. This story of a small Vietnamese girl's relationship with her grandmother and the experience of her grandmother's death is full of gentleness and warmth. Preschool–grade 3.

Michael Dorris, photographs by Joseph C. Farber, *Native Americans: 500 Years After,* Thomas Y. Crowell, 1975. A must book, even though expensive, for a home or school library. It includes hundreds of photographs of Native Americans, and gives children a realistic picture of Native American people today. Middle grades and older children.

Richard Erdoes and Alfonso Ortiz, eds., illustrated by Richard Erdoes, *American Indian Myths and Legends,* Pantheon, 1984. This is a valuable collection of legends and myths from many Native American people, organized around various themes, for example, tales of human creation, tales of the sun. Grades 6 and up.

Muriel Feelings, *Jambo Means Hello, Swahili Alphabet Book,* Dial Press, 1974. This is an introduction to Swahili words. The illustrations by Tom Feelings are outstanding and evoke warmth and dignity. Young children.

Muriel Feelings, *Moja Means One, Swahili Counting Book,* Dial Press, 1971. In this book the reader is given an introduction to counting from one to ten in Swahili. The illustrations are exceptional. Both of these books will help to dispel any stereotypes children have about the fearsomeness of Africa and African people. Young children.

Shirley Graham, *Julius Nyerere: Teacher of Africa,* Julian Messner, 1975. An outstanding biography, written for junior high age and up, that not only shares the story of one of Africa's greatest leaders, but also provides a wealth of information on basic African history and value systems. Older children.

Eloise Greenfield, illustrated by George Ford, *Darlene,* Metheun, 1980. A disabled girl enters into the fun while on a visit to her aunt and uncle.

Eloise Greenfield, *First Pink Light,* Thomas Y. Crowell, 1976. Greenfield and illustrator Barnett team up to present a warm, enjoyable story of a small boy's desire to stay up until his daddy gets home. The reader can't help but be drawn into the love in the family. The "family" includes immediate and extended family, because the father has just returned home after spending time with a sick grandmother. The red and gray pencil illustrations add to a feeling of belonging and simple joy. Young children.

Eloise Greenfield, illustrated by Carole Byard, *Grandma's Joy,* Putman, 1980. When Rhondy's Grandmama is forced to move because she can no longer pay the rent, Rhondy assures her all will be well because she still has her "joy" — Rhondy. Warm, loving illustrations. Grades 2–4.

Eloise Greenfield, *Honey, I Love and Other Love Poems,* Thomas Y. Crowell, 1978. Beautiful illustrations, filled with sensitivity and pride, set off this collection. The poems cover a range of experiences, people, and emotions springing directly from a child's everyday life. Many of the themes would be understandable by preschoolers. Young children.

Eloise Greenfield, *Mary McLeod Bethune,* Thomas Y. Crowell, 1977. The black-and-white illustrations in this book exude dignity and are so fitting in a story about Mary McLeod Bethune. The author tells of this courageous woman's fight for her people with simple eloquence. Middle grades.

Eloise Greenfield, *Paul Robeson,* Thomas Y. Crowell, 1975. This biography of Robeson is "must" reading. It tells simply of his many and varied accomplishments as well as his political activism, and what he had to endure because of it. Robeson is definitely an important hero for children to become acquainted with at an early age. Middle grades.

Eloise Greenfield and Lessie Jones Little, with materials by Patti Ridley Jones, illustrated by Jerry Pinkney, plus family photographs, *Childtimes: A Three Generation Memoir,* Crowell, 1979. Eloise Greenfield, her mother, and her grandmother demonstrate the continuity of the African-American family through the experiences of three strong, loving, and talented women. Grades 5 and up.

Eloise Greenfield and Alesia Revis, *Alesia,* Philomel Books (Putnam), 1981. This is one of the few books with a positive message about a person of color who is disabled. Alesia is Black and she tells her story beautifully, without self-pity and with a great deal of honesty and vitality. Grades 5 and up.

Dianne Homan, illustrated by Mary Heine, *In Christina's Toolbox,* Lollipop Power (P.O. Box 1171, Chapel Hill, NC 27514), 1981. This book is an excellent introduction to tools, how they are used and how to care for them. The last illustration shows Christina putting her toolbox next to her mother's. Preschool–grade 3.

Margo Humphrey, *The River That Gave Gifts,* Children's Book Press, 1978. In this Afro-American story, four children in an African village make special gifts for an elder who is going blind. Beautiful colors. Preschool–grade 3.

Selected by Hattie Jones, *The Trees Stand Shining,* Pied Piper Books, 1971. A fine collection of Native American poetry for children. The selections are good for reading aloud. Beautiful watercolor illustrations. Young children.

June Jordan, *Fannie Lou Hamer,* Thomas Y. Crowell, 1975. Beautifully sensitive illustrations mark this biography, written in an exceptionally powerful style. The story is a strong statement about racism and the effects of racism. It chronicles the efforts of one woman. It also conveys hope because of her strength and the positive effect of what happens when people band together to fight in a community-building way. Middle grades.

Peggy Kahn, illustrated by Enola Johnson, *The Handy Girls Can Fix It,* Random House, 1984. An enjoyable tale showing the flexibility of sex roles. Four girls set up a fix-it shop, the envy of two little boys. Reverse role models show that girls can also be looked up to and admired for their skills. Preschool–grade 2.

Athena V. Lord, *Spirit to Ride the Whirlwind,* Macmillan, 1981. Set in the spring of 1836, this is the story of Binnie Howe, a 12-year-old girl who goes to work in the new textile mill in Lowell, Mass. When wages are cut, Binnie has to make some agonizing decisions about forming a union and striking. Grades 7–up.

Cruz Martel, *Yagua Days,* Dial Press, 1976. Martel's story is about a Puerto Rican boy living in the U.S. who goes to visit his parents' home town in Puerto Rico. Besides a simple description of "yagua days," the book includes some good stereotype countering in terms of physical appearance. The illustrations convey excitement and strength. Young children.

Sharon Bell Mathis, illustrated by Leo and Diane Dillon, *The Hundred Penny Box,* Viking, 1975. Mike's great Aunt Dew is 100 years old and he cares about her very much. Intermediate level.

Inez Maury, illustrated by Lady McGrady, *My Mother the Mail Carrier/Mi Mamá la Cartera,* Feminist Press, 1976. This bilingual story of the relationship between a 5-year old and her single mother is also an anti-sexist story. The mother and child truly rejoice in each other.

Patrica McKissack, *Martin Luther King, Jr.: A Man to Remember,* Children's Press, 1984. This biography of Dr.

King presents him as very human, while facing the issue of racism. Grades 6 and up.

Milton Meltzer, illustrated by Catherine Noren and Morrie Camhi, *The Hispanic Americans,* T. Y. Crowell, 1982. A very readable account of the life of Puerto Ricans, Mexicans, and Cubans in the United States. Grades 7 and up.

Betty Miles, *Around and Around Love,* Knopf, 1975. This wonderful book, with beautiful black-and-white photos, shows love as valid in all ways between all kinds of people. Good multicultural mix in the photos. Preschool–grade 3.

Miska Miles, illustrated by Peter Parnall, *Annie and the Old One,* Little Brown, 1971. Through her grandmother, a respected Navajo elder, Annie learns a valuable lesson about growth and change and death. Grades 2–4.

Simon J. Ortiz, *The People Shall Continue,* Children's Book Press, 1977. Strikingly bold and colorful illustrations and a rhythmic text make this a good book to read to children. It contains lots of information which can be presented to young children little by little. Ortiz presents somewhat of a panorama of Native American history. Usage of the term "the People" indicates pride and identity. The creation stories are also very useful with young children. Middle grades.

Letty Cottin Pogrebin, ed., *Stories for Free Children,* Mc-Graw, 1982. A collection of nonsexist, multicultural stories based on the *Ms.* magazine feature of the same name. All ages.

Beatrice Siegal, *Alicia Alonso: The Story of a Ballerina,* Frederick Warne, 1979. The biography of the famous Cuban ballerina gives the reader glimpses of Cuban history as well as a personal story of struggle against sexism, the physical disability of blindness, and the hardship of learning to survive in a new culture. Grades 8–12.

Norma Simon, illustrated by Dora Leder, *Why Am I Different?* Albert Whitman and Co., 1976. Differences in physical make-up, personality, and culture are presented to give children an understanding of others. Ages 4–8.

Elberta H. Stone, illustrated by Margery W. Brown, *I'm Glad I'm Me,* G. P. Putnam's Sons, 1971. A young Black child goes through all kinds of things "he'd like to be" (tree, bird, cloud, etc.) and ends by saying "I'm glad I'm me." Charcoal illustrations, rich in detail, add a sense of dignity to the story.

Mildred D. Taylor, *Song of the Trees,* Dial Publishing Company, 1975. This story of a Black family during the 1930s gives penetrating insights into the effects of discrimination and racism on real people. Much food for thought and discussion with children in this novel. Middle grades.

Joyce Carol Thomas, *Black Child,* Zamani Productions, 1981. The poetry in this book revolves around the themes of pride in African Heritage, self-pride, family-love. The illustrations by Tom Feelings, as always, are exquisite. Grades 4 and up.

Marlo Thomas, *Free to Be, You and Me,* McGraw Hill, 1974. This compilation of stories, poetry and songs, dialogues, essays, is a delightful way to introduce the more serious realities of how sexism limits the development of young men and young women. It is especially valuable for young children, but will be enjoyed by all ages.

Yoshiko Uchida, *A Jar of Dreams,* Atheneum, 1981. This is a story of an eleven-year-old Japanese-American girl living in California during the Depression. The book counters stereotypes about Japanese-Americans and promotes a sense of positive self-concept. Grades 5–9.

Vera B. Williams, *Something Special for Me,* Greenwillow, 1983. Portrays a close extended family whose small savings in a jar will provide a birthday present for the little girl. The author attempts to make the reader sensitive to the struggles and decisions inherent in being poor, while not romanticizing poverty. Preschool–grade 3.

Lawrence Yep, *Child of the Owl,* Harper and Row, 1977. This is a beautifully sensitive story of a Chinese-American girl, Casey, who begins to mature as she grows in her understanding of Chinatown and what it means to be Chinese. Grades 6–8.

Lawrence Yep, *Dragonwings,* Harper and Row, 1975. Through the story of Moon Shadow and his relation with his father, this book gives an in-depth look at the rich traditions of the Chinese community in a hostile world. Grades 6–9.

Claudia Zaslavsky, illustrated by Jerry Pinkney, *Count on Your Fingers African Style,* Thomas Y. Crowell, 1980. Through a simple text and engaging illustrations, this book teaches numbers and counting and gives the reader a glimpse of several different African peoples. Preschool–grade 2.

Media

Free to Be You and Me by Marlo Thomas, record.

Teen/Adult Video Resources

For Canadians, an excellent source of a wide variety of audio-visual resources for teens is *Creative Resources.* This is a 24-page resource guide addressing ten key teen issues, from school, careers, and work to media, communication, self-esteem, and chemical abuse. It is produced by Youth Corps, an outstanding Christian youth program in Ontario that provides workshops, retreats, service projects, and other services. Contact Dwyer Sullivan at Youth Corps, 80 Sackville St., Toronto, Ontario M5A 3E5, Canada; tel.: 416-863-6702.

Perhaps the most helpful resources to counteract the manipulative impact of "glamorous" videos, toys, and ads are other videos. The following films/videos are some of the most helpful:

Amazing Grace and Chuck. 1987. The story of Chuck, a 12-year-old who gives up baseball as a protest against nuclear weapons. His lonely act of courage eventually touches others, including pro basketball star Amazing Grace. Although a highly unlikely story, it moves youth and adults to see the power of courageous witness and the difference each person can make.

Karate Kid II. Presents an image of "enemy love," as the karate instructor overcomes the hostility of a life-long "enemy." An excellent counterpoint to the notion that only violence is effective in dealing with conflict.

The Mission. A 1986 Academy Award winner. A moving portrayal of what it means to "accompany the poor," of resistance to injustice, and of the choice between non-violence and violence in such resistance.

Platoon. Another 1986 Academy Award winner graphically and realistically shows the impact of war on soldiers and civilians alike. A powerful account of the Vietnam War.

Roses in December. This story of Jean Donovan, one of the four U.S. women martyrs in El Salvador, is but one of many films and documentaries available from peace and justice media centers like Maryknoll Films (Maryknoll, NY 10545).

Silkwood; Gandhi; Norma Rae; Marie. Four of the best depictions of people who took courageous stands for justice and who can inspire our youths. Many video rental outlets have them all.

CHAPTER 14

Two Non-U.S. Experiences

Christian Family Peace Weekends

A Christian community in Ontario, Canada, known as the "Sharon Core Team," has been conducting what they call "Christian Family Peace Weekends" for years. Two members of this team, Dwyer and Sheila Sullivan, are the Ontario coordinators for the Parenting for Peace and Justice Network. With several other members of their team, they have developed an elaborate explanation of their program and process.

It is excerpted here in some detail because it may be helpful to other program planners. While their program is more elaborate in its organizational structure than most other PPJ-related programs and involves many more people in the planning than most PPJ teams are able to attract, its core components should be considered as part of any PPJ-related program.

Components

1. HOSPITALITY

See p. 19 above for an extensive description of their welcoming activities.

2. GUEST SPEAKER

The core team selects the weekend theme. The guest speaker chooses the mode of presentation. The presentation is followed by a few moments of silent reflection, dialogue with the speaker, and then dialogue in numbered groups, outside wherever possible.

3. WORKSHOP SESSIONS

There are fewer workshop sessions than in the other models described in this guidebook, so there is more time available for other (more intergenerational) components. But these weekends do incorporate a variety of workshop options to give participants an opportunity to meet their individual needs.

Each workshop is an open intergenerational activity, although at that time, activities are planned for 0- to 4-year olds, 5- to 8-year olds, and 9- to 12-year olds. Some workshops are more suitable for teens and adults, but, with parental permission, the children may participate. Children have a habit of cutting through the barriers and going for the core! These workshops are held mainly outdoors.

The workshop can consist of, for example, a presentation and a dialogue, a slide show and a question-and-answer period, a written exercise on inner self, community building through games, or video presentations. Each facilitator has the option to choose his or her own method of presentation. The agenda contact person makes sure that whatever format is followed, the right atmosphere and the proper tools are available (for example, paper, pencils, video, mike, extra cords).

Through the guest speakers and workshop facilitators, the participants have become aware of the world beyond self, family, community. Many become aware of lay ministries beyond their present environment. Young people have participated in programs in the Dominican Republic and Haiti. Many have become involved in inner-city programs, prison visitation, the peace movement (for example, a weekly vigil at a factory that builds component parts for nuclear warheads, Parenting for Peace and Justice, Pax Christi, protest through music).

Others work with unwed mothers, single parents, abused children, alcoholics, bereavement groups, youth groups, the disabled, and the elderly. The awareness alone is a stretching, growing experience. For some, it becomes their profession.

4. CREATIVITY, SPORTS

After the workshops on Saturday afternoon, we have a number of intergenerational activities. Creativity is stressed; we often make a banner based on the theme. Swimming and after-dinner baseball are always appreciated. Somehow, the baseball score always comes out 42 to 42!

5. DANCE

Our dance is under the stars or in the barn. It is a mixing and meshing of workers and participants, solo dancing and group dancing, the wheelchair person with the able-bodied, the very young with the very old — a real celebration!

6. CANDLELIGHT

This ceremony is a time for the glorious recognition that we are one with the universe. Around 10:15 p.m., we gather on the side of a hill. At the top of the hill is a bonfire. Through the words and music, we recognize our uniqueness, our oneness with Christ, with God. As each candle is lit from the "Christ-candle," we become the stars on earth. We link arms in unity after a short dialogue in small groups. The group then moves toward the campfire to join in singing and laughter.

7. WORSHIP

Our worship is an experience of great creativity, as we use, for example, drama, pantomime, music, creative expressions with thank-you's for gifts received. It is also a time for appreciating racial harmony. The 5- to 8-year-olds greet the worshippers in many languages, including sign language. They challenge the group to repeat the theme in international sign language. As an added bonus, many of the worship leaders have been missionaries or are visitors from other countries.

Most importantly, as many participants as possible are incorporated into the worship in leadership roles, especially women and youth. Inclusive language is stressed. The worship should represent the culmination of the sense of joy felt throughout the weekend.

"MC" Responsibilities

You are in charge of the weekend agenda:

- to begin each session *on time* — gather people at specified locations.
- to introduce sessions, people, and activities.
- to be available to answer questions.
- to know who are the speakers, workshop facilitators, resource people, and members of each committee in charge during the weekend.

Sample Schedule

1. FRIDAY EVENING

7:00: ARRIVAL, REGISTRATION, SET-UP TENTS

8:00: HOT DOG SUPPER

9:00: CALL TO THE BARN: MUSIC AND SINGING

MCs: Welcome everyone to Sharon — Announce theme and explain. Make sure everyone has registered. — Call people from different places. — Go through the highlights of the Big Agenda Poster posted in the barn. — Know who the guest speakers are.

10:00: INTRODUCE THE DRAMA

10:30: CLOSE OFF

Give instructions for getting into groups according to group numbers. — Teens stay in the barn. — Tell about break later and bonfire. — Stress bedtime and rising time. — Chapel at 7:45. — Introduce the leader of the morning jogging. — Keep noise down after 11:00.

2. SATURDAY MORNING

7:30: JOGGING

7:45: WORSHIP IN THE CHAPEL

8:00: BREAKFAST

9:00: GATHER IN THE BARN: MUSIC AND SINGING

MCs: Good morning everyone. — Tell on who made noise last night. — Run down morning agenda briefly.

10:30: DIALOGUE

MCs: Ask for two minutes after speaker is finished. — No one leaves the barn, please! — Facilitate question period for 15 minutes. Don't let the same person ask questions all the time.

10:45: BREAK INTO SMALL GROUPS

MCs: Ask the group leaders to come forward and get their numbers. — People follow them outside in front of the barn.

11:30: BREAK FROM SMALL GROUPS

12:00: LUNCH

3. SATURDAY AFTERNOON

1:00: BARN: MUSIC

MCs: Announce creativity and carnival after the workshop. — Ask person in charge of creativity to introduce what they will do. — Get volunteers for ring masters. — Ask for workshop facilitators to come forward, get their workshop posters, and introduce themselves and their workshop. — Break into workshop groups.

3:00: CREATIVITY AND PREPARATION
       FOR CARNIVAL

MCs: Call for those who wish to participate in Sunday Liturgy and meet with the Liturgy Committee. — Call representatives from Music, Teens, and Kids Committees. Encourage people to join in the creativity, young and adults alike.

4:30: CARNIVAL

5:30: ADULT SWIM TIME

4. SATURDAY EVENING

6:00: SUPPER

7:00: BASEBALL

Core Team Reflection (1/2 hour) during the baseball game.

8:00: GATHER IN THE BARN: SING-ALONG.

Presentations by kids or teams arranged beforehand.

MCs: Make necessary announcements (lost and found, etc.). — Run through the evening agenda, candlelight person may wish to speak. — Ask people to go outside the barn for the dance.

8:30: DANCE

10:00: BREAK

10:15: CANDLELIGHT CEREMONY

10:45: HOT CHOCOLATE AND COOKIES, BONFIRE

11:00: LIGHTS OUT

All quiet in tent and cottage areas.

5. SUNDAY

7:30: JOGGING

8:00: BREAKFAST

9:00: GATHER IN BARN: MUSIC AND SINGING

Practice songs for worship.

MCs: Good morning everyone. — Give morning run down. — Ask Kids Committee to take kids away. Ask adults to stay. — Member of Agenda Committee gives a brief history of Sharon and a pep talk asking volunteers to join us next year. — Invite everyone to our All Day in September and our Advent Day in December. — Member of the Liturgy Committee introduces the Liturgy Workshop and describes the creative things done during previous weekend liturgies. — People go outside and join their original group for the Liturgy Workshop. — Remind group leaders to get copies of liturgy readings and pencils for their members as they step out. — Agenda Co-ordinator distributes sheets for those interested in joining the Sharon Core.

9:30: SMALL GROUPS FOR LITURGY WORKSHOP

10:45: BREAK FOR WORSHIP

11:00: WORSHIP

A member of the Liturgy Committee welcomes all and reads an introduction of the Liturgy.

12:00: LUNCH

1:30: PACK AND CLEAN

3:00: DEPARTURE

Committees and Team Responsibilities

Food Committee (10-12 members): One-two meetings required...One person in-charge per week...Plan menu...Order food...Obtain extra people to help serve and prepare...Buy cleaning materials and first aid supplies...Prepare and serve meals...Clean up kitchens.

Teen Committee (6-8 members): Four-five meetings required...One person in charge per weekend ...Arrange reflection on talks...Help prepare scripture reading on Sunday...Outreach...Plan activities for kids (0–12) and teens (13–up) to help integrate them into the weekend...Help out on other committees when free.

Children Committee (17-20 members): Five-six meetings required...One person in charge per weekend for each age group (0–4, 5–8, and 9–12)...Prepare programs for these three age groups ...Know where the children are...Babysitting...Supervise their swim time and assist lifeguards...Coordinate to help parents have free time for workshops, discussions, etc.

E.E.C. — Engineering Environmental Control (6–10 members): One-two meetings required...One person in charge per weekend...Look after garbage...Set up tents, water jugs, bonfire, tractor and Mass benches...Set up for arrival and organize arrival and departure...Set up for Mass...Cook for barbecue and light fires...Johns...Parking...Supervise, maintain, and run swimming pool...Organize set up/clean up details before and after weekend.

Music Committee (8–10 members): Eight-ten meetings required...One person in charge of music and one person in charge of equipment per weekend ...Pick songs for the weekend according to theme. Prepare song books for weekends...Arrange lots of practice to allow new people to learn songs and work together...Tapes for background/wake up music and Saturday night dance. Dance tapes... Prepare music for Mass and Bonfire...Set up, maintain, and operate sound equipment.

Creativity Committee (5–6 members): One-two meetings required...One person in charge per weekend...Plan for crafts to be done...Arrange and gather up supplies and materials needed...Set up arts and crafts and clean up...Creativity session Saturday afternoon, for example, banner-making, head bands, necklaces.

Registration Committee (6–12 members): One-two meetings at home, one day per week at office until after weekends...Gather registration forms ...Book people into weekend...Book core team on weekend...Assign tents...Assign rooms in cottage to handicapped and ill...Assign helpers for the handicapped...Cancellations...Waiting list... Name tags, pins and marker cards for tags...Group facilitators for discussions...Arrange to have help for registrations on Friday night.

Candlelight Committee (6–8 members): Four-five meetings required...One person in charge per weekend...Prepare candlelight readings...Make music tape for candlelight...Set up and organize supplies (candles) or equipment needed after and gather same as required.

Outreach & Hospitality Committee (6–8 members): Five-six meetings required...One person in charge per weekend...Invite groups and individuals who might benefit from the weekend...Conduct publicity evenings and slide shows to groups and parishes ...Be responsible for them on the weekend (disabled, ethnic)...Greet people on Friday coming in ...Say goodbye Sunday afternoon...Be aware of those not participating and encourage them to join in.

Drama Committee (8–10 members): Eight–ten meetings required...One person in charge per weekend...Prepare drama on the theme...Supply and maintain all materials and props required...Coordinate with Agenda Committee regarding the weekend agenda.

Agenda Committee (8–10 members): Four–five meetings required...One person in charge per weekend...Prepare weekend agenda...Prepare workshops for Saturday...Responsible for the Saturday morning speaker, MCs, and facilitators for workshops for the weekend...Follow-up resource people by writing letters of thanks and arrange for stipends if necessary.

Liturgical Committee (4–5 members): Three-four meetings required...One person in charge per weekend...Arrange for priest on the weekend (well in advance)...Arrange for stipends if needed...Reflect on Mass readings and come-up with "images" for weekend liturgy and notify priest (some prefer to do it themselves)...Meet with representatives from Teen, Children, and Music Committees on Saturday to plan for Sunday Mass...Arrange for readers, gift-bearers, and ministers of communion...Prepare altar supplies and priest's vestments if required.

Special Needs Committee (6–8 members): Three–four meetings required...One person in charge per weekend...Provide assistance and take care of participants who are handicapped or with disabilities...Be responsible for them during the weekend...Provide awareness, training, and outreach for volunteers who are qualified or who are willing to learn how to properly take care of people with special needs.

You are invited to attend

A CHRISTIAN FAMILY PEACE WEEKEND

At Regina Mundi Farm — Sharon, Ontario
Approximately 45 Miles North of Toronto

FOUR FUN-FILLED WEEKENDS THIS SUMMER

June 26th to 28th   *July 10th to 12th*
July 17th to 19th   *July 24th to 26th*

AT UNBELIEVABLY LOW COSTS PER WEEKEND

- *$30 for individuals, $20 for students*
- *$70 per family with less than 5 children*
- *$75 per family with more than 5 children*

HIGHLIGHTS

- *People, Love, Joy, Peace*
- *Drama, Music, Laughter*
- *Talks, Workshops, Group Sharing*
- *Swimming, Jogging, Nature Walks*
- *Co-Op Games, Ball Games, Exercises*
- *Carnival, Barn Dance, Creativity*
- *Candlelight, Bonfire, Hot Chocolate*
- *Barbecued Hot-Dogs, Hamburgers, Cheese*
- *Outdoor Buffet, Coffee, Tea, Cookies*
- *Birds, Sunshine, Blue Sky, Fresh Air*
- *Tents, Trailers, Cottages*
- *Peace Bridge, Singing Brook, Willow Tree*
- *Chapel, Mass, Creative Liturgy*

CALL US TODAY! *Or better still, complete the enclosed Application Form and mail to us with your payment. Registration will be accepted on a FIRST-COME, FIRST-SERVED BASIS!*

COME, DARE TO DREAM...

at the Christian Family Peace Weekends at Sharon.

A Friendly Invitation

The Sharon Core Group invites you to come and be a part of the Christian Family Peace Weekends at Regina Mundi Farm this summer, in Sharon, Ontario.

We welcome individuals, families, single parent families, young and old, teens and children, nuns and priests, those with special needs, or anybody who wishes to experience a fun-filled weekend centered in Jesus and the Christian Family.

Our Theme This Year is—
COME, DARE TO DREAM...

We challenge you to join us in dreaming our vision as a community of Love, Forgiveness and Justice . . . and we WELCOME YOU to be a part of this vision.

The goals of the weekend are threefold:

- To strengthen both family life and the Christian community.

- To pray and celebrate together in an atmosphere of love, peace and friendship.

- To provide an opportunity for dreaming, creating and building together.

Schedules & Fees

Each weekend starts at about 7 p.m. on Friday, and ends at about 3 p.m. on Sunday. The dates for the weekends this year are:

* June 26 to 28	* July 10 to 12
* July 17 to 19	* July 24 to 26

Registration will be accepted on a FIRST-COME, FIRST-SERVED BASIS, with a limit of 230 people for each weekend. Please pass the word on to all other persons who may want to come for the first time.

The prices for the entire weekend are:

- $30 for individuals, $20 for students

- $70 per family with less than 5 children

- $75 per family with more than 5 children

Enclose your payment in the attached application form. Note that 25% of your payment is non-refundable after May 15, 1987.

We are aware that the above categories and fees may not cover everyone's situation and financial capabilities, accordingly, those who are able to pay more are cordially invited to make a contribution. This' will allow those with financial restraints an opportunity to also attend a weekend.

All meals are provided, and non-alcoholic beverages are served at certain times during the weekend. In-between meal snacks are your responsibility.

Tents

We are really short of good tents. We encourage you to bring your own tent if at all possible. Available tents will be assigned on a first-come, first-served basis. Anyone with a good tent (we have enough with rips, holes and tears, ourselves) and who would be willing to donate it to us, please contact Joe van Pinxteren at 284-4213.

Dare Others to Come

We encourage you to reach out not only to your friends and family but also to others beyond your family who might really appreciate the Christian Family Peace Weekends.

These might include those who are physically or mentally handicapped, others who are poor or who have been wounded in some way and are in need of the experience and a sense of community support. Please dare others to come!

If you have any questions or concerns about anything at all, please do not hesitate to call the Youth Corps office at 863-6702 or Marg Martin at 884-0287 or Pat Fannon-Lally at 466-2569.

Family Camping:
The Extended or Church Family,
by Lola and Ian Mavor

Camping has sometimes been regarded as mainly for children and teenagers, but participation in Family Camping can help break that image. We have shared in the leadership of many Family Camps over the years and have been impressed by the growth, learning, and enrichment that can take place through them.

Our approach has been to take seriously the rich images that are part of the word "family" and to make that a focus of the program. This usually means taking steps to develop a sense of being a family group and to nurture the intergenerational potential that is available. While each camp would be planned to meet the particular situation of the group involved, there are some patterns that provide a starting point from which to adapt to fit in with what is wanted.

Most Family Camps are planned by parishes or congregations in the hope that they can develop their sense of being a community of people across the age range. This tends to be implied by the use of such terms as "the church family." If the camp is developed by running separate programs for different age groups, much of the potential of the camp experience is lost. In contrast, our approach is to encourage a balance of together times and of special-interest times to give everyone a sense of participation.

We also recognize that when adults learn with children there is often a greater freedom to experiment with creative teaching methods that might feel awkward to adults when they are just with their peers. This could include the use of simple and spontaneous activities, such as showing pictures, telling stories, singing action songs, participating in

Mrs. Lola Mavor serves as a Consultant in Adult and Family Ministries for the Queensland Synod of the Uniting Church in Australia and is also the Regional Associate for Effectiveness Training programs. She has developed a range of programs in relation to marriage and family life and is concerned with issues related to the role of women in church and society.

Rev. Dr. Ian Mavor is Master of King's College at the University of Queensland and also serves as Dean of the Brisbane College of Theology. He completed his doctoral studies at Teachers College, Columbia University, and Union Theological Seminary in New York.

simple dramas or simulations, making posters or banners, creating forms of artwork, and using homemade puppets.

A "FAMILY" MODEL FOR CAMPING

A Family Camp provides an opportunity for affirming the family groupings that are present as well as enriching people's ideas about what constitutes a "family." One pattern that we have used on many occasions and which has always proved valuable was the creation of "extended families" within the total camp population. This pattern would be established early in the camp and used for a range of activities. At the same time, care is taken to avoid any rigidity in the use of the extended families and at meal times everyone sits where they please. This allows for other patterns of friendship to be strengthened in the course of the camp.

If a camp runs from Friday evening until Sunday afternoon, the first time of being together as a total group could be used to establish the family groupings and to gain a sense of being a community. This could be helped by "ice breakers" such as singing, milling, greeting as many people as possible, and organized fun.

FORMING EXTENDED FAMILIES

The "extended families" can be based on the nuclear families that are part of the camp and then augmented by adding others to them. Start by identifying the groupings in which at least one parent and one child, up to about 16 years of age, are present. This allows for both one- and two-parent families to serve as the nucleus of an extended family and to provide the family name. Often these groups can be identified before the camp on the basis of enrollments.

The intention is to form families of eight to twelve members and, at times, it may be necessary to link together pairs of nuclear families, to form a "Smith-Jones" family or a "Robinson-O'Reilly" family to which others can be added as follows.

Some signs are displayed for the roles played by members of an extended family, such as "nephew," "niece," "aunt," "uncle," "grandfather," "grandmother," "mother-in-law" or "father-in-law." The remainder of the camp participants are asked to decide which of these roles they wish to adopt in the extended families. They then write their names on slips of paper which they fold and place near one of the signs.

Next, a member of each nuclear family is asked to select slips of paper from the various roles until all are distributed. Some supervision may be helpful here to ensure a reasonably even spread, but, as in real life, there is no single combination for an extended family and some variations in size are appropriate. This can also allow for later arrivals to be fitted into a family group during the camp.

Once the extended families are formed it is important to provide time for them to develop a sense of belonging to one another. They could be asked to take time to find out more about one another, to develop a family motto, to create a poster that acknowledges each one of them as part of the family and to create a simple ritual that affirms their oneness as a family. The mottoes and posters could then be presented to the camp as a whole, to reaffirm the sense of being a total community.

ALTERNATE PROCESS

In some situations where the balance of numbers seemed to create problems for this system, we have used an alternate approach. This allows for the creation of families without any group serving as the nucleus. While this can be done quite simply, it tends to lack the bonus of affirming normal family groupings that are present.

For this process a more random allocation takes place and the result is perhaps more like a small tribe than a family. All present are arranged in a long line from the tallest to the shortest, after which they count off to create the number of groups required. Thus, if there are fifty participants and each group is to have ten members, they are counted into fives. They are then asked to group together by the numbers allocated. Unless the total group is too small, this method tends to create "families" that contain both male and female members and a range of ages.

Once again it is important to spend time in developing the sense of being a group. In this case that could include the selection of a shared name and the adoption of the particular roles that might be found in an extended family.

PROGRAM PATTERNS

The processes described here can be adapted to a range of formats, but have usually been applied to a weekend camp situation.

Friday Night: While each camp has to be planned individually, most commence after the evening meal Friday night, with the starting time depending on the distance to be travelled. The focus of that evening would be on becoming a community and forming families, with scope also for devotional activities as part of that process. This could run from 7:30 to 9:00 p.m. or 8:00 to 9:30 p.m. and be followed by refreshments. Some groups then have further activities for those who want to stay up later, thus reducing noise levels in the sleeping areas.

Once the families are established, we explain their purpose and our hopes for their contribution to the weekend. We also ask each family to arrange an activity for a social night on Saturday and to plan a segment for the family worship on Sunday morning.

Saturday Morning: On Saturday morning we usually have two study times, each of some 75 minutes and with an emphasis on participatory methods of learning. Our preference is to have everyone above about 8 years of age involved in the first study time, but to arrange alternative activities for children below high school age during the second study.

Saturday Afternoon: Saturday afternoon provides an opportunity for recreational activities such as swimming, walking, and volleyball. These need not involve the family groupings beyond asking them to check that everyone has some plan and that no one is left out. Some further encouragement might also be given to ensure that the families are planning their contributions for the evening program and the Sunday worship.

Saturday Evening: The leadership for Saturday evening can often be provided by the older teenagers who are present, as long as they are given due warning of what is expected. If there is a youth fellowship for this age group, that request can be passed to them as part of the planning of the camp. Again, the evening can be split into two parts by a refreshment break about the time that the younger campers are put to bed. While the first part of the program would seek to involve everyone, the latter part could provide options from which they can choose.

Sunday Morning: We have always tried to have

a eucharistic celebration; our preferred time is before breakfast on Sunday. Unless there is a problem with the weather, we usually hold this out of doors, sitting on rugs or on the grass. In this we try to express the imagery of Jesus feeding the crowds, which particularly in John's Gospel is given sacramental significance.

By asking everyone to sit in their family groups we affirm the sense of belonging somewhere while being part of the whole. We also try to ensure that children are more than spectators at an adult event. For our tradition, within the Uniting Church in Australia, it is permissible for all ages to share in the communion and this fits in well with the rationale of the camp.

Another important element in the Sunday morning program is a time of family worship. We have found that when the family groups are encouraged to contribute, and are provided with a block of time for planning and rehearsal, they make a lively contribution to the worship. In turn, they are enriched by their participation. Presentations have often included singing, mime, dance, role plays, the use of posters and banners, and the dramatic reading of Bible passages.

One pattern is to ask that every group have something planned by Sunday breakfast for reporting to the worship leader. This allows time to deal with any overlaps and also for the suggestions to be organized into a coherent order of service. In this, our preference is to leave the families free to choose what they want to do rather than planning the order and allocating tasks. After breakfast there can be a time for final preparations, a refreshment break and then the structured time of worship. With careful coordination, there can still be time for other recreational activities before lunch.

Sunday Afternoon: The final gathering for the close of the camp can be another time of family interaction and parting, so it is important to have this before some start to leave. This is usually early Sunday afternoon. One simple act of affirmation that we have used is to pin a sheet of paper on each person's back and to ask everyone to move around writing affirmative comments on one another's sheets. Another activity involves some ritual enactment to indicate the transition from camp to home and to assist the debriefing of the family structure created for the camp.

In camps with a focus on the place of children in the church we close by enacting several ways of viewing the church. First we ask the adults to form a circle facing inwards, while the children move away, to depict a church with no place for children. We then ask the children to stand around outside the circle as "spectators" of adult activities. Then we place them in the middle of the circle, as sheltered and nurtured but without a real contribution to make. Next the children joined the circle of adults, so that a larger circle is required and all are part of it, even though this might make it less unified. Finally, everyone turns outward and joins hands, depicting a church in which all ages have a place and each supports the other, and where people are orientated outward toward the world. This then provides a physical awareness as a basis for a form of commissioning to send people on their way.

STUDY ACTIVITIES

Many options are available for intergenerational learning, including the following:

Family Circles: Provide each person with a sheet on which are drawn a series of circles and ask them to write the name of one of their family members in each circle. Then ask them to write:

- something you appreciate about that member;
- something you really enjoy doing with him or her and the last time you did it together;
- some areas where you would like to improve your relationship with that person.

Families and God: Work through the following tasks:

Individually:
- List five things you look for in a family.
- List five things a family might expect of its members.
- Read Ephesians 3:14–21.
- What meanings does it have for you to think of God as a parent?

In discussion groups of five:
- What "parent" qualities would you like to add to the ways most people think of God?

- What qualities of life might be linked to "the nature of God" (Eph. 3:19).

- How might these qualities be expressed in a family? in the church?

  In pairs:

- What difference would it make if your life was filled with "the nature of God"?

- What can be done to improve the life of your family?

- What difference would it make if members of your family took faith in God seriously?

Our Church: Write five ideas on each of the following topics, then find out what someone else has written and share your thoughts. Next, work in small groups to prepare petitions addressed to an appropriate council of the local church urging some specific action that you would be willing to support.

- Five things I like about our church.

- Five things I'd like to see improved.

- Five things I could do to make it better.

Shalom Box

The *shalom* box can be a helpful reminder of the various ways we experience *shalom* and are building *shalom* in our homes, neighborhoods, and world. The box can also remind us to pray for *shalom*. Thus, the *shalom* box should be placed in a prominent place, perhaps on the dinner table.

While *shalom* boxes can come in many shapes and sizes, a shoe box is a good size. Decorate the outside of the box with pictures that symbolize specific ways you have experienced *shalom*.

These might include pictures or photos of family, close friends, special places, people who inspire you to work for *shalom,* an individual or family "partner" in another country, or prisoner with whom you correspond. Symbols might include peace and justice buttons you have worn or the logos of groups you support.

Place items in the box that are signs of hope for you that God is building *shalom.* These could include flags from Canada, the United States, the Soviet Union, or a peace crane (see Worksheet 15). Also appropriate are special "love tokens" or gifts from family members or friends, mementos from a special vacation or other occasion, letters from peace and justice or hunger groups or others asking for help.

Build the *shalom* box gradually, involving as many members of the household as possible in its creation and updating. Rotate items and pictures, if necessary, once the box is full, so that it maintains some freshness and does not become taken for granted. Refer to it during mealtime prayer. Write out action decisions made during and after the PPJ program and place them on or in the box as a reminder to implement those decisions.

Gifts of Shalom

God's Gifts of Shalom to Our Family

Identify with words or pictures specific instances when you have experienced God's gift of shalom as a family — however you define "family" for yourself.

Our Gift of Shalom to Others

Identify with words or pictures specific ways your family has been an agent of God's shalom to others, whether in your immediate family, your community, or the global family.

A Reflection on Shalom

The central vision of world history in the Bible is that all of creation is one, every creature in community with every other, living in harmony and security toward the joy and well-being of every other creature....

That persistent vision of joy, well-being, harmony, and prosperity is not captured in any single word or idea in the Bible, and a cluster of words is required to express its many dimensions and subtle nuances:

- love
- loyalty
- truth
- grace
- salvation
- justice
- blessing
- righteousness

But the term that in recent discussions has been used to summarize that controlling vision is *shalom.*

Both in current discussion and in the Bible itself, it bears tremendous freight — the freight of a dream of God that resists all our tendencies to division, hostility, fear, drivenness, and misery.

Shalom is the substance of the biblical vision of one community embracing all creation.

It refers to all those resources and factors which make communal harmony joyous and effective. Ezekiel in a visionary passage expresses its meaning:

I will make with them a covenant of Shalom and banish wild beasts from the land, so that they may dwell securely in the wilderness and sleep in the woods.

And I will make them and the places round about my hill a blessing; and I will send down the showers in their season; they shall be showers of blessing.

And the trees of the field shall yield their fruit, and the earth shall yield its increase, and they shall be secure in their land.... They shall no more be a prey to the nations, nor shall the beasts of the land devour them; they shall dwell securely, and none shall make them afraid.

And I will provide for them plantations of Shalom. (Ezekiel 34:25–29a)

The origin and the destiny of God's people is to be on the road of *shalom,* which is to live out of joyous memories and toward greater anticipations.

[From Walter Brueggemann, *Living Toward a Vision,* United Church Press, 1976.]

God's Promise of Shalom

Father, may they be one in us,
as you are in me and I am in you,
so that the world may believe
it was you who sent me.
I have given them the glory you gave to me,
that they may be one as we are one.
With me in them and you in me,
may they be so completely one
that the world will realize
that it was you who sent me
and that I have loved them
as much as you loved me.

(John 17:21–23)

But now in Christ Jesus
you who once were far off
have been brought near in the blood of Christ.
For he is our peace,
who has made us both one,
and has broken down the dividing wall of hostility,
by abolishing in his flesh
the law of commandments and ordinances,
that he might create in himself
one new person in place of the two,
so making peace,
and might reconcile us both to God
in one body through the cross,
thereby bringing the hostility to an end.

(Ephesians 2:13–16)

Until the Spirit is poured upon us from on high,
and the wilderness becomes a fruitful field
and the fruitful field is deemed a forest.
Then justice will dwell in the wilderness,
and righteousness abide in the fruitful field.
And the effect of righteousness will be peace,
and the result of righteousness,
quietness and trust for ever.
My people will abide in a peaceful habitation,
in secure dwellings,
and in quiet resting places.

(Isaiah 32:15–20)

God shall judge between the nations,
and shall decide for many peoples;
and they shall beat their swords into plowshares
and their spears into pruning hooks;
nation shall not lift up sword against nation,
neither shall they learn war any more.

(Isaiah 2:4)

For behold, I create new heavens and a new earth;
and the former things shall not be remembered
or come into mind.
But be glad and rejoice for ever
in that which I create....
I will rejoice in Jerusalem,
and be glad in my people;
no more shall be heard in it the sound of weeping
and the cry of distress.
No more shall there be in it
an infant that lives but a few days,
or an old man who does not fill out his days,
for the child shall die a hundred years old,
and the sinner a hundred years old shall be accursed.
They shall build houses and inhabit them;
they shall plant vineyards and eat their fruit.
They shall not build and another inhabit;
they shall not plant and another eat;
for like the days of a tree
shall the days of my people be,
and my chosen shall long enjoy
the work of their hands.
They shall not labor in vain,
or bear children for calamity;
for they shall be the offspring
of the blessed of the Lord,
and their children with them.
Before they call I will answer,
while they are yet speaking I will hear.
The wolf and the lamb shall feed together,
the lion shall eat straw like the ox;
and dust shall be the serpent's food.
They shall not hurt or destroy
in all my holy mountain, says the Lord.

(Isaiah 65:17–25)

Behold, the days are coming, says the Lord,
when the plowman shall overtake the reaper
and the treader of grapes him who sows the seed;
the mountains shall drip sweet wine,
and all the hills shall flow with it.
I will restore the fortunes of my people Israel,
and they shall rebuild the ruined cities
and inhabit them;
they shall plant vineyards and drink their wine,
and they shall make gardens and eat their fruit.
I will plant them upon their land,
and they shall never again be plucked up
out of the land which I have given them,
says the Lord your God.

(Amos 9:13–15)

Our Family Names

MEMBERS OF OUR FAMILY   **MY NAME IS SPECIAL BECAUSE:**

_____

_____

_____

_____

_____

_____

_____

A good name is more desirable than great wealth,
the respect of others is better than silver or gold. (Proverbs 22:1)

OUR FAMILY CREST

Family Names

Most people in the European countries had only one name until about nine hundred years ago. As the towns and villages became larger and the population increased, it became difficult to distinguish between persons with the same name, so a second name was added.

Most last names in Europe were chosen from four different sources: a persons' occupation, the area where one lived, one's father's name, or a personal characteristic. For example, the names Smith, Taylor, Cook, and Mason became the last names of persons in those occupations. Names such as Brooks, Hill, Townsend, and Lake were used to denote location. Names ending in *son* or *sen* were derived from the father's first name, such as Jackson, Swensen, or Johnson.

Some people with unusual characteristics might be given a last name such as Short, Stout, Fox, or Longfellow. After a few generations these "sur" names became fixed and have been carried down to the present time.

[From *Home,* sponsored by the Archdiocesan Office of Religious Education, Dubuque, Iowa.]

Parents:

- Share what information you know about your surnames. Perhaps you know whether it has changed through the years. In what country did it originate? Locate that country on a globe or world map.

- Share with your children how you selected their names (for example, the name is that of a special friend or family member, the name has a special meaning).

- Look up the meaning of your family members' first names. Share how you feel about your "discovery."

Peace Pie and Trouble Cake

PEACE PIE RECIPE	TROUBLE CAKE RECIPE
1. _____	1. _____
2. _____	2. _____
3. _____	3. _____
4. _____	4. _____
5. _____	5. _____
6. _____	6. _____
7. _____	7. _____
_____	_____
_____	_____
_____	_____

Construct the recipe for each of the above by choosing from the ingredients below. Write in the necessary ingredients, using each one time only. Then add other ingredients not listed below that you think are also part of the recipes for "peace pie" and "trouble cake."

A. Take time to learn and think about a problem before deciding.

B. Hit someone when you feel bad.

C. Decide rules together.

D. Have a big kid be boss.

E. Decide what to do about a problem before you learn all the facts.

F. Listen to another person.

G. Consider how the other person feels.

H. Yell in a mean way.

I. Talk to someone about how you feel.

J. Take turns telling about a problem.

K. Holler and don't listen to what another person wants to say.

L. Use a kind tone of voice.

M. Have only one person tell about a problem.

N. Insist your ideas or ways are the best.

Case Studies in Creative Conflict Resolution

1. PRESCHOOL

Amy is 4 and Suzy is 3. Amy has been building a tower of Lego blocks. Suzy comes in and for several minutes they work together in the building process. Then Suzy decides to knock down the tower. Amy pushes Suzy down. Suzy hits Amy. Then follows lots of screaming, hitting, and biting. You are the parent who has been working in the other room as this situation has developed. What do you do?

2. ELEMENTARY SCHOOL

About 5:00 on a Tuesday afternoon, 9-year-old Tommy and his friend Sean headed down to the basement to play, with Tommy's 7-year-old brother David close behind, apparently to check on the security of his things. Sure enough, I (the father) heard the rattling of the car hubcap David had found earlier. Loud voices soon joined the rattling, followed shortly by cries. I went downstairs and found Tommy punched and David bitten, both telling me the hubcap was theirs. What would you do?

3. JUNIOR HIGH SCHOOL

The scene is a home in Kansas. Aaron, who is 13, is a passionate football fan. His favorite team is playing in the Superbowl. Joshua, 11, will occasionally watch a game, but football is not one of his prime interests. Fishing is Joshua's passion. It is Superbowl Sunday. The two boys get into a heated argument when Joshua insists he has a right to watch his favorite half-hour sports program (which this Sunday is featuring Kansas bass fishing) even though it conflicts with part of the Superbowl coverage. Joshua refuses to go upstairs to watch the family's 13-inch black-and-white TV, because the program guide says some special underwater footage is "don't miss" viewing for people who love bass fishing. What would you do?

4. PARENT–TEEN

Tom McHugh is 17. On Monday afternoons he and two of his classmates participate in a special service project designed by their school. They work for two hours at a nearby child-care center. Their usual routine is to stop at one boy's home for a sandwich and then go to the center. On this particular Monday, they decided they didn't feel like going to the center. They spent the afternoon eating, watching TV and playing video games. Mary McHugh, Tom's mother, had told Tom she would pick him up at the center at 3:00 that afternoon to take him to track practice at school. From there he was going to get a ride to a nearby McDonalds where he begins work at 5:00. Around 2:30, Tom called his mother to tell her he didn't need the ride to track practice because one of the other boys would drop him off as they left the center. Mary said fine and reminded him that she would pick him up at McDonalds at 8:30. But at 8:30 Tom wasn't there. The manager told her that Tom had called in sick. When she got home and made a few calls, she discovered that he hadn't been at track practice or at the center and was with his friends eating pizza at the home of a girl from their class. At about 10:00 Tom walked into the house with his Mcdonalds uniform on. You are Mary. What would you do.

5. ADULT–ADULT

If you have participants for whom the above case studies would not be helpful and who would prefer discussing adult-adult conflicts, provide this option. After instructing the other groups on how to proceed with their case studies, have each member of this adult-adult group identify in silence a specific conflict situation they are or were recently engaged in that they would like some feedback on from the group. Have each person describe this conflict briefly, without any comments from others. Have the group decide which conflict to discuss first. Give that person a chance to elaborate on the conflict before opening it up to others' questions or suggestions. If time permits, move to a second conflict mentioned and repeat the process.

1. If you were the adult involved, what do you think you should do and why?

2. List some important elements in the creative resolution of this (and other) conflicts.

Conflict Resolution Skills

Directions: *Recall a typical family conflict. On the left below, make a list of the behaviors that tend to make your family disagreements "worse." On the right below, make a list of those behaviors that help get a disagreement settled with the least amount of hurt.*

HURTFUL

e.g., name calling, labeling

_____

_____

_____

_____

_____

HELPFUL

e.g., listening carefully to all sides

_____

_____

_____

_____

_____

If you have time today (or later at home), here are some questions for further thinking:

1. Describe how well your family solves problems together.

2. Think of your behavior that has been hurtful and for which you wish forgiveness. (The family extends forgiveness with a verbal or nonverbal gesture.)

3. Think of one recurring family conflict that you would like to work on in a new way after you go home today.

Family Meetings: A Key to Conflict Resolution

Some Do's

1. Schedule them regularly, so there is some predictability. Otherwise the children will not trust the process.

2. Schedule them at the most convenient time for all members of the family.

3. Make the agenda available to everyone (having a piece of paper posted where everyone can see it to write items on helps considerably; otherwise children forget what they want to discuss).

4. Include agenda items that involve family plans, family fun events, family service opportunities; don't limit the agenda to problems and conflicts only.

5. Combine the family meeting with things that "taste good" (e.g., a special dessert, a family game or fun night, a trip to the ice cream store).

6. Rotate leadership so that children get a chance to develop their leadership skills.

7. Be sure that decisions are clear, tasks are assigned, consequences are identified when necessary, and that a "check-in" time has been identified (i.e., a time to evaluate how well a particular solution is working).

8. Give everyone a chance to speak; help less verbal members of the family get their points across.

9. Whenever possible, consider the children's agenda items early in the meeting, so that they experience the process working for them.

Some Don't's

1. Don't try to cover every item on a large agenda if some family member(s) are having a hard time staying with the process; consider continuing the meeting the next evening.

2. Don't vote on possible solutions; try to come to a consensus. If that isn't possible at the time, carry the item over to the next meeting. Sometimes it works to ask a lone "hold-out" on a decision if they would be willing to go along with what the others propose for a limited amount of time and then evaluate it.

3. Don't always settle on the first solution proposed; brainstorm alternatives before deciding on one.

4. As adults, don't always be the first to speak to an item and don't criticize brainstormed possibilities or the language the children use unless it is hurtful to others; strong feelings need to be expressed.

Family Covenant:
Helps in Making Family Agreements

Step One: Be realistic. Think in terms of what can really happen, knowing what you do about the family members involved. What will we focus on?

Step Two: Spell it out. What is the agreement in specific terms? "Our family will have a family meeting every Friday evening from 5 to 7 p.m. This will include a special meal, an enjoyable family activity, and time for us to discuss openly areas of conflict within our family."

Step Three: What will it look like? If behavior needs changing in your family, how can the change be visibly noticed? Rather than saying, "Marsha will be more helpful around the house," Marsha's behavior is easier to measure if the covenant is worded: "Marsha will make her own bed, hang up her clothes, and keep her room neat."

Step Four: Time limit. What amount of time are we giving our family members to accomplish the agreement. A month? A week?

Step Five: How is it going? A covenant and agreement always need to be nurtured along the way. Every so often gather as a family to check on how well the agreement is going. How often will we check?

Step Six: Covenant Celebration. Agree on something special to do as a family, such as a picnic, a movie, going out for a pizza, if everybody keeps his or her part of the covenant.

[Adapted from "The Family Covenant" in *Try This: Family Adventures Toward Shalom,* Discipleship Resources.]

A Family Reconciliation Service

Children and Parents

- Do I make an effort to see the members of my family as good people? Do I look for that goodness in them when we disagree?

- Am I stingy with my "things," my time, my thoughts and feelings, my attention with my family?

- How much time do I spend with my family? Is it enough to express a sense of commitment to them as a priority in my life?

- Am I open in my communication in the family? Do I speak kindly yet openly about what I think and feel?

- Do I appreciate my family? Do I tell individual family members what I like about them or do I concentrate more often on what I don't like?

- Do I try to resolve conflict or do I rush to judgment? Am I sarcastic with family members? When we argue, do I use things I know about family members to hurt them? Am I careful about the use of other family members' property?

- Do I make unrealistic and perhaps uncharitable demands on the family's finances? Do I give my "fair share" to the family's upkeep (help with projects, pay back loans, make some sacrifices)?

- Am I open to sharing prayer as a family? Do I willingly participate in liturgical observances? Do I risk sharing my doubts where faith is concerned?

- Do I listen to other family members? As a parent, do I operate on the false premise that "children are to be seen and not heard"? Do I seek out my children?

- As a child or adolescent, do I make an effort to talk openly with my parents?

- Do I stay open, as a parent, to my children's questions and doubts? As a child or adolescent, do I respect my parents' experience?

- Am I overly strict and harsh as a parent? Do I discourage my children? Do I play my children off one against another? Do I express genuine concern for my children? As a child or adolescent, do I make an effort to see where my parents are "coming from"?

- Do I compliment my children or am I afraid of "giving them a big head"? Do I see my children through God's loving eyes? As a child or adolescent, do I tell my parents what I like about them?

Family as a Whole

- As a family, have we given into consumerism?

- Do we see ourselves, as a family, needing to take responsibility for our neighborhood?

- Do we foster prejudice or bigotry as a family?

- Are we interested in the welfare of others beyond our own family circle?

- Are we involved in any active way, as a family, in feeding the hungry and clothing the poor?

- Are people able to look at us, as a family, and say "see how they love one another...and others"?

- Do we see a connection between learning to be peace-filled as a family and world peace? Do we understand that peace-filled means more than being conflict-free?

- Do we see ourselves, as a family, as needing to be interested and active in bringing about world peace?

- Do we promote war or peace, stewardship or consumerism, equality or prejudice in the gifts we give and the lifestyle we live as a family?

- Are girls and boys, men and women equally valued in our family?

A Suggestion

Each family member write out a hurt they have been holding on to. Ask those who might like to share (either in the group or with the person involved in the hurt alone) to do so. *Focus on wanting to forgive and be forgiven*, not blaming or justifying. After the sharing or if there is no sharing, use a large ashtray or bowl to burn the papers (as a sign of forgiveness and new beginning.)

[By Michael and Joan Hoxsey; excerpted from their Youngstown Ohio Family Life Department newsletter, *The Family Knight*, March 1987.]

Soviet Faces

*Who has set loose
the thought that we should
oppose each other?*

MATTHEW 5:43–48

You have heard that it was said, You shall love your neighbor and hate your enemy. But I say to you, Love your enemies and pray for those who persecute you, so that you may be sons of your Father who is in heaven; for he makes his sun rise on the evil and on the good, and sends rain on the just and on the unjust. For if you love those who love you, what reward have you? Do not even the tax collectors do the same? And if you salute only your brethren, what more are you doing than others? Do not even the Gentiles do the same? You, therefore, must be perfect, as your heavenly Father is perfect.

[Photos are from the color slide show *Forbidden Faces*, Fellowship of Reconciliation, Box 271, Nyack, NY 10960. Caption quotes are reprinted from *To a Siberian Woodsman*, by Wendell Berry, from his volume *Openings*, © 1968, by permission of Harcourt, Brace, Jovanovich.]

There are very few of us in [North] America who are able to see the faces of Soviet children, of Soviet workers, or old people or students. [Let us] see the faces of one another, especially the faces which are forbidden us, forbidden our eyes and forbidden our hearts.
— Daniel Berrigan

I WANT TO LIVE

I want to live and not to die,
I want to love and not to cry.
I want to feel the summer sun,
I want to sing when life is fun.
I want to fly into the blue,
I want to swim as fishes do.
I want to stretch out a friendly hand to all the
      young throughout the land
I want to fight for what is right
against deceit — against despair —
against hunger everywhere.
I want to live...I want to live!
No atom bomb annihilate my shining world!
I want to love and not to cry...
I want to live and not to die.

[The author of this poem, a young girl, recited it in English and them in Georgian to a group of Americans visiting School 53 in Tbilisi in April 1984.]

*Who has imagined your death negligible to me
now that I have seen these pictures of your face?*

U.S.–U.S.S.R. Reconciliation Possibilities

1. Order a quantity of the F.O.R. U.S.-U.S.S.R. friendship bookmarks. Give them to friends, teachers, students. Ask your public library to offer them to readers as they check out their books.

2. Correspond with a pen-pal in the Soviet Union through Russian Pen-Pals, International Friendship League, 22 Batterymarch St., Boston, MA 02109; tel.: 617-523-4273. Children, ages 7–15 years, who want a Soviet pen-pal should send their letter to Kids Meeting Kids Can Make a Difference, Box 8H, 380 Riverside Dr., New York, NY 10025.

3. Make the peace cranes to send to a child, family, church, or school in the Soviet Union. Arrange this through the Fellowship of Reconciliation or the Peace Crane Project, St. Peter's Church, 619 Lexington Ave., New York, NY 10022.

4. Read about Russian history, culture, people, or a Russian novel and discuss it with family, friends, others. *Fast Train Russia*, by Jay Higginbotham (Dodd, Mead & Co.), is one simple account of a North American's visit to the Soviet Union and his encounters with Russian people. *What About the Russians?*, edited by Dale Brown (The Brethren Press), is a collection of essays by North American Christians wrestling with how they as Christians are called to relate to the people and policies of the Soviet Union.

5. Subscribe to *Soviet Life* (a monthly magazine similar to *Life*). Write the Soviet Embassy, 1706 18th St., N.W., Washington, DC 20009, to subscribe. Or subscribe to the U.S.-U.S.S.R. Bridges for Peace Quarterly Newsletter (Box 283, Norwich, VT 05055), for U.S.-U.S.S.R. exchange possibilities, resources, and organizations to contact.

6. Encourage your school systems to teach Russian history, culture, and language.

7. Arrange for a recent visitor to the Soviet Union to speak to your congregation or community groups.

8. Write letters and petitions to United States, Canadian, and Soviet leaders (address the latter to Soviet Union Embassy, 1706 18th St., N.W., Washington, DC 20009), calling for greater efforts at disarmament negotiations, increased trade, and other exchanges between our countries.

9. Get small flags from these countries to display in your home as a reminder to pray and work for peace. See if your school or church would display these flags as a part of an international understanding program or exhibit. Flags are available wherever UNICEF materials are sold.

10. Pray daily for the people of the Soviet Union and for better understanding between our countries. Use the "The World Peace Prayer" (p. 56) as one possibility.

11. As a further reminder to pray and work for reconciliation and to assist our prayer, place a picture of Russian people in an appropriate place in your home or work place. Encourage others to do the same.

12. Construct a bulletin board display about the Soviet Union and its people for your school or church. Invite others to add to this bulletin board display.

13. Contact Ground Zero (P.O. Box 19049, Portland, OR 97219), about their program of pairing North American cities with similar types of cities in the Soviet Union. Share this information with local civic and church leaders to see if you can get broader support for such a project.

14. Contact F.O.R. or the Institute for Soviet-American Relations (2738 McKinley St., N.W., Washington, DC 20015; tel.: 202-244-4725) about people-to-people exchanges and tour possibilities.

15. Write a letter to the editor of a local paper, calling for both disarmament negotiations and people-to-people effort, mentioning one or more of the reconciliation possibilities described above.

[From *Hope Springs from God;* reprinted with permission of James McGinnis, author, and the United Church Press, publisher.]

Contact the Fellowship of Reconciliation, Box 271, Nyack, NY 10960, for their brochure on all their "U.S.-U.S.S.R. Reconciliation Program" ideas.

Folded Paper Cranes

- Make each crease as exact and as firm as possible.

- Don't give up! It might take more than one try
  to complete a successful crane!

1. *Use a perfectly square
   piece of paper;
   make 4 exact creases;
   unfold after making each crease.*

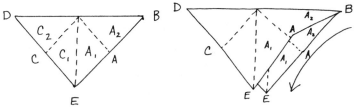

2. *Fold on a diagonal crease. Face point E toward you.
   Lift side A at point A and tuck section A_2 inside section A_1,
   bringing point B inside and down to point E.*

3. *Repeat with side C. Lift side C at point C
   and tuck section C_2 inside section C_1,
   bringing point D inside and down to point E.
   Crease C_3 folds down inside vertically along
   center line F of the diamond (see Figure 4).*

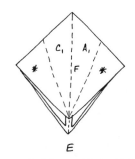

4. *Keep open end of diamond (point E) facing down.
   Fold top outside halves (*) of sides A_1 and C_1
   along the dotted lines to center line F.
   Turn over and repeat,
   so that all points meet at open end (point E)
   and you have a kite-shaped figure.*

5. *Fold top section G back and forth
   over the front and back,
   making a firm crease
   along the dotted line.*

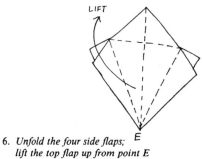

6. *Unfold the four side flaps;
   lift the top flap up from point E
   to form a canoe-like figure (see Figure 7).*

Folded Paper Cranes (cont.)

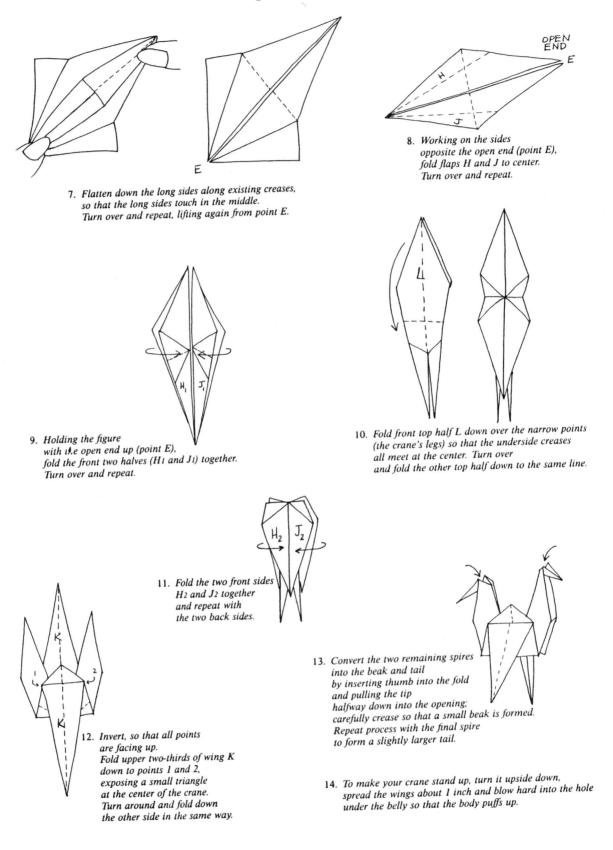

7. Flatten down the long sides along existing creases, so that the long sides touch in the middle. Turn over and repeat, lifting again from point E.

8. Working on the sides opposite the open end (point E), fold flaps H and J to center. Turn over and repeat.

9. Holding the figure with the open end up (point E), fold the front two halves (H1 and J1) together. Turn over and repeat.

10. Fold front top half L down over the narrow points (the crane's legs) so that the underside creases all meet at the center. Turn over and fold the other top half down to the same line.

11. Fold the two front sides H2 and J2 together and repeat with the two back sides.

12. Invert, so that all points are facing up. Fold upper two-thirds of wing K down to points 1 and 2, exposing a small triangle at the center of the crane. Turn around and fold down the other side in the same way.

13. Convert the two remaining spires into the beak and tail by inserting thumb into the fold and pulling the tip halfway down into the opening; carefully crease so that a small beak is formed. Repeat process with the final spire to form a slightly larger tail.

14. To make your crane stand up, turn it upside down, spread the wings about 1 inch and blow hard into the hole under the belly so that the body puffs up.

Guidelines for Involving Children in Social Action

1. Invite the children regularly to join us in social action. They are capable of understanding a lot, if we take time to share with them. They can co-sign letters with us, join us occasionally at meetings or vigils. But invitation means giving them the freedom to say "no." And it means incorporating the children into deciding how the family will involve itself in social action.

2. Expose the children to people who are the victims of injustice, to people who are working for change, and to a wide variety of situations. This deepens their understanding of injustice, or what needs to be done and how to make a difference. It touches our hearts and moves us to want to act more courageously. Inviting people into our homes; looking for books, TV shows, movies music that touch children; finding places in our own community as well as elsewhere (when we travel) that expose children to justice concerns are all possibilities.

3. Seek out actions that are within children's capabilities. Actions involving sharing our home are "safer" and more understandable for younger children. Building on previous experiences rather than multiplying new ones helps. Quality is more important than quantity. Some social action campaigns provide opportunities in which children have a specific role. Recognizing and respecting the children's needs means tailoring our time expectations to them and being flexible.

4. Integrate social action with fun. We want our children involved because *they want* to be there, not because we forced them. Making the activity fun includes several possibilities — combining action with an event that is fun, finding "doing" and "making" roles for the children (rather than observer roles), and especially joining with others, particularly with other children.

5. Integrate social action with faith. Prayer helps us experience social action as part of the very substance of our faith. It helps us (1) know that Jesus walks with us, (2) unite with the whole Body of Christ, and (3) experience deeper family unity. This integration involves our nurturing a sense of wonder and unity in children through experiencing God's gift of creation, making prayer a part of our social action, and incorporating social action into the liturgical year.

THE IMPORTANCE OF COMMUNITY

The support of others helps us overcome our fears. Working with other families increases the effectiveness of our social action. Working with others provides both accountability and challenge. The example of others challenges us to live more faithfully. It is easier to run away, as it were, when no one else is around. Finally, working with other families often provides the necessary ingredient of enjoyment. Having other children along makes a real difference in many cases.

PREPARING CHILDREN FOR SOCIAL ACTION

1. Promote our children's self-esteem and self-confidence. Affirming our children, giving them a chance to stand up in public, and encouraging leadership opportunities are ways we can increase their willingness to take risks later on.

2. Relate to our children's needs and interests. When we invite them into our larger world, our children need to know that we are interested in their own world of school, sports, music, and play, and that we love them where and as they are.

3. Help our children develop as "caring" persons. The issues are secondary, especially at first. The heart is primary. Encouraging them to care for each other, for the environment, for their grandparents, for pets, for their toys — this prepares them to care for others who need help.

How Are We Global Peacemakers?

Already Doing	Possible Next Steps
Promote interracial harmony	
Promote global inclusiveness (e.g., host a foreign student)	
Pursue a simpler, more ecologically sound lifestyle	
Participate in direct service or solidarity projects (e.g., Quest for Peace in Nicaragua)	
Engage in (public) acts of protest or resistance	
Engage in political action or advocacy	
Educate children or others about these issues and values	
Pray, fast, or do other sacrificial acts for peace	

Global Peace Bingo Card

a.	b.	c.	d.
_____ name	_____ name	_____ name	_____ name
e.	**f.**	**g.**	**h.**
_____ name	_____ name	_____ name	_____ name
i.	**j.**	**k.**	**l.**
_____ name	_____ name	_____ name	_____ name
m.	**n.**	**o.**	**p.**
_____ name	_____ name	_____ name	_____ name

Find someone who:

a. Has talked about nuclear war with other people at home.

b. Has seen the movie *Gandhi.*

c. Has read the book *Sadako and the Thousand Paper Cranes.*

d. Has written a letter to the President about peace.

e. Has had a bumper sticker on their car about peace.

f. Has worn a button about peace.

g. Has ever been to a peace rally.

h. Has read a book about Martin Luther King.

i. Has prayed for world peace.

j. Has been to the United Nations building in New York.

k. Has a pen pal in another country.

l. Has given money for some project in another country.

m. Has made a paper crane.

n. Has made a poster or sign about peace.

o. Has been on a world hunger walk.

p. Knows the name of the president of the Soviet Union.

Simple Gifts, a Shaker Hymn

'Tis a gift to be simple
'Tis a gift to be free
'Tis a gift to come down where we ought to be
And when we see ourselves in a way that's right
We will live in a valley of love and delight
When true simplicity is gained
To live and to love we will not be ashamed
To laugh and to sing will be our delight
Till by laughing and singing we come round right.

REASONS FOR A SIMPLER LIFESTYLE

"The essence of voluntary simplicity is living in a way that is outwardly simple and inwardly rich. This way of life embraces frugality of consumption, a strong sense of environments which are of a more human scale, and an intention to realize our higher human potential — both psychological and spiritual — in community with others."
                                                                                                (*Alternatives Catalogue*)

- *Naturalistic:* helps us appreciate the serenity of nature, its silence, the changes of the seasons, and its creatures.

- *Symbolic:* promotes solidarity with the world's poor and reduces the hypocrisy of our current overconsumptive lifestyle.

- *Person-oriented:* affords greater opportunities to work together and share resources with one's neighbors.

- *Ecological:* reduces our use of resources, lessens pollution, and creates an awareness that we must live in harmony with our world.

- *Health:* lessens tension and anxiety, encourages more rest and relaxation, reduces use of harmful chemicals, creates inner harmony.

- *Economic:* saves money, reduces the need to work long hours and increases both number and quality of jobs.

- *Spiritual:* allows time for meditation and prayer and rejects materialistic values.

- *Social:* induces frustration with the limited scope of individual action and incites us to move to social and political action levels.

[From *99 Ways to a Simple Lifestyle.*]

What Can We Do About Stewardship?

	Already Doing	Possible Next Steps
Food	1. _____	1. _____
	2. _____	2. _____
	3. _____	3. _____
Energy	1. _____	1. _____
	2. _____	2. _____
	3. _____	3. _____
Transportation	1. _____	1. _____
	2. _____	2. _____
	3. _____	3. _____
Recreation	1. _____	1. _____
	2. _____	2. _____
	3. _____	3. _____
Clothes	1. _____	1. _____
	2. _____	2. _____
	3. _____	3. _____

FROM CHIEF SEATTLE (1850s)

Teach your children what we have taught our children, that the earth is our mother. Whatever befalls the earth, befalls the children of the earth. If we spit upon the ground, we spit upon ourselves. This we know. The earth does not belong to us; we belong to the earth....

One thing we know, which the White man may one day discover — our God is the same God. You may think now that you own Him as you wish to own our land; but you cannot. He is the God of *all* people, and His compassion is equal for all. This earth is precious to God, and to harm the earth is to heap contempt on its Creator....

So love it as we have loved it. Care for it as we have cared for it. And with all your strength, with all your mind, with all your heart, preserve it for your children, and love...as God loves us all.

Living Green: 101 Things You Can Do to Promote Green Values

The Green movement is more than just a political ideology. Green values also involve how we live everyday. This list is for those who have the "Green spirit" and would like to incorporate it further into our lives.

1. Recycle paper, glass, and metal
2. Recycle motor oil
3. Use cloth diapers
4. Reuse egg cartons and paper bags
5. Avoid using styrofoam — it can't be recycled
6. Avoid disposable plates, cups, and utensils
7. Use rags instead of paper towels
8. Use paper bags, not paper towels to drain grease
9. Give away rather than dispose of unneeded items
10. Use the back of discardable paper for scratch paper
11. Be responsible and creative with leftover food
12. Use water from cooking vegetables to make soup
13. Mend and repair, rather than discard and replace
14. Invest in well-made, functional clothing
15. Buy bulk, unpackaged goods
16. Purchase goods in reusable or recyclable containers
17. Buy organic, pesticide-free foods
18. Avoid highly processed foods
19. Eat foods that are low on the food chain
20. Compost your food scraps
21. Grow your own food (even small kitchen gardens!)
22. Volunteer to start or help with a community garden
23. Support local food co-ops
24. Discover where the food and goods you buy come from
25. Buy locally grown produce and other foods
26. Use glass and steel cookware rather than aluminum
27. Volunteer to maintain local parks and wilderness
28. Buy living Christmas trees
29. Plant trees in your community
30. Learn about the plants and animals in your region
31. Discover your watershed and work to protect it
32. Oppose the use of roadside defoliants in your area
33. Use non-toxic, biodegradable soaps and detergents
34. Use non-toxic pest control
35. Buy products that don't support animal testing
36. Keep hazardous chemicals in spillproof containers
37. Put in a water-conserving showerhead
38. Take shorter showers
39. Turn off the water while you brush your teeth
40. Put a water conservation device in your toilet tank
41. Learn where your waste and sewage goes
42. Learn where the energy for your home comes from
43. Support your local utility's conservation program
44. Hang your clothes out to dry
45. Be sure your home is well insulated
46. Weather-seal your home thoroughly
47. Heat your home responsibly, with renewable energy
48. Don't burn green wood
49. Put a catalytic converter on your wood stove
50. Turn off lights when not in use
51. Turn down your hot water heater
52. Lower your thermostat and wear warmer clothes
53. Buy energy efficient electrical appliances
54. Drive a fuel efficient car that uses unleaded gas
55. Keep your engine well-tuned
56. Conserve gas by walking, bicycling, and carpooling
57. Shop by phone first, then pick up your purchases
58. Use rechargeable batteries
59. Research socially responsible investments
60. Support local credit unions
61. Support local shops and restaurants, not chains
62. "Adopt a grandparent" from the local senior center
63. Volunteer to cook for senior citizens
64. Become a Big Sister or Brother to a child in need
65. Hold a community potluck to meet your neighbors
66. Pick up litter along highways and near your home
67. Sponsor a clothes swap
68. Become involved with community projects & events
69. Organize or participate in community sports
70. Be responsible for the values you express
71. Participate in sister city and cultural exchanges
72. Educate yourself on global and Third World issues
73. Learn about the cultural diversity of your bioregion
74. Spend time visualizing global peace
75. Learn how your legislators vote and let them know your views
76. Be an active voter and attend "Town Meetings"
77. Vote for candidates who support Green values
78. Become involved with your child's school
79. Encourage your child's natural talents and interests
80. Organize or join a neighborhood toy co-op
81. Put toxic substances out of reach of children
82. Teach your children ecological wisdom
83. Listen your children's needs and support their dreams
84. Discourage the use of violent toys in your household
85. Communicate openly with your friends and co-workers
86. Acknowledge someone who provides quality service
87. Work to understand people with different views and values
88. Be conscious of the struggles of oppressed people
89. Work to unlearn cultural sexism and racism
90. Acknowledge spirituality in yourself and others
91. Donate blood if your health permits
92. Explore ways to reduce the stress in your life
93. Practice preventative health care
94. Exercise regularly and eat wisely
95. Bring music into your life
96. Learn about the medications you put into your body
97. Practice responsible family planning
98. Learn first aid and emergency procedures
99. Take time to play, relax, and go into nature
100. Decrease TV-watching & increase creative learning
101. Have fun and be joyful

[This list will be expanded into a calendar with a Green idea for each day of the year. Please send comments and suggestions to Mary-Clayton and Christoph Enderlein, 11064 Exeter Ave., N.E., Seattle, WA 98125, or call 206-362-5577]

Cooperative Crafts

Gift Certificate: Brainstorm a list of "gifts" that family members can give to people that are things to do with or for another person, not things to buy. For example, a promise to help a parent with a particular chore once a week; free tutoring for a friend who has difficulty with a particular subject; setting aside a special time to play with a younger brother or sister just what they want to play.

Family Puzzles: Each family is given an envelope prepared for them that contains the number of puzzle pieces that corresponds to the number of people in their family. When the puzzle pieces are put together they make up an $8\frac{1}{2} \times 11''$ sheet. On each puzzle piece, the individual person draws pictures of things that are characteristic of him or her. (Small children will need some help, but all family members are included.) After the individual pieces are completed, the family puts their puzzle together and pastes it onto a blank sheet of paper.

Shalom Banner: Using scraps of paper, trace hand prints. Put your name on your hand print and glue it onto the banner.

Family Banner or Windsock: Have available paper, streamers, marking pens, and stencils. Each streamer on the windsock could affirm contributions by a family member in the areas of peace and justice. There are many variations for this project.

Paper Crane Chains: Make paper cranes after sharing the story of "Sadako and the Thousand Cranes." These can vary in size and color and be strung together in chains or mobiles and given as a gift.

Shalom Box: Decorate the outside of a box with pictures that symbolize ways your family has experienced shalom or are building shalom. Inside the box can be placed items that are signs of hope that God is building shalom. Build the shalom box gradually, involving as many members of the family as possible in its creation and updating.

Family Peace Dove: Cut the shape of a large dove out of cardboard or posterboard. From white construction paper, trace the shape of one hand of each member of your family. Put the person's name on the hand and glue it on the dove to make its feathers. Have this in a place such that each time a guest comes into your home they many "sign in" and become part of your Peace Dove.

Shakertown Pledge Worksheet

Recognizing that the earth and the fullness thereof is a gift from our gracious God, and that we are called to cherish, nurture, and provide loving stewardship for the earth's resources, and recognizing that life itself is a gift, and a call to responsibility, joy, and celebration, I make the following declarations:

	Already Doing	**Could Do**
1. I declare myself to be a world citizen.		
2. I commit myself to lead an ecologically sound life.		
3. I commit myself to lead a life of creative simplicity and to share my personal wealth with the world's poor.		
4. I commit myself to join with others in reshaping institutions in order to bring about a more just global society in which each person has full access to the needed resources for their physical, emotional, intellectual, and spiritual growth.		
5. I commit myself to occupational accountability, and in doing so I will seek to avoid the creation of products which cause harm to others.		
6. I affirm the gift of my body and commit myself to its proper nourishment and physical well-being.		
7. I commit myself to examine continually my relations with others, and to attempt to relate honestly, morally, and lovingly to those around me.		
8. I commit myself to personal renewal through prayer, meditation and study.		
9. I commit myself to responsible participation in a community of faith.		

Have–Need Checklist

Directions

1. Draw a circle around each thing below that you really need —
   something you would find it hard to live well without.

2. Draw a line under all the things you actually have.

3. Put a check in front of the things you believe a child in a developing country cannot do without.

4. If you have fewer checks than circles, write in this blank the things you circled but did not check.

   _____

5. Look over all the items that are underlined only. These are the things you have but could do without —
   right? List here the three underlined items it would be hardest for you to give up.

   _____

6. Write here the three that would be easiest for you to do without.

   _____

- air conditioning
- wearing the latest styles
- a college education
- being a part of the church
- pets
- expensive food for pet
- sports
- a family to belong to
- stereo
- Christmas presents
- television
- TV without ads
- candy
- contact with nature
- health
- hair dryer/curler
- hearing or playing music
- playground

- throwaway bottles, cans
- more than five shirts or blouses
- water
- several close friends
- housing
- bike
- paper plates/styrofoam cups
- daily newspaper
- dishwasher
- meat every day
- three meals a day
- opportunities to travel
- more than ten toys
- bath every day
- minibike
- doctor/dentist
- quiet place to be alone
- trip by bus

Ten Objects Exercise

Scenario: Your residence is on fire. All the people and pets are safe. You may safely return to save ten items. List the items and describe them briefly keeping the following issues in mind:

- The value of the item (sentimental or economic)
- How long you have had it
- Its uniqueness or replaceability (would you/could you)
- Why it was chosen over other things

Now think about how your life would be changed without these items. Would it? Are there either or both positive and negative changes that would occur?

For an exercise in choice when more time is available the scenario can be changed to one in which the family is moving to a distant land with a limit on how many items they can take with them.

This can be done as an individual exercise with each person allowed to choose a certain number of items or as a group decision where all members of the group must agree to the choice. The exercise might be done at home where the whole family can walk around together and actually review all their belongings by sight and touch.

Racial Background Sheet

The questions below refer to your own racial experiences and background. There are no right or wrong answers.

1. What is the racial composition of the people with whom you work? With whom you and/or your children go to school?

2. What has been the racial character of your own educational experiences (e.g., racial identity of fellow students)? Of your children's educational experiences?

3. Have any previous living or working experiences put you in contact with a significant number of people from a racial group other than your own? (If there are many of these experiences, list just the last three.)

4. What notable black person do you admire the most:

   - Locally?

   - Nationally?

5. Answer question 5, substituting:

   - Hispanic (local; national)

   - Native American (local; national)

   - Asian (local; national)

6. Using the scale below, how would you assess your own racial experiences and background?

Totally your own race									*Totally multi-racial*
1	2	3	4	5	6	7	8	9	10

   - Where would you like to be on that scale five years from now?

   - What one thing can you do now to move toward that point?

7. Name one person or experience that has had a significant positive effect on changing your racial attitudes.

Checklist for My Home

1. Check pictures and other visual representations in your home. Are they multiracial?

   - Total number? ____
   - Native Americans? ____
   - Blacks? ____
   - Asians? ____
   - Hispanics? ____
   - Whites? ____

   Do you think any of the visuals reflect a stereotype of a particular racial group? Which racial group?

2. Are musical selections from a variety of racial groups available in your home? Remember, pictures on record jackets are another source of visual images for children. Are the pictures on your record jackets multiracial?

3. Check the reading materials that come into the home. List them in terms of the racial identity of the people pictured on the cover in one month:

   - Total number of magazines? ____
   - Blacks? ____
   - Asians? ____
   - Whites? ____
   - Native Americans? ____

4. Do you subscribe to any minority periodicals (for example, *Ebony, Ebony Jr., Akwesasne Notes*)? How many?

5. Does your circle of friends include people from other racial groups? In other words, do your children see a multiracial group of people come into your home?

6. Consider the following to help yourself and your children become more critical of the kinds of images of different racial groups gained through television, movies, advertising, etc.

   - How many TV series have Blacks? ____ Hispanics? ____ Asians? ____ Native Americans? ____ In leading roles? ____

   - How many commercials feature people from the following racial groups: Blacks? ____ Whites? ____ Native Americans? ____ Hispanics? ____ Asians? ____

   - How many TV shows depict minorities in stereotyped roles? How many commercials?

   - Apply similar criteria to movies, magazines, newspapers, and store advertising (for example, a Pontiac dealer that depicts a be-feathered Indian saying, "Me heap'em Big Trader!"). How many stereotypes did you find?

   From your analysis of TV, advertising, etc., what conclusions can you draw in terms of:

   - numbers of minorities portrayed?
   - stereotyped portrayals?

7. Consider the positive role models of various racial groups you provide for your child. Think in terms of those who are considered "important people" from a child's perspective (doctors, dentists, teachers, etc.). Establishing positive role models from varied racial groups could be one of your criteria in choosing these people for your children. List the professionals your child sees according to race: Asians? Native Americans? Whites? Blacks? Hispanics?

8. Do you and your children go to plays, musical performances, and art exhibits that help them to understand a variety of cultural experiences?

9. Families might select places for outings or trips on the basis of what effect the event will have on forming racial attitudes. (For example, a "Wild West" amusement park motif often includes stereotypic and possibly frightening images of Native Americans.) Think back over your family entertainment in the past six months. Can you recall any outings that may have presented stereotyped images of minorities to you and your children?

10. Consider where you live, where you shop, where your children attend school, and where your family worships in terms of the people with whom you and your family interact on a day-to-day basis. Is it a racially isolated existence?

Wesley

My name is Wesley. I am seventeen years old and am in my senior year in a suburban high school, East Ridge High. The student body in our school is mostly Black. I am also Black. I play on the varsity basketball team. We have one of the better teams in the area, maybe even in the state.

In one of our early games this season we played another suburban school that is all White, Madison Park High. Before the game started, I looked up and saw one of the Madison Park students sitting in the stands with a white Ku Klux Klan hood over his head. I was surprised, to say the least. I noticed that he and another student handed the hood back and forth before and during the game. Several of my teammates noticed it too. Sometime in the second half, we saw an adult talk to the students, and then the hood disappeared.

We talked about the incident with our coach and then with our principal after the game. Our coach and principal decided to go to the principal of Madison Park. After talking to him, they told us that he had apologized for the two students and had assured them that "the behavior of those two students was not racially motivated." I wonder what he means by that?

1. Why do you think the Madison Park students were wearing the hood?

2. How would you feel if you were Wesley?

3. What do you think the Madison Park administrator meant by his remark? Do you agree?

4. If you were a parent of a Madison Park student, what would you do about the incident?

Kwanza

If you get tired of saying "Merry Christmas," try saying *"Habara gani?"* (Har-bar-ree Gah-nee). That's Swahili for "What's happening?" "What's happening?" is a new kind of celebration that began as a harvest festival in Africa. Kwanza means "first," and the traditional festival was held when the first harvest was brought in from the village fields. It was a time for giving thanks, taking stock of your life, and making plans for the future.

Kwanza begins on December 26. The celebration has seven days. On the first day the correct answer to "What's happening?" is *Umoja* (Oo-mo-jah), which means "unity." on that day a family might look at old photographs and talk about old times and things they are proud of in their family. Each of the next six days of the celebration honors a different principle:

- *Kujichagulia* (Koo-gee-cha-goo-lee-ah): taking charge of your life

- *Ujima* (Oo-gee-mah): working together for the good of all

- *Ujamaa* (Oo-jah-mah): business cooperation

- *Nia* (Nee-ah): purpose

- *Kuumba* (Koo-um-bah): creativity

- *Imani* (Ee-mah-nee): faith

Each family decides together on special ways to celebrate these themes.

Some important decorations are a part of every Kwanza celebration. One of them is the *mkeka* (M-kay-kah), a straw mat that represents history and tradition, the foundation on which everything rests. On the *mkeka* is a *kinara* (Kee-nar-ah), a holder for seven candles, or *mishumaa* (Mi-she-mah), representing the seven principles of Kwanza. Sometimes decorations make the *kinara* look like the stalk of a tree or plant to remind Black persons of their one beginning. Also on the mat is an ear of corn, or *muhindi* (Moo-hin-dee), which represents the children of the house, who are the hope for the future. A bowl holds many kinds of fruit, called *zawade* (Zah-wah-dee), or gifts.

Some families also place on the mat or in the bowl small gifts for everyone in the family, which cannot be opened until the last day of the festival. These should be small handmade items, things with a special meaning, or promises that will help the person through the next year.

The colors red, black, and green are the favorites for Kwanza decorations and gifts. Red stands for the blood of Black people shed for hundreds of years; black for the color of Black people; and green for the land.

Each day during Kwanza the family gets together, lights the candle for that day, and talks about the principle for the day. Then they pour a drink into the ground to honor their ancestors. (City families use a basket filled with earth).

On the last day — January 1 — the family has a feast, or *karamu* (Kar-rah-mu). They eat nuts, vegetables, and fruits to remind them of an African and American Southern tradition of offering these foods on New Year's Day. There is singing and dancing to African music and lots of joy and laughter. Together families rejoice over the good year gone and the good year that is coming, because everyone, in celebrating Kwanza, has promised to try to make tomorrow brighter.

The Story of Kwanza, by Safisha L. Madhubuti, illustrated by Murry N. De Pillars, Third World Press (7424 S. Cottage Grove Ave., Chicago, IL 60619), 1977, is a good explanation of Kwanza for young readers.

For a fuller explanation of the origin and the specifics of the celebration rituals for Black American families, consult "How I Came to Celebrate Kwanza," by Omonike Weusi-Puryeai, in *Essence,* December 1979, pp. 112ff.

Family Task Chart

Families work together to create a chart representing their own families:

Jobs Mom does:

Jobs Dad does:

Jobs Brother does:

Jobs Sister does:

Circle those jobs listed that all do. Box those jobs listed that only boys do.
Underline those jobs that only girls do.

Talk as a family about why these jobs are performed by the family members indicated. Decide
on ways sex-role stereotyping can be challenged in your home. You may wish to share your
chart and "challenges" with the other families.

Family Vignettes

Story 1: Bobby

Bobby is seven years old. He likes to ride his bike, play with his dog, listen to records, play with trucks with his friends. He would also like to take ballet lessons. He went to a ballet with his parents and was impressed by the obvious strength and agility of the dancers. He would like to be able to dance like that, too. His parents are confused. There are no other boys in the neighborhood who are taking ballet. Bobby knows that the rest of the class would be girls. He says he doesn't care.

What should his parents do?

Story 2: Saundra

Saundra is fifteen years old. She enjoys school, loves to read poetry, plays a little guitar, and is beginning to enjoy trying her hand at cooking. She is a new member of the cheerleading squad. However, she has some reservations about being a cheerleader. First of all, she thinks there should be as big a cheerleading squad for the girls' basketball and volleyball teams as for the boys' teams. Second, she does not think that the cheerleaders should be expected to bake cookies for the boys on the teams, decorate their locker rooms, put stars on the front doors of their homes, and generally be seen in a supportive role. Most of the other girls on the cheerleading squad feel she should not rock the boat. Saundra has asked her parents for their advice.

What should her parents say?

TV Monitor Sheet

The images of both women and men offered to us by TV are narrow in their scope and dangerous, especially to young minds groping to define what it means to be a man or a woman. Answer the following questions for yourself and then with your children.

1. How many women have major TV roles? minor roles? (Perhaps the family could log its TV watching for a week and write down the numbers; see the chart below.)

2. Use of sex and the woman's body:

   • What percentage of women playing roles on the shows we watch are exceptionally attractive? How does this compare to the percentage of men? (Total number of shows: ____; number of exceptionally attractive women: ____; number of exceptionally attractive men: ____.)

   • How often are the women characters attired in clothes that have obvious sexual connotations? Note specific examples of shows.

   • In how many commercials is a women's body used as a decoration? Note specific examples, and estimate what percentage of the total commercials use this technique.

3. What personal qualities are reflected through characterizations of men and women on TV? Are these qualities shown primarily in one sex? (For example, leadership: male or female? Compassion: male or female? Clear thinking in emergencies: male or female?) Note some of these characteristics on a sheet of paper, and then note the number of times they are exhibited in men and in women. Note specific examples.

4. List the occupational roles of men and women as depicted in the shows you see in a week.

5. How often does a man use violence to solve a conflict? Note the total number of conflicts, and then the number of violent resolutions of conflicts.

6. Do any of the show's make an attempt to deal with injustice toward women? With changing sex roles? List examples.

7. How many times are women made to appear incapable or inferior intellectually to men? Note specific examples.

8. How many times does a man solve a problem for a woman?____. How many times does a woman solve a problem for a man?____.

9. How many times are male characters evaluated according to:

   • the amount of money they have (what percent of male characters are in this category?)

   • the amount of prestige their occupation has (what percent of male characters are in this category?)

   • how "tough" they are (what percent of male characters are in this category?)

Give examples of these.

Name of Show	Number of Major Male Characters	Number of Major Female Characters	Number of Minor Male Characters	Number of Minor Female Characters

Attitudes About People with Disabilities

How do you feel about the poster?

Do you feel that the poster pictures a real situation?

Are disabled people capable of loving relationships with others?

What does the caption mean: "See me as a person. It's important to both of us"?

See me as a person.
It's important to both of us.

NATIONAL HANDICAPPED
AWARENESS WEEK

A public education project
of the Easter Seal Society

Interest Form — How Can We Help You?

I/we would like to be kept informed about any future Parenting for Peace and Justice events:

_____ yes   _____ no.

I/we are interested in meeting on an on-going basis with:

_____ other single parents
_____ other parents of preschool children
_____ other parents of elementary-aged children
_____ other parents of teens and grown children
_____ group of adults nurturing children of various ages

I/we are interested in future presentations, programs, or discussion groups (family support group) on the topics of:

_____ cooperation, conflict resolution, discipline in the home
_____ helping children deal with the violence in the world around them
_____ helping children/families deal with consumerism, peer pressure, stewardship
_____ developing healthy racial attitudes in our children
_____ how families can work for world peace
_____ how families can integrate social concerns with prayer and worship
_____ other (please name other topics you would like us to organize a presentation or program around):

Name _____ Phone _____

Address _____

....

I/we would like to receive the bi-monthly PPJN Newsletter on a regular basis ($15/year). Make checks payable to:

Institute for Peace and Justice: PPJN
4144 Lindell Blvd. #122
St. Louis, MO 63108

Name _____ Phone _____

Address _____

What Can Families Do About Racism?

1. **Inform yourself about racism**

   Two classics about institutional racism are *Institutional Racism in America* by Louis L. Knowles and Kenneth Prewitt (Prentice-Hall, 1969) and *Blaming the Victim* by William Ryan (Vintage Books, 1976). For more regular updating, subscribe to the *Bulletin* of the Council on Interracial Books for Children, 1841 Broadway, New York, NY 10023 ($15 a year for eight issues), and the "Civil Rights Journal," a news service of the United Church of Christ Commission on Racial Justice (weekly 3-page bulletin, no charge; 105 Madison Ave., New York, NY 10016). Subscribe to a Black, Hispanic, Asian, or other ethnic newspaper in your community.

2. **Talk about current events**

   Talk within your family specifically about events that have racial implications. Encourage children to ask questions and draw conclusions.

3. **Celebrate racial justice heroes**

   Lift up for yourselves and your children the lives of people of color, past and present, who have fought and continue to fight for racial justice. Enjoy the learning by surrounding it with a party or other enjoyable event (for example, a birthday party for Martin Luther King). Suggested heroes: Rosa Parks, Chief Joseph, Cesar Chavez, Jesse Jackson, Harriet Tubman.

4. **Utilize holidays and cultural events**

   Many communities have cultural events (dance, theater, art) that provide information as well as real insights into the culture, history, and life of different racial groups. Holidays (for example, Martin Luther King's birthday, Kwanza, Cinco de Mayo, Chanukah) can also be times for us to learn more about the values of other peoples.

5. **Never use or allow racially derogatory terms**

   Children need to know that comments and/or jokes that belittle or insult the racial ancestry of any person or group are absolutely unacceptable in our homes. It is also important for them to see us confront other adults about their language.

6. **Check TV programming**

   Children can be brought into our discussions about TV shows. We can look at the simple question of numbers: how many TV series have Blacks? Hispanics? Asians? Native Americans? We can also discuss the kinds of roles: are people of color shown in positive or in stereotypic ways? (For example, are Blacks shown in warm, loving family situations or as perpetrators of crimes?)

7. **Look at your voting patterns**

   Political candidates at all levels need to be evaluated in terms of their stance and activity against racism in all forms. Children can be part of discussions about these candidates, about our voting decisions and the reasons for those decisions. In some communities, working on voter registration drives is a concrete way of putting into practice concern about the ability of all people to participate in the political system.

8. **Write letters to the editor**

   In every community there are racial incidents that occur as well as ever-present economic and political realities that reflect the institutional dimensions of racism (for example, high unemployment, infant mortality, difficulties in voter registration). Families can let their opinions be known in the community through letters that could be signed by the whole family.

9. **Involve yourself in community projects**

   It is important for both adults and children to be involved in projects in which the leaders are people of color.

10. **Stand with the victims**

    Even though the circumstances vary from one community to another, there are always opportunities to add our voices to those fighting against the impact of racism, whether at school board meetings, city council hearings, court procedures, or vigils. At times these situations may be appropriate for the participation of children.

What Can Schools and Churches Do About Racism?

1. Multiculturalize learning materials

Curriculum review is a big issue for schools and school districts. Learning materials should include the culture and history of all racial groups. A curriculum screening committee can be trained to detect bias and to help individual teachers as well as students to detect the bias themselves. Posters, A-V materials, and libraries (school and church) provide wonderful opportunities to celebrate a multicultural world.

2. Evaluate hiring practices

A multicultural staff makes a strong statement to members of a congregation or to students and their parents. In the broadest sense, this includes full- and part-time employees, volunteers, consultants, and outside speakers. National church offices for racial and cultural affairs, minority business councils, Black and Hispanic newspapers, and Black college placement offices are often aids in this kind of recruitment.

3. Offer educational events that deal with racial justice

Schools and churches need to have school assemblies, adult and children's Sunday school, parish educational nights, film festivals, etc. that focus on racism, prejudice, and the effects of racism and economic injustice. In-service staff development sessions for faculties are crucial for ongoing education.

4. Look at business practices

Suppliers of products and services can be evaluated in terms of their concern for racial and economic justice. Doing business with firms owned and operated by people of color or firms that have a good track record in affirmative action makes a statement to the entire church or school community.

5. Multiculturalize worship

The music, prayers, children's devotions, visuals, content of services of reconciliation, etc. that are part of the worship life of the church community can reflect the heritage of a variety of races and cultures.

Resources

Lois Stalvey, *The Education of a Wasp,* Bantam Books, 1971. A personal view of a White person's coming to a realization of the realities of racism.

Lois Stalvey, *Getting Ready,* Bantam Books, 1974. A penetrating look at racism in a big city school system and how a family deals with it.

James and Kathleen McGinnis et al., *Educating for Peace and Justice,* Institute for Peace and Justice, 1985. See vol. 1, units on Multicultural Education and Racism. This manual is oriented toward teachers but has many suggestions that are immediately adaptable to the home.

Kathleen and James McGinnis, *Parenting for Peace and Justice,* Orbis, 1981. Includes a chapter with many ideas about how to multiculturalize family life.

Filmstrip: *Childcare Shapes the Future: Anti-Racist Strategies,* Council on Interracial Books for Children (1841 Broadway, New York, NY 10023). This filmstrip/tape resource explains clearly how racism affects very young children and offers strategies for change.

Video: *Building Shalom Families: Christian Parenting for Peace and Justice.* This is a comprehensive parenting program on two video cassettes. It assists participants in dealing with important issues confronting today's families, including the issue of racism. Available from the Institute for Peace and Justice, 4144 Lindell Blvd. #122, St. Louis, MO 63108.

A Selection of Prayers from the Soviet Union

Russian Orthodox Christians pray the following beautiful prayer every Sunday morning, indeed every time they gather to celebrate the liturgy. They have been doing so for nearly a thousand years! The deep concern for peace that it evidences is not new, but has been central in Christians' prayers and actions from the beginning. This ancient prayer illustrates that, for it has been part of the worship of all Eastern Orthodox Christians across the centuries. It is in fact the prayer that begins the Liturgy of St. John Chrysostom, which they use throughout the year.

This prayer could take on a very special significance if Christians in the United States and the Soviet Union prayed the same prayer for peace as they gather to worship their common Lord. It is especially appropriate as we celebrate the Lord's Supper. This prayer has been adapted by Dr. Bruce Rigdon, professor at McCormick Theological Seminary.

Leader: In peace let us pray to the Lord.

People: Lord have mercy.*

Leader: For the peace from above and for our salvation, let us pray to the Lord.

People: Lord have mercy.

Leader: For the peace of the whole world, for the welfare of the holy churches of God, and for the unity of all people, let us pray to the Lord.

People: Lord have mercy.

Leader: For this holy community of faith and for those who with faith, reverence, and love of God enter herein, let us pray to the Lord.

People: Lord have mercy.

Leader: For our pastors, for all clergy, for all who bear office in the church, for all of the people of God in all times and places, let us pray to the Lord.

People: Lord have mercy.

Leader: For the president of the United States of America and all civil authorities, for the leaders of all nations, and for those who serve in the United Nations, let us pray to the Lord.

People: Lord have mercy.

Leader: That God will aid them and grant them wisdom and strength to struggle for justice and peace.

People: Lord have mercy.

Leader: For this community, for every city and land, and for the faithful who dwell in them, let us pray to the Lord.

People: Lord have mercy.

Leader: For healthful seasons, for abundance of the fruits of the earth, and for peaceful times, let us pray to the Lord.

People: Lord have mercy.

Leaders: For travelers by sea, by land, and by air, for the sick and the suffering, for refugees and the homeless, for prisoners and their salvation, for the poor and the needy, let us pray to the Lord.

People: Lord have mercy.

Leader: For our deliverance from all tribulation, wrath, danger, and necessity, let us pray to the Lord.

People: Lord have mercy.

Leader: Calling to remembrance our mothers and fathers in the faith, with all of God's saints let us commend ourselves and each other and all our life unto Christ our God.

People: To you, O Lord.

Leader: O Lord our God, whose power is beyond anything that we can imagine, whose glory is greater than our ability to know, whose mercy knows no limits, and whose love toward humankind is deeper than our capacity to understand: do, O God, in your tender compassion look upon us and upon this holy community of faith and grant us and those who pray with us your rich blessings and benefits. For unto you are due all glory, honor and worship: to the Father and to the Son and to the Holy Spirit: now and ever and unto ages of ages.

All: Amen.

---

*The expression "Lord have mercy" (*Kyrie Eleison* in Greek) in this prayer is not necessarily a plea for forgiveness. It is instead a proclamation of one's faith in the presence and power of God.

Shalom Chaverim

Shalom, My Friend *Shalom Chaverim*	Partners touch left palms, push back and forward gently.
Shalom, My Friend *Shalom Chaverim*	Same action with right palms.
Till We Meet Again *or* May Peace Be With You *Lahit Raot*	Hug left shoulders.
Till We Meet Again *or* May Peace Be With You *Lahit Raot*	Hug right shoulders.
Shalom, Shalom	One puts out hands, palms together. Other covers outstretched hands with his or her hands.

Throughout the song the partners look — and sing — directly at each other, wishing each other peace. One pair begins and then picks new partners; then the four each pick new partners from the group.

Each time everyone picks a new partner until everyone is involved. It is amazing how quickly everyone is involved, showing how quickly we can spread peace from one to another.

I Still Have A Dream,
by Martin Luther King, Jr.

If there is to be peace on earth and goodwill to all, we must finally believe in the ultimate morality of the universe and believe that all reality hinges on moral foundations. Truth crushed to the earth will rise again. No lie can live forever.

I tried to talk to the nation about a dream that I had had. And I must confess to you today that not long after talking about that dream, I started seeing it turn into a nightmare.

Yes, I'm personally the victim of deferred dreams, of blasted hopes. In spite of that, I close today by saying, I still have a dream.

Because, you know, you can't give up in life. If you lose hope, somehow you lose that vitality that keeps life moving. You lose that courage to be....As we continue to hope for peace on earth and goodwill to all, let us know that in the process we have cosmic companionship.

And so today I still have a dream. People will rise up and come to see that they are made to live together as brothers and sisters. I still have a dream today that one day every person of color in the world will be judged on the content of their character rather than the color of their skin; and everyone will respect the dignity and worth of human personality; and brotherhood will be more than a few words at the end of a prayer, but the first order of business on every legislative agenda.

I still have a dream today. Justice will roll down like waters and righteousness like a mighty stream.

I still have a dream today — that war will come to an end, that individuals will beat their swords into plowshares and their spears into pruning hooks, and nations will no longer rise up against nations. Neither will they study war any more. I still have a dream.

[Christmas Sermon, Ebenezer Baptist Church, December 24, 1967, filmed by the Canadian Broadcasting Co. and included in the video *Trumpet of Conscience*.]

Other Resources from the Institute for Peace and Justice

EDUCATING FOR PEACE AND JUSTICE, 1985 Edition

BY JAMES MCGINNIS, KATHLEEN MCGINNIS, AND OTHER CONTRIBUTORS

Volume 1: National Dimensions

12 Units ($14.25, 304 pages)

- Nonviolent Conflict Resolution
- Case Studies in Nonviolence
- Institutional Violence
- Peace and Justice in Schools
- Peace and Justice and the Law
- Poverty in the U.S.
- Sexism
- Racism
- Disabled People
- Older People
- Advertising/Stewardship
- Multicultural Education

Volume 2: Global Dimensions

8 Units ($14.25, 320 pages)

- World Hunger
- Global Poverty and Development
  (Case Study on El Salvador)
- Global Interdependence
- U.S. Foreign Policy
  (Case Studies on the Philippines and Nicaragua)
- Sadako and the Thousand Paper Cranes
  (Readers' Theater Version)
- U.S. – U.S.S.R. Relations
- The Military and U.S. Life
- War and Alternatives

Volume 3: Religious Dimensions

6 Units ($14.25, 240 pages)

- Today's Peacemakers
- Peace and Justice
- The Prophets
- Gospel Culture Contrasts
- Peace and War
- Service Programs

All volumes contain:

- explanation of EPJ methodology
- a list of helpful organizations

Each unit of all 3 volumes contains:

- development of the basic concepts of the theme
- teaching strategies for all age levels
- a wide variety of action possibilities,
  both within the school and in the larger community
- short student readings and worksheets
- bibliography of further teacher and student resources
- directions on teaching the unit

All 3 volumes: $37.00 (price includes postage)

BUILDING SHALOM FAMILIES:
CHRISTIAN PARENTING FOR PEACE AND JUSTICE

A comprehensive parenting program that assists participants in dealing with important issues confronting today's families. By using creative visuals, music, stimulating presentations, prayerful reflections, and practical "how to" sessions, the video enables the participants to experience the McGinnises and their important message of how to build peace in the home. There are visual backgrounds for the McGinnises' input, which include documentary footage and still shots. Also included are short reflective pieces incorporated into the sessions that provide a fuller sensory experience of the themes.

BUILDING SHALOM FAMILIES (1986) is a complete video package containing the following materials for program leaders:

- two 120-minute 1/2" VHS videotapes
- a 32-page guidebook
- the *Parenting for Peace and Justice* book
- worksheets and action brochures

  ☐ The Building Shalom Families Program — complete kit: $149.95 (plus $5 U.S. mailing)

  ☐ "Peacemaking in the Home" Tape — 72 minutes with introductions and seven segments: $30.00

  ☐ Additional sets of the guidebook, worksheets, action brochures, catalogues: $8.00

FAMILY ENRICHMENT MATERIALS

- **PARENTING FOR PEACE AND JUSTICE** (Orbis Books, 1981) is Kathy and Jim McGinnis's account of their own family experience and that of twelve other families in making justice and peace an integral part of family life. Chapters are Stewardship/Simplicity, Nonviolence in the Family, Helping Children Deal with Violence, Multiculturalizing Family Life, Sex-Role Stereotyping, Family Social Action, Prayer and Parenting, and How the Church Can Encourage Families. ($10.50)

- **NURTURING CHILDREN IN A WORLD OF CONFLICT** is an excellent short introduction to "Parenting for Peace and Justice." Multiple copies are available at 25 cents each for 1–9, 20 cents each for 10 or more.

- **STARTING OUT RIGHT: NURTURING YOUNG CHILDREN AS PEACEMAKERS,** by Kathy McGinnis and Barbara Oehlberg (Institute for Peace and Justice and Meyer-Stone Books, 1988) adapts the original PPJ book to families with pre-school age children. ($12.20)

- **HELPING KIDS CARE: HARMONY-BUILDING ACTIVITIES FOR HOME, CHURCH AND SCHOOL,** by Camy Condon and James McGinnis (Institute for Peace and Justice and Meyer-Stone Books, 1988), comes complete with step-by-step directions, detailed illustrations, easy-to-find props, focused discussion questions, and lists of additional resources. ($11.20)

- **CHILDREN AND NONVIOLENCE,** by Janet and Robert Aldridge (Hope Press, 1987), recounts the Aldridges experience raising ten children to be peacemakers. ($10.50)

- **CONFLICT PARTNERSHIP,** by Dudley Weeks (Transworld Productions, 1984), offers adults very practical techniques for nonviolent conflict resolution applicable to family, work, and community conflict situations. ($10.50)

- **FAMILIES IN SEARCH OF SHALOM** is a 100-frame 10-minute filmstrip introducing the PPJ themes and their Judeo-Christian foundation. It has three new versions, adapting the script to Jewish, Black, and Hispanic audiences. ($29.00)

- **EXPANDED PHIL DONAHUE SHOW VIDEOTAPE** includes a 3-minute segment on family meetings as well as segments on how family support groups operate, on the PPJ Network, the *Families in Search of Shalom* filmstrip, and the 45-minute highly entertaining Donahue Show on PPJ. ($45.00)

PPJ NETWORK

The PPJN is a network of families, family life leaders, and others working with families with three main goals: to help families

- understand how forces like violence, racism, materialism, and sexism affect them
- find ways of resisting these forces
- do this as a whole family and with other families.

The PPJN is currently working through local PPJ coordinators and ecumenical local teams in some 150 U.S. and Canadian cities, plus 16 national Christian denominations. Families and leaders from other religious and moral traditions are also part of the PPJN. The PPJN offers a variety of services, from leadership training workshops and family enrichment experiences to linking families in the same area in "family support groups."

PPJN NEWSLETTER

The Newsletter, a six-times-a-year resource, provides practical suggestions for family action, "parent-to-parent" reflection on efforts to live PPJ values, information on written and AV resources for both adults and children, suggestions for integrating family social action and prayer, and details about up-coming events (PPJ workshops, family camps, training events, etc.).

Each issue of the newsletter focuses on a particular theme (for example, non-violence in the home, toys, families and the nuclear threat, families confronting racism). There are columns written by single parents and grandparents ("Grand-parenting for Peace and Justice"!), and others.

Members of the PPJN are strongly encouraged to share through the newsletter their own stories about applying PPJ to their family situation.

For a listing of all PPJ resources and information on how to become part of the PPJN and receive the PPJN newsletter and other mailings, send a self-addressed stamped envelope to:

Parenting for Peace & Justice Network
Institute for Peace & Justice
4144 Lindell Blvd., Room 122
St. Louis, Missouri 63108
Tel.: 314-533-4445

For more information about
the Institute for Peace and Justice,
the Parenting for Peace and Justice Network,
and to order IPJ resources, write or call:

Institute for Peace and Justice
4144 Lindell Blvd., Room 122
St. Louis, Missouri 63108
Tel.: 314-533-4445